DREAMe

THE U.S. WAR

ON

IMMIGRANT

LATINX

CHILDREN

Arturo Jiménez

DREAMers Nightmare
THE U.S. WAR ON IMMIGRANT LATINX CHILDREN

Arturo Jiménez

President Obama and the Trump Administrations have failed the DREAM'ers and DACA recipients. Immigrant children stuck in legal limbo are living a nightmare.

Immigration on the U.S. Southern Border is a humanitarian crisis that has overwhelmed our border patrol and blocked our courts with a flood of dreamer migrants seeking asylum from the violent Northern Triangle of Central America fleeing human rights abuses. Conditions at the border are a powder keg. This book puts faces to the Immigration issue, looks at the causes, and affect and searches for solutions.

This book is a work of nonfiction. It aims to start a discussion and dialogue to resolve the issues outlined by the author. Names have been changed where appropriate to protect the innocence of the unaccompanied migrant children.

First addition Published 2019 By Arturo Jiménez. Arturo Jiménez.com

Photograph and image credits appear in the book.

Editors, research and referencing Cheri Lucking and Peter Lucking | ContentBrandingSolutions.com
Cover, graphics, and book design by Peter Lucking | ContentBrandingSolutions.com

DREAMers Nightmare
THE U.S. WAR ON IMMIGRANT LATINX CHILDREN

ISBN: 9781693665455 First Edition: 2019

Arturo Jiménez Immigration Law

Advocate • Immigration Attorney • Counselor at Law • 303-455-1809 • jimenezimmigrationlaw.com

"The bosom of America is open to receive not only the Opulent and respectable Stranger, but the oppressed and persecuted of all Nations And Religions; whom we shall welcome to a participation of all our rights and privileges, if by decency and propriety of conduct they appear to merit the enjoyment." - George Washington

Dedicated to my Grandmother Eulalia "Lily" Calderón,
known as a child, as "Lali" Lopez
December 19, 1923 - May 8, 2017.

As the matriarch of the family, she taught the family
politics and gave us our voice.

Lily's inspiring Mexican American life began in Trinidad,
Colorado, as a child of immigrants, born in the U.S. by chance.

The family worked the farmers' field circuit from the 1920s
through the Great Depression, from Mexico to Nebraska,
overnighting in pig pens, hen houses or living out of their car.

Lily initially attended a racially segregated school for
Mexicans, Hispanics, and Mexican Americans in Colorado until
our Great Grandfather demanded that she be enrolled in a
normal American school as she was a United States Citizen.
She never lost her ties to Mexico visiting her parents'
homeland of Mexico many times.

Lily did her part in World War II as a Riveter with her sister Neri in the Glenn L. Martin Company's bomber factory in Nebraska.

She lost her brothers in the war, one in England in a bomber crash, and the other who was a war photographer in Japan.

After marrying our grandfather, Gabriael Calderón, Lily lived in the U.S. and Mexico.

Lily became a bi-lingual educator in the local public schools and an activist for La Leche League advocating for breastfeeding moms and their babies in Denver.

Raised a Catholic, she took issues with the Pope's governance and left to join the Russian Orthodox Church.

She was a gifted painter who loved her family of fourteen children, (eleven surviving) thirty grandchildren and 25 great-grandchildren.

She was and is our family inspiration.

Contents

THE IMMIGRATION QUIZ

Take the Immigration quiz to test your knowledge immigration.

1. **Does the United States deport innocent children?**

    Yes - or - **No**

2. **What President deported more children than any other president in U.S. History?**

    A. President Ronald Reagan

    B. President George H.W. Bush

    C. President Bill Clinton

    D. President George W. Bush

    E. President Barack Obama

    F. President Donald Trump

3. **Senators from what political party first introduced the DREAM Act into Congress?**

    A. Republicans

    B. Democrats

    C. Green Party

4. **How many times has the DREAM Act been introduced into at least one chamber of Congress?**

    A. 2 times

    B. 5 times

    C. more than seven times

5. **Are DACA and the DREAM Act the same thing, or are they different?**

6. **Does DACA lead to Permanent Legal Status and eventual Citizenship?**

7. **What is the most recent military coup, takeover of a nation's government, in which the United States has acknowledged involvement?**

    A. Venezuela

    B. Nicaragua

    C.   El Salvador

    D.   Honduras

8. **Which President last signed a law to expand the wall on our Southern border with Mexico?**

    A.   President Ronald Reagan

    B.   President George H.W. Bush

    C.   President Bill Clinton

    D.   President George W. Bush

    E.   President Barack Obama

    F.   President Donald Trump

9. **Are the children who have arrived at our Southern Border considered "Dreamers" by those sponsoring the DREAM ACT?**

10. **Which is the last president to sign a law granting some level of "amnesty" by offering Legal Permanent Residence and a pathway to citizenship to those who entered the U.S. unlawfully?**

    A.   President Ronald Reagan

    B.   President George H. W. Bush

    C.   President Bill Clinton

    D.   President George W. Bush

    E.   President Barack Obama

    F.   President Donald Trump

11. **Which political party controlled both the Senate, the House of Representatives and the Presidency yet failed to pass legislation benefiting immigrants?**

    A.   Democratic Party

    B.   Republican Party

    C   OTHER

12. **What are the three countries in the so-called Violent Northern Triangle from which tens of thousands of children are arriving at our Southern Border?**

    A.   El Salvador

    B.   Nicaragua

    C.   Guatemala

    D.   Honduras

    E.   All of the above

    F.   A. C. and D

13. Do you believe that a wall on the Southern border might solve some of our immigration problems?

Answers are at the back of the book.

Arturo Jiménez

FROM THE AUTHOR

The Search for Resolution on Immigration

I wrote this story to share my knowledge and firsthand experience as a family immigration lawyer, father, and advocate for child immigration rights.

If you are a Republican or Democrat, whatever your beliefs on the immigration issues are, I can bet you that 95% of all people will be wrong when it comes to the truth behind the migrants, the law, and immigration issues.

If you are a middle-class mom from Middle-America like many women in my family, or a working-class dad like many of my younger cousins, a white-collar worker in a downtown financial district, a grandchild of a sharecropper, or a third-generation Latino like me who really just wants to know the issues, and maybe, if the opportunity presents itself, have enough knowledge to start a conversation about what our country could do to alleviate the immigration situation, then this book is for you.

There will be those of you who don't fit into any population niche or category that is easy for the media to address. What if you voted for President Donald Trump and are convinced that you would do so again? What if you are on the opposite side of the spectrum and you voted for Hillary Clinton or even for Bernie Sanders? What if you cannot vote at all because you are a Legal Permanent Resident, or you are here without any legal immigration status? Does this book serve a purpose for anyone or everyone? I believe you will find it does—not because I can give you all the answers—rather because you will have a basis to start this conversation with other people from a very human point of view. At the same time, I intend to provide enough information and references to support the facts.

This work is not based on a religious nor on a political party platform. To the contrary, you may find that this book challenges many of the notions that arise from those corners while acknowledging that it will take work from all groups in every direction to craft solutions to the immigration question and the humanitarian crisis at our Southern Border.

Perhaps some of you may feel that the immigration issue will take care of itself. After all waves of immigrants came to our shores and borders over the last one hundred and fifty years before the founding of the United States, to five hundred years ago when the first groups of European migrants arrived in the Americas. It has worked out well for everyone, or has it?

Many of these prior immigrants have been integrated one way or another into the United States, sometimes dragged through a muddy process of forcible name changes, loss of language, and relegation to working the worst jobs. Prior immigrant integration into the United States does not begin to account for the descendants of African slaves who were forcibly removed from their homes and in most instances sold into generations of slavery in the Americas by opposing victorious tribal leaders for profit. (Klein, 1999)

Thus, you may state the obvious question: Didn't all of our families' ancestors have to go through some level of ugly second-class status—maybe even something worse than what we see on television today? You may be one of the many people who feel like everyone has to start someplace and most immigrants have to start at the bottom to work their way up as many of our parents who may have toiled in sweatshops, fields of vegetables, shipyards, and meatpacking plants. Well then, you may ask yourself why this situation is different?

Possibly you might know one of the many millennials that supports immigration reform for those teenage immigrant "DREAM'ers" who were brought here as children, grew up next door and shared a locker and a crush on the same Hollywood movie star throughout high school. At the very least it is curious what is happening to children inside as well as at the doorways to our country.

Perhaps you have glanced at the news and noticed the scenes of toddlers, elementary-aged children caged and crowded in tent cities, herded by the hundreds and guarded by uniformed government officers.

I believe that we all realize that the basic discourse of whether or not to build a wall along the southern border of the U.S. does not begin to address *why* we have created concentration camps for kids from Central America, *how* this came about, and *what* we plan to do next. Whether we build a wall or not has no bearing on these inhumane realities.

On a positive note, people from diverse backgrounds and with different political orientations have begun to question our treatment of children in the United States. Additionally, even the average American who may not be a fiscal conservative might wonder if our taxpayer-funded government is using our hard-earned cash for a worthy cause.

Thankfully, there is a small, growing chorus of religious leaders, including the Evangelical Christians, and Catholics who are questioning if we are doing right by our values to shelter, and care for the most vulnerable of immigrants.

Republicans and Democrats are joining with Independent and Libertarian-minded thinkers who have begun to openly question if our haphazard treatment of children is possibly the most glaring example that our sprawling government is truly out of touch with the American spirit in the 21st century.

Americans from many different walks of life are finding a common concern for the treatment of immigrant children. Many, like me, believe that this issue will define "America" because our humanity is at stake. I urge you to please read on and inform yourself of the facts through stories of real children along with references to facts from both sides of the political aisle, including official government sources.

Who are these children who have become to be known as the so-called "DREAM'ers?" Most DREAM'ers were brought to the U.S. by their parents or arrived alone. They had no part in the decision as to where they should grow up. Their situation is different from adults because they cannot advocate for themselves.

If you have ever had a dream that turned from ultimate happiness to a spiraling nightmare, then you know it is time to wake up and look around the room to make sure that we are still in one piece.

PROLOGUE

The Search for Truth:
U.S. Meddling in Latin America

Every U.S. President has intervened in Latin American nations. The unintended consequence of this intervention is the migration of children and families from Central America to the United States for the last 40 years.

To understand the crisis of undocumented, or "illegal," mass migration of humanity from the Northern Triangle of Central America (NTCA), which includes El Salvador, Guatemala, and Honduras, we must take note of U.S. history in the region.

Should the United States of America assume some responsibility for the mass migration of children from countries with social, economic, and political unrest? Perhaps well-documented covert actions, imperialism rhetoric from the U.S. helps us to reframe this question as: How much responsibility should the U.S. assume?

President James Monroe, in 1832, stated that Latin America was within the United States' "sphere of influence." Europe was to cease from colonizing and interfering with the region. This concept became known as the Monroe Doctrine.

In 1845, Manifest Destiny, the concept was adopted by the United States. This concept embodies the belief that the U.S. was destined by God to spread its boundaries, as well as its particular form of democracy and economy, from the Atlantic to the Pacific and across the entire North American continent.

The combination of these two concepts has guided U.S. interventionism down to the Panama Canal and beyond into South America. The countries that have felt the brunt of this new form of blessed colonialism are the countries of the NTCA.

El Salvador, Guatemala, and Honduras have endured a long list of direct interventions into their political and economic affairs since the 1800s.

One of the most notorious examples of U.S. intervention was the establishment of a military training school for Latin American soldiers allied with the United States. "The School of the Americas" was first created in Panama in 1946 to continue the official policies that had begun with the Monroe Doctrine and Manifest Destiny. It became commonly referred to as the "School of the Assassins." Today the school is officially called the Western Hemisphere Institute for Security Cooperation (WHINSEC) and is located at Fort Benning near Columbus, Georgia.

This book will focus on the recent past beginning in the 1980s from which tens of thousands of migrants, many of them unaccompanied children, have arrived in the U.S. seeking asylum from the region's sadistic civil wars and pervasive gang violence.

This book takes the position that the U.S. has, in large part, directly caused the migration of children to our Southern Border. The intention was and is to protect and bolster U.S. interests in the region; however, the unintentional outcomes require our attention.

Additional historical references and research can be found on my website at The Search for Truth: U.S. Meddling in Latin America for readers who desire a detailed chronological history starting with the Monroe Doctrine that outlines the U.S. intervention in these sovereign nations. The following is a summary to put the book in this historical perspective.

El Salvador's worst "Decade of Terror" and human rights abuse starts with the assassination of Archbishop Oscar Romero and four American nuns in 1980. Roberto D'Aubuisson, a graduate of the U.S. "School of Assassins," is believed to have ordered Romero's death and is the principal politician who is the proponent of death squads throughout El Salvador's civil war.

In the twelve years that followed, over 75,000 people die in El Salvador, mostly innocent civilians, who were brutally executed by U.S.-trained Salvadoran soldiers. The terror will escalate with the death of six Jesuit priests in 1989 committed by the Atlacatl Battalion, also graduates of the U.S. "School of Assassins."

"Over 1 million became refugees or internally displaced persons. Arbitrary detentions, death squad killings, 'disappearances,' bombardments of urban areas and other acts of brutality directed primarily against civilians were attributed to the Government or to irregular groups that supported or sympathized with it.

FMLN [rebels of the Farabundo Marti National Liberation] were also responsible for murder and violence, assassinating mayors and judges and committing acts of sabotage against electric power stations, telephone and electricity lines, public transport, commercial establishments, and other important community targets." (United Nations 1995, p. 7-8)

Download or read the United Nations El Salvador 1990-1995 (Boutros-Ghali, 1995)

The U.N. intervention in 1990 resulted in the United Nations Observer Mission in El Salvador (ONUSAL), which helped to facilitate formal peace accords in 1992 and observed democratic elections two years later.

This sad period of El Salvador's history is well covered in Myra Gomez' book Human Rights Abuse in Cuba, El Salvador, and Nicaragua: *A Sociological Perspective on Human Rights Abuse.*

Meanwhile, in the neighboring Central American nation of Nicaragua, rebels called the Sandinistas, led by Eden Pastora and Daniel Ortega, overthrow the authoritarian military dictator Anastasio Somoza in 1979. That year, the U.S. completes a delicate transfer of the Panama Canal back to Panama, but the U.S. still controls the waterway.

During the watch of President Ronald Reagan, Central America becomes the "killing field of the 1980s." In Guatemala, 440 Mayan villages of men, women, elderly, and children are annihilated by the Guatemalan army between 1981 and 1983. This era is known as "The Guatemalan Silent Holocaust" as the indigenous Mayans in Guatemala endure torture, sexual violence, genocidal massacres and other crimes against humanity under the dictator Efrain Rios Montt.

In 1981, President Reagan authorized the CIA to help bring arms into El Salvador. That same year, Reagan gave the CIA official authorization to create an anti-Sandinista paramilitary force known as the "Contras" in Nicaragua, earmarking $19 million in special funding. (Gómez, 2003, p.139) (Gilbert, 1988, p.164)

Reagan's order allows the CIA to support the Contras with arms, equipment, and money to overthrow the Sandinistas. The Contras trained and operated out of neighboring Honduras and also used airstrips in El Salvador to carry out their activities in Nicaragua.

That same year in the neighboring nation of El Salvador, the U.S. "School of Assassins" graduates, the Atlacatl Battalion murders 900 men, women and children as they scorch the village of El Mozote to the ground.

Investigative journalist Mark Danner reviewed hundreds of CIA and other government documents to expose the cover-up by the U.S. government of their role in supporting the massacre. See his article "The Truth of El Mozote," The New Yorker. (Danner, 1993).

In 1982, the U.S. Congress passed the first Boland Amendment barring the use of government funds to overthrow the government of Nicaragua or from provoking a war between Honduras and Nicaragua.

The Second Boland Amendment passed by Congress in 1986 loosened the restrictions on the CIA. That same year it was revealed that the U.S. government sold arms to Iran to fund the Contras in Nicaragua. At this time, the CIA acknowledged that there were drug deals between traffickers selling cocaine in the U.S. and the Contras to raise money for the overthrow of the Nicaraguan government during the First Boland Amendment, named for its author Massachusetts Congressman Edward Boland (D).

"There are instances where the CIA did not, in an expeditious or consistent fashion, cut off relationships with individuals supporting the Contra program who were alleged to have engaged in drug trafficking activity or take action to resolve the allegations." (Congressional Hearings, 1998) .

Total Southwest Border Apprehensions

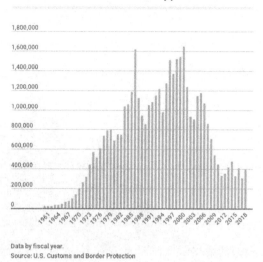

Data by fiscal year.
Source: U.S. Customs and Border Protection

According to the *1999 Statistical Yearbook of the Immigration and Naturalization Services*, VI. ENFORCEMENT, page 3 of that chapter *"Southwest Border apprehensions were an **all-time record 1,615,844 in the fiscal year 1986** and then decreased three consecutive years immediately following enactment of the Immigration Reform and Control Act (IRCA) of 1986.*

If you compare the Southwest Border apprehensions to the total aliens Apprehended on Chart L below from the *Immigration and Naturalization Services, VI, ENFORCEMENT* there is a clear correlation of displaced Latin American people to the Reagan's Administrations activities in the Latin-speaking nations in Central and South American countries.

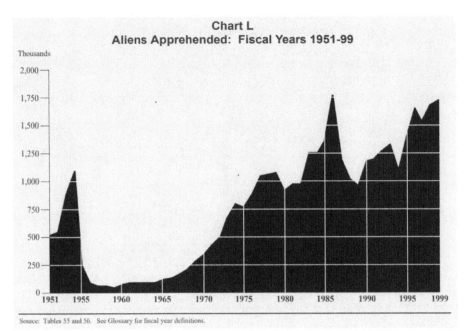

In 1987, the "Espuipulas II Accord" emerged from Costa Rica's president Oscar Arias Sanchez' peace plan in 1987. The accord was signed by the presidents of Guatemala, El Salvador, Honduras, Nicaragua, and Costa Rica. The Norwegian Nobel Peace Prize Committee believed the Esquipulas II Accord would open the way for hope and a prosperous future which could replace the years of bloody conflict with an open, trusting peaceful society in Central America.

In 1990, the U.S. Congress passed a quiet law that established the Special Immigrant Juvenile Status (SIJS) for immigrant children who suffered abuse, abandonment, or neglect by one or both of their parents. This SIJS benefit would become especially significant in 2014 during President Obama's administration.

In 1991 through 1992, President George H. Bush designated nationals of El Salvador living in the U.S. without permission the protection of Temporary Protected Status (TPS) as the country recovers from their protracted civil war.

In 1993, President Bill Clinton promoted legislation and signed a bill to construct a wall along our Southern border between Tijuana, Mexico and San Ysidro, California for 13 miles at the cost of $39 million.

In 1994, Mexico, Canada, and the U.S. sign the North American Free Trade Agreement or NAFTA. The agreement hurts small-plot farmers in Mexico who cannot compete with the cheap U.S. mass-production prices and government subsidies of U.S. farmers. U.S. corporations begin leaving the United States territory and building massive factories South of the Border as a result of NAFTA. Later the U.S. signs a similar agreement with Central American nations called CAFTA.

Image Source: © Barry Deutsch | Barry Deutsch

In 1996, the Oslo Accords were signed in Guatemala ending the 36-year civil war. However, the broker of the peace accords, a Catholic Bishop Juan Jose Gerardi was murdered with a cinder block at his home in 1998. A graduate of the U.S. "School of Assassins," Colonel Byron Lima Estrada was convicted of the murder in 2001.

The quick stroke of President Clinton's pen solidified the Illegal Immigration Reform and Immigrant Responsibility Act (IIRAIRA) in 1996. This Clinton-era bill criminalizes immigrants and put into place permanent bars for immigrants starting in 1997.

Those Clinton-era laws resulted in countless separations of families from their U.S. citizen spouses, children and parents for seemingly harmless acts such as returning to the home country after being in the U.S. for a year or more without permission. Minors over age 16, who in error, believed that they were U.S. citizens by birth would now be permanently barred from receiving legal status.

In 1997, Congress passed the Nicaraguan And Cuban Adjustment and Relief Act (NACARA) allowing Nicaraguans, Cubans, Guatemalans, and Salvadorans the ability to pursue legal permanent residence instead of awaiting Asylum.

In 1998 Hurricane "Mitch" hits Honduras and Nicaragua with devastating force. President Clinton authorizes Temporary Protected Status for their nationals living in the U.S. while the countries rebuild. Later President Trump tried to end this designation in 2019, but a Federal Judge has blocked the termination pending a lawsuit.

In 2000, Alfonso Portillo became president of Guatemala. Later in 2010, he is arrested for embezzlement for money laundering of $2.5 million through U.S. banks, later is freed from a U.S. jail.

In 2000, about 750,000 Mexicans cross without permission at our Southern Border when former president Bill Clinton was in power. That year US/Mexico border apprehensions reach 1,643,679; which is a record for the most apprehensions in history.

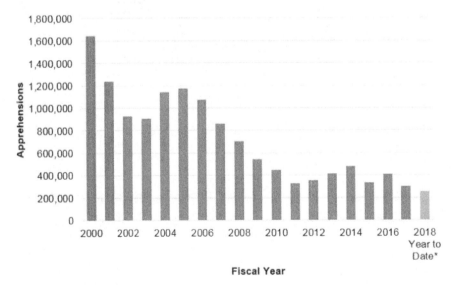

Sources: U.S. Border Patrol, "U.S. Border Patrol Monthly Apprehensions (FY 2000 - FY 2017)," accessed Feb 4, 2019, www.cbp.gov/sites/default/files/assets/documents/2017-Dec/BP%20Total%20Monthly%20Apps%20by%20Sector%20and%20Area%2C%20FY2000-FY2017.pdf; U.S. Customs and Border Protection (CBP), "Southwest Border Migration FY2018," updated June 6, 2018, https://www.cbp.gov/newsroom/stats/sw-border-migration.

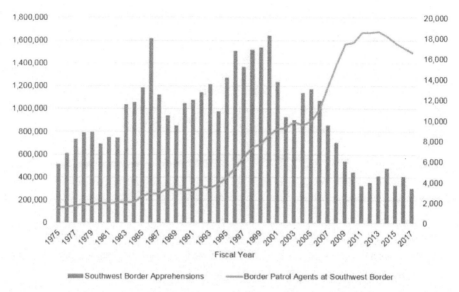

Fiscal Year

▬▬ Southwest Border Apprehensions   ▬▬Border Patrol Agents at Southwest Border

Sources: CBP, "United States Border Patrol Southwest Family Unit Subject and Unaccompanied Alien Children Apprehensions Fiscal Year 2016," updated October 18, 2016, www.cbp.gov/newsroom/stats/southwest-border-unaccompanied-children/fy-2016; CBP, "Southwest Border Migration FY2017;" CBP, "Southwest Border Migration FY2018."

The George W. Bush-era began with hope for Latinx immigrant children who were raised in the U.S. as the DREAM (Development, Relief, and Education for Alien Minors) Act was first introduced into Congress and co-sponsored by Utah Republican Senator Orin Hatch in 2001. It would provide a pathway to Legal Permanent Residence for nearly 1 million immigrant children and young adults. It failed more than seven (7) times in Congress and still has not been passed as of September 2019.

In early 2001, President Bush, like his father did in 1991, provided Temporary Protected Status to Salvadorans living without permission in the United States while El Salvador recovered from a devastating earthquake. President Trump later sought to end this TPS designation in 2019, and it is currently in litigation in Federal Court.

The Terrorist Attack on New York in 2001 prompted the formation of the Department of Homeland Security after almost 3,000 American lives were lost in attacks by Middle Eastern men who had entered legally as students and tourists. They had overstayed their visas approved by the U.S. Department of State and the Immigration and Naturalization Service.

Soon after the commencement of military action sending U.S. armed forces to Afghanistan for Operation Enduring Freedom in 2001, President Bush and Congress sought to reform the executive agencies in charge of the U.S. immigration laws.

Attention went immediately to our Southern Border although none of the perpetrators were alleged to have come into the U.S. through the land border with Mexico and all had arrived legally with the approval of the U.S. government.

The Homeland Security Act of 2002 had a massive impact on immigration. The American Immigration Lawyers Association Section-by-Section Summary covers all the aspects clearly and can be read on their website.

This Act resulted in a complete reorganization of federal agencies over immigration and the beginning of the strict implementation of the Clinton-era laws that turned immigrants, adults and children alike, into criminals overnight for minor actions.

A little-known provision in the Homeland Security Act of 2002 designated immigrant children who arrived without a parent in the United States as Unaccompanied Alien Children, or UACs. The Act provided for the placement of such children in foster care through the newly created Department of Homeland Security and the existing U.S. Department of Health and Human Services (HHS).

To complicate this huge reboot of U.S. immigration enforcement between three gargantuan federal bureaucracies, Bush called for domestic enforcement by the military. In 2006, President Bush gave a speech about "illegal immigration" and called for the short-term deployment of up to 6,000 National Guard troops in a supporting role for the Border Patrol along the U.S.-Mexico Border.

In 2006, President Bush signed legislation to construct a "wall" along 700 miles of the Southern border and to provide for a "virtual barrier" along the entire 2,000 miles of the border with Mexico.

David Martin of The Migration Policy Institute (MPI) wrote an interesting article titled Immigration Policy and the Homeland Security Act Reorganization: An Early Agenda for Practical Improvements, discussing his concerns:

"Among the key points of concerns related to this massive reorganization are: the unified immigration policy structure; the uncoordinated legal advice between various agencies; the needless creation of the Ombudsman Office; the respective authorities of the Attorney General and the Secretary

of Homeland Security; and the extensive powers over immigration matters vested to the Attorney General." (Martin, 2003)

The last concern, "the extensive powers over immigration matters vested to the Attorney General," has proved to be epic in 2018 and 2019, allowing President Trump's administration to direct his many Attorney General appointees to announce a "Zero Tolerance" policy for re-entry into the U.S. of immigrants.

Furthermore, President Trump has utilized this power to severely limit the availability of Political Asylum for immigrant children who fear persecution and torture in their home countries. Like Presidents Bush and Obama, Trump has directed the agencies under his control to focus their heavy hand on immigrant children at the Southern Border who are from the Northern Triangle of Guatemala, El Salvador, and Honduras.

In 2008, Honduras democratically elected president, Manuel Zelaya allied with the Leftist government of Venezuela and implements social programs to address poverty, education, and health in Honduras. Later in 2009, the recently elected President Obama tasks Secretary of State Hillary Clinton to protect U.S. interests in Honduras.

The Bush Era ends in 2009, with the notorious T. Don Hutto Detention Facility scandal near Austin, Texas. The allegations echoing dark deeds, stark conditions, and sexual abuse of immigrant women with small children placed there by Immigration Customs and Enforcement (ICE). The allegations would not be the last of accusations that would extend to physical and sexual abuse of immigrant children in private-run detention centers.

In 2009, the U.S. backed a military coup d'etat to remove Zelaya as President and Honduras quickly becomes the country with the highest murder rate in the world by 2011 through 2013 due to the destabilization and spread of U.S.-based criminal syndicates the Mara Salvatrucha, or MS13 the most notorious street gang in the Americas expanding their influence from El Salvador into Honduras.

In 2011, the U.S. facilitated the election of Otto Perez Molina as president of Guatemala as the Mexican drug cartel "Los Zetas" expands into Guatemala. The Zetas are formed and founded by ex-military soldiers trained by the United States.

In 2012, Latin America suffered 134,519 homicides which is about 31% of the world's total murders.

In 2013, former Guatemalan dictator Efrain Rios Montt was convicted of genocide for the massacres of Mayan villages in the early '80s.

In 2014, a "surge" of over 60,000 Unaccompanied Alien Children or UACs arrive at the U.S. Southern border with Mexico. Most of these "surge" children are from Honduras. Many are from Guatemala, El Salvador, and Mexico. President Obama moves quietly and swiftly to deport the children from nations in the Northern Triangle of Central America.

Many of former President Obama's policies towards the swift detention and removal of children did not come to light until President Trump re-employed and expanded federal enforcement to detain and remove children at the border and inside the U.S.

oxymoron

Particularly, President Trump has sought to terminate Obama's popular executive policy of Deferred Action for Childhood Arrivals (DACA) implemented in 2012.

That policy allowed children who had arrived at a young age and completed schooling in the U.S. to have their deportation "deferred" for an unspecified time. DACA is not the much sought after DREAM Act that gives these children, known as DREAM'ers their opportunity for permanent legal status.

Since 2016, President Trump has dedicated much of his efforts to construct a massive barrier "wall" on the Southern Border as he singles-out Central American refugees to limit their access to U.S. political asylum protection.

In 2017, Latin America's murder rate accounted for 38% of all homicides in the world. Thousands of fatherless children and families continue to flee the Northern Triangle for sanctuary in the U.S.

In 2017, President Trump authorized the military to send troops to the border. In 2018, migrant caravans with thousands of refugee's gathered for safety and started walking towards Mexico on their way to the U.S. They are fleeing the turmoil in Latin America.

In 2019, in response to the migrant caravans, President Trump orders Border Patrol, ICE, and the Mexican government to keep Central American refugees including men, women, and children in camps on the Mexican side of the border through a Migrant Protection Protocol, known as the "Wait in Mexico" policy.

Over 50,000 Central American refugees are waiting 6 to 9 months at major port entries along the Southern Border. Over 400,000 unaccompanied minors and families with children were apprehended so far in 2019 according to Kao and Lu's article How Trump's Policies are Leaving Thousands of Asylum Seekers Waiting in Mexico published in The New York Times August 18, 2019.

There are many reasons that Latinx children have decided to flee to the United States. U.S. foreign policy doctrine to protect national interests have created migration from the chaos of war, clandestine interference with sovereign government and rampant abuse by corrupt Central American governments or groups that those governments are unwilling or unable to control.

Arturo Jiménez

INTRODUCTION

Victims of Wars: The River of Lost Children

In 2019 the asylum seekers from the violent Northern Triangle of El Salvador, Guatemala, and Honduras poured across the U.S. border through Mexico seeking sanctuary. Flooding our system with a mass of humanity and our officials with a mountain of paperwork, blocking our straining courts with mounting dockets of humanitarian cases.

The trickle of asylum seekers began with the secret CIA Guatemalan Coup in 1954 to sterilize the "Red Infection." The stream gained strength in the '70s with the rise to power of the Medellín cartel in Columbia helped by U.S. covert operations.

El Salvador's twelve-year war of the '80s ravaged the population claiming the lives of seventy-five thousand (75,000) men, women, and children, and creating over one million refugees.

The river of humanity seeking asylum began to flow with the civil unrest of the '80s, and the so-called "War on Drugs" in Latin America led by the U.S. President Ronald Reagan's Administration.

Immigration swelled by decades of civil war and U.S. intervention in the violent Northern Triangle of El Salvador, Guatemala, and Honduras, bordered by Nicaragua to the south with Costa Rica and Panama, and the shoulder nations of South America, Ecuador, Columbia, and Venezuela.

The U.S. trained and backed "freedom fighters," unleashed the dogs of war, violence, corruption, kidnapping, rape, rampant crime, and human trafficking in the violent northern triangle area of Central America. U.S. intervention in multiple wars has caused a flood of families of refugees and asylum seekers, many of them innocent children who fled north to seek the shelter and safety of the United States of America.

"By 1986 Southwest Border apprehensions were at a record 1,615,844." According to the 1999 Statistical Yearbook of the Immigration and Naturalization Services, Chapter VI. ENFORCEMENT, page 3.

President Obama and Secretary of State Hillary Clintons' staunch support of the 2009 Honduran military uprising was a U.S.-led strategy that manipulated dissidents, people in business, and the Hondurans, to remove the democratically elected president Zelaya and install a military dictator.

Hillary Clinton wrote in her hardcover autobiography, Hard Choices, published in 2014.

"We strategized on a plan to restore order in Honduras and ensure that free and fair elections could be held quickly and legitimately, which would render the question of Zelaya moot and give the Honduran people a chance to choose their future,"

It is interesting to note that that the quote and its associated discussion disappeared from paperback addition, during editing!

In 2014 the number of unaccompanied children asylum seekers apprehended on our southern borders surged dramatically to sixty-seven thousand three hundred and thirty-nine (67,339). Children from the violent Northern Triangle, El Salvador, Guatemala, and Honduras joined hands with Mexican toddlers desperate for shelter from gang violence, organized crime, and crippling poverty began the two thousand three hundred and fifty-odd (2,350) mile march north for life to the United States. (Renwick, 2018)

The United Nations High Commission for Refugees outlined the issue with first-hand accounts of refugees fleeing in their report, *Women on the Run* (United Nations High Commissioner for Refugees, 2015)

"Tens of thousands of women – traveling alone or together with their children or other family members – are fleeing a surging tide of violence in El Salvador, Honduras, Guatemala, and parts of Mexico."

Few listened or even read the dramatic heart-wrenching *Women on the Run* report and account of children caught in the detention cages, their terrifying stories of the purgatory inflicted on the migrants who help clarify why many have been forced to flee their homelands.

Migrants flee from their oppressive governments, transnational criminal organizations, rape, assault, extortion, family disappearances, and death threats. Migrants endure murder or family abductions often unable to comprehend or repress the violence they are left with no choice but to run for their lives. To flee the living nightmare of reality.

"El Salvador, Guatemala, and Honduras have consistently ranked among the most violent countries in the world, according to the World Economic Forum."

The long trek to the U.S. is an ordeal for adults who are exploited by unscrupulous "coyotes," beaten, raped, and too often killed along the way. The journey to safety is a journey through hell, imagine that journey for a child.

Imagine your child, grandchild, niece or nephew walking from the jungles of Central America across multiple countries, with strange foreign languages, violent thugs, a journey full of antagonist's wrought with danger. This description provides the visual of an epic fantasy nightmare movie like "Wrong Turn" or "Vacancy," the nightmare is real.

Like the movies when at last sanctuary has been grasped and the heroine is about to succeed, we have a twist of fate. The dreamer searching for sanctuary is caged and shackled, humiliated as a slave of a political and judicial system that has lost its way, treated without dignity or humanity in a living nightmare.

This book will explain the untold humanitarian story of children refugees from Central America. Refugees from a war that has been waged by many presidents both American and South American on immigrant children the investigation of the cause, and the search for a solution.

President Obama's Administration flooded by unaccompanied child refugees, swiftly but quietly enacted a deliberate policy to deport a vast majority of these children back to their countries of origin. The plan was intended to send a message to the region now known as the Northern Triangle.

That message was to tell the parents and government officials directly "not to send your kids to the United States and to take care of your problems in your own country."

The policy did not work, and all three Central American countries continued to send what the 43rd president, Bush administration disparagingly labeled "Unaccompanied Alien Children" (officially referred to as the UAC's). Also, a growing number of single-parent and two-parent families began to flee to the United States to escape burgeoning criminal "gangs" that are unrestrained by or, as some allege are in collusion with, the governments of those countries.

Obama's successor President Donald Trump continued the policy albeit in a more celebratory manner. President Trump's personally making the situation a centerpiece to his "Zero Tolerance" policy. What has become well known during the Trump administration are the shady detention camps first implemented by Obama. Many of these camps furnishings feature canopy tents draped over cages of children. Trump just reinstated the tent city slums, the inhumane detention camps.

Humanitarian Rights Abuse Closes Tent City

Image Source: 3TV/CBS 5

Historically controversial tent detention facilities in the U.S. have been shut down for humanitarian and cost reasons.

Tent city's closure saving Maricopa County millions (Gorden, 2018)

Paul Penzone, the Maricopa County Sheriff, announced his decision to close Tent City Tuesday. "Closing "Tent City Jail," the Lightning rod of controversy will save taxpayers millions." FOX 10's Matt Rodewald and Matt Galka reported, in team coverage. Watch the video

"Inmates were often subjected to extreme heat; conditions some called inhumane. Sheriff Penzone labeled them as "unacceptable" Wednesday. "Which leads to certain circumstances such as health issues, safety issues and sometimes lawsuits," Penzone said.

It is interesting to note that after 24 years of operation, one of the reasons for the closure is operation costs of the facility versus a standard facility.

If these types of facilities are not regarded as humanitarian for our incarcerated adults, why are these facilities acceptable for Children? Why are we putting children in them?

If tent cities abuse the human rights of U.S. Criminals, what scars do they leave on innocent minors, children taken prisoner, kidnaped from their parents, and families?

What image of America does this portray?

"There is still no plan on how to reunite parents with children." (Merchant, 2018).

The real question is, why were they separated against their will in the first place? The action of separation is believed by many to be tantamount to kidnapping and abduction.

Sofi, a 3-year-old baby girl, traveling with her grandmother who was seeking asylum, was ripped from adult care at a port of entry in El Paso, Texas, last June. The Customs and Border Protection official Brian Hastings in a hearing before the Senate Homeland Security and Governmental Affairs

Committee on June 26, 2019, could not determine if she was a "criminal or national security threat." Seriously!

Little Sofi was separated from her grandmother and family for forty-seven days until the Trump administration, forced by court order, to reunite them.

As Representative Jerry Nadler stated during that hearing, "deporting a parent without their child is literal kidnapping." (Stahl, 2019). Why is separating a family from their children without their permission any different?

If you or I stole a child from our neighbors, we would be kidnapping. Was Little Sofi in need of protection? No. That child had the protection of her grandmother.

Image Source: Photo by Mike Blake/Reuters

"Immigrant children housed in a tent encampment, shown walking in single file at the facility near the Mexican border in Tornillo, Texas, on June 19, 2018."

Trump says asylum seekers will live in tent cities before their day in court.

"We're catching. We're not releasing... We are going to put tents up all over the place... We are not going to build structures and spend all of this, hundreds of millions of dollars," he said... "We are going to have tents... They are going to be very nice, and if they don't get asylum, they get out." Mr. Trump stated during an interview on **Monday** night on <u>The Ingraham Angle 10/29/18 | Fox News Today, October 29, 2018.</u>

President Trump's nationalist dictatorial "Zero Tolerance" Policy upped the ante on detained families and openly separated parents and children into different sections of these camps and in many instances, into completely different facilities.

Most recently, Trump's focus has been to prevent caravans of tens of thousands of migrants from the Northern Triangle from entering the U.S. border completely.

The "Zero Tolerance" Policy *"Stiffened U.S. Approach to Illegal Border Crossings Will Separate Families" Under the new policy, adults may be detained while asylum cases are considered... The policy punishes illegal aliens who arrive in the U.S. illegally and deters migrants from applying for asylum."* (Caldwell, 2018).

President Trump orders 5,200 active-duty troops to US-Mexico Border *(Copp, 2018).*

It appears that Trump's ordering of the National Guard to protect the border was an echo from 2006 when President Bush gave a speech that called for the short-term deployment of up to 6,000 National Guard troops in a supporting role along the U.S.-Mexico border.

The 5,200 active-duty troops would join about 2,100 National Guard forces sent by Texas, California, New Mexico, and Arizona earlier this year to bolster the border.

In defiance of court orders that prohibit long-term detention of children or families; President Trump's administration had ordered troops to "harden" the border. Orders were issued to use lethal force on men, women, and children "If necessary" harkening back to the *Wild West* when territorial governors ordered troops with bayonets to police elderly and children of the so-called *Indians* of the plains.

The Trump administration has fingered Flores v. Reno, or the "Flores Settlement," as its reason for "forced separations of parents from children" to prosecute them. The "Flores Settlement," provides a twenty-day limit for detaining children and requires the government to release children from immigration detention without unnecessary delay to their parents, other adult relatives, or licensed programs.

The Trump administration claims they are unable to detain families together, families who have parents who are in the process of being criminally prosecuted for illegal entry. This claim means that the Trump administration believe they must separate the children and send them to the Department of Health and Human Services as "unaccompanied alien children."

The processing system to help these children become legal permanent residents is backlogged and broken. Customs and Border Protection officials are making decisions under duress; their patience and professionalism stretched to the breaking point.

President Trump's wall is -0.01% of the budget. Why not use the dollars to solve the problem? Five billion dollars will go a long way to help solve the backlog and the reason that these children came in the first place.

While both Democrats and Republicans engage in a media war to blame the other party and demonize either side, 14,000 immigrant children who have arrived alone without parents remain in camps and institutions that now spread across the United States. These children are the victims of the war on immigrant children.

It is time for us to stop treating children as pawns in the game of politics.

The humans on the ground enforcing these laws trying to act humanely within an inherently inhumane system

Image Source: © Peter Lucking | contentbrandingsolutions.com

CHAPTER 1

Does Our Country Deport Little Children?

It was the first year into the 21st Century for me as a young immigration attorney, and a typical day at the U.S. Immigration Court in Denver, Colorado. About forty immigrants were in the waiting room. Six or seven of them were able to hire a private attorney. A few others were able to be added onto a long waiting list for a volunteer advocate by applying through one of the few nonprofit groups in the Denver area.

I was one of those attorneys sitting in the waiting room with my client. I was discussing legal strategies for immigrants detained without bond with a friend and mentor named Jim Salvator.

Jim Salvator was about my father's age at the time he had long hair tied back in a hurried ponytail. He wore a bolo tie and cowboy boots. He was also waiting at court with his client.

Most of the immigrants waiting for court appearances were adults; some were accompanied by their families. A few had brought their small children, who were born in the U.S. Most of them were from Mexico as they sat stoically barely blinking as they waited their turn with the patience of an owl.

At dusk, the children began singing a nursery rhyme in English. "Ring-a-ring o' roses, A pocket full of posies, A-tishoo! A-tishoo! We all fall down."

There were a couple of Central American folks—the Guatemalans with their round Mayan faces, and Salvadorans with their bravado demeanor. Also, there was one African couple, a father, and son from Nepal, and a middle eastern man. There was a worried murmur of conversations mostly concerning the fate of each immigrant with the judge.

Suddenly, all song and conversations stopped, and everyone turned to see two tall, menacing burly immigration agents walking on both sides of a terrified child in a baggy oversized orange jail jumpsuit.

The boy in the orange jumpsuit had to be no older than 7 or 8 years old. The young boy was shackled like a slave, his feet in chains that dragged across the floor and his hands were in cuffs. He was shaking, his demeanor dejected. Wide eyes full of fear and sadness, red with tears stared pleading as he shuffled along.

We all watched in disbelief as he was shoved into the courtroom ahead of everyone by the armed broad-shouldered immigration agents.

"No one allowed in. The courtroom will be closed for this proceeding," announced the court guard as he unlocked the door and held it open for the agents dressed in the unmistakable green INS uniforms.

The year was 2001, and the Department of Homeland Security had not yet come into existence.

I, along with almost everyone else, was in shock and did not know what to do or say. The child was alone in a living nightmare. I had a general feeling of helplessness watching that frightened little boy, shuffling through the waiting room with his head down. I was sitting right in front of where they passed, so I had an unobstructed view of his little brown eyes, large, red, and sad.

Most assuredly, I thought this little boy or any boy or girl did not deserve this harsh treatment. I thought of my children, what would I do for them in this situation?

My client, a middle-aged woman in her thirties, a mother of children, broke the silence.

"Que va a pasar a este niño?" She asked in Spanish. She wanted to know what would happen, but I did not know what to tell her.

I was numb with shock, images of slaves flashed chillingly through my mind. Then something remarkable happened.

Jim Salvator stood up and said: "Let's go see what's going on."

He rose and strode over to the court door, and I followed him inside. The judge was in his black robe and was sitting atop on a raised wooden deck that looked like an elegant boat's deck.

The little boy was sitting, at the table for immigrants, in front of the judge along with the two guards. At another table, the INS government attorney was in the middle of his one-sided argument to deport the youngster.

A wooden gate separated us closed to the front of the courtroom.

The judge interrupted the government attorney, covered his recording microphone with his hand, and told us, "I'm sorry, but no one is allowed in here during this proceeding. You'll have to wait outside."

My friend Jim politely, but sternly asked the judge, "Does this young man have an attorney?"

The judge paused for a few seconds. Perhaps he was surprised by the question or impressed by Jim's insistence to obtain an answer. By the time the judge answered "no," Jim had made his way through the gate and up next to the boy who was still shyly looking at the ground.

"Then I will represent him," Jim stated.

The Judge again hesitated as the large guards looked at the INS attorney, and they all looked at each other, not knowing what to do. The boy had legal representation that the court would otherwise not have provided, even though he was a minor.

Jim sat down at the table. When the judge finally gathered his wits, he ordered me to leave the courtroom.

The other attorneys were gathered just outside the door of the courtroom and stopped me like a group of reporters asking their questions all at once.

"What's going on? What happened? What is Jim doing in there? Was that little kid really in chains?"

I explained to them that Jim told the judge that he was representing the boy.

We were all very proud of our colleague for standing up and offering to provide a frightened minor with representation and hope.

Jim told me later that he requested removal of the shackles and cuffs from the boy. He was, after all, harmless and a minor. The Judge agreed.

All four came out of the courtroom as the agents whisked the youngster and his new attorney downstairs.

Although I had been practicing immigration law for over two years at that point, I had never seen anything like that poor little abandoned fellow being brought in like a dangerous criminal.

I had no idea that ICE would treat children in such a manner so far from the border. We were well into the interior of our country—in Denver, Colorado, for God's sakes!

That day I learned a valuable lesson about the treatment of children by immigration authorities. Note, that would not be the first or last time that my friend and mentor Jim Salvator would show me how to step up and be an advocate.

This book is about the children stuck in the limbo of our immigration laws, broken families, and the political battle between the two major political parties of the nation.

Do We Deport Little Children? Yes!

President Obama Started using wide-scale detention, deportation, and removal of immigrant families back to their countries of origin in 2014. President Trump "Zero Tolerance" policies are a harsher continuation of those set up by his predecessor.

It is important to understand the legal implications of removal versus return.

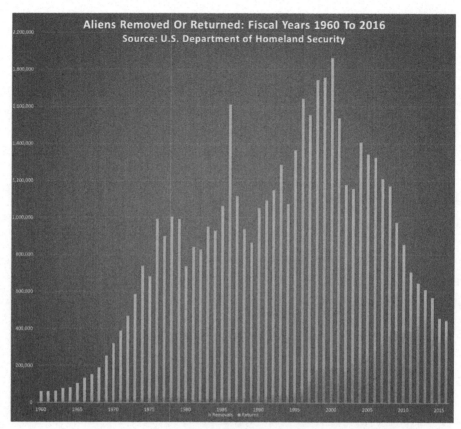

Aliens Removed Or Returned: Fiscal Years 1960 To 2016
Source: U.S. Department of Homeland Security

Data: (DHS D. o., 2016) Graphic: © Peter Lucking | ContentBrandingSolutions.com

Removal is "the compulsory and confirmed movement of an inadmissible or deportable alien out of the United States based on an order of removal," according to the Federal Government definition.

Removals have consequences that hold the individual legally accountable for their actions.

Removal has key legal implications; an automatic five- or 10-year ban on applying for re-entry into the country. If the individual is apprehended a second time, they could face criminal incarceration and a 20-year or lifetime ban from re-entry.

Return, or "the confirmed movement of an inadmissible or deportable alien out of the United States not based on an order of removal," according to the Federal Government definition. Formerly referred to as a "voluntary departure."

Return is far more lenient, giving you time to "Pack up and go" and enabling very short restrictions to re-entry, or no restrictions at all if one has been in the U.S. for less than 180 days.

National Public Radio (NPR) incorrectly reported, "Obama Administration Deported Record 1.5 Million People... in his first term" (Dade, 2012) spreading a confusing rumor, which was spun incorrectly by many political media reporters. The ICE report that is referenced in this article clearly shows arrests and removals, not deportations.

Counter to widespread belief Obama Does Not Hold the Record for Deportations! But Obama's Record is Much Worse.

The DHS chart shown below indicates this is incorrect President Clinton tops this number by a large margin at 6,922,376 (DHS, 2016), the total deportations (The number of Removals + Returns = Deportations).

- Deportations by President is the total number of removals and returns:
- President Ronald Reagan 1981 – 1989 (R) Total deportations 8, 275,853
- President George H. W. Bush 1989 – 1993 (R) Total deportations 4,161,683
- President Clinton 1993 – 2001 (D) Holds the record for total deportations 12,290, 905
- Bill hit the jackpot in 2000 with 1,864,343. I knew there was a reason I did not trust him.
- President George W. Bush 2001 - 2009 (R) Total deportations 10,328,850
- President Obama (D) 2009 – 2016 (D) Total deportations 5,281,115

The Obama Administration forcefully "Removed," (Removals) 1,574,544 people in his first term, and yes that is a record.

- **Obama holds the record for "Removals," 3,094,208** compulsory deportable aliens out of the United States between 2008 to 2016. For political reasons, he started to scale back enforcement of "Removals" in the last two years of his administration to position the Democrats in a better position for the election.

Obama holds the record for "Removals," that carries a more severe legal penalty!

- **Deportation Separated Thousands of U.S.-Born Children From Parents In 2013:** ICE in April reports to the Senate Appropriations Committee and the Senate Judiciary Committee, as required by law confirmed the authenticity of the two reports, which layout 72,410 removals of immigrants who said they had one or more U.S.-born children in 2013.

- Ten thousand seven hundred (10,700) parents had no criminal convictions, although they may have fit other ICE priorities for removal, according to the reports.

Read the ICE Report Deportation of Aliens Claiming U.S.-Born children

Ask yourself, what are the "Build a wall" and Trade Wars truly about?

Under President Trump's executive order; it is much easier to separate and deport families and children, and it meets his personal nationalistic and philosophical goals.

- President Trump signs an executive order to rescind the 1997 federal court decision under the "Flores Settlement" that strictly limits the government's ability to keep children in immigration detention.

The Flores Settlement requires the federal government to do two human things:

- Place children with a close relative or family friend "without unnecessary delay," rather than keeping them in custody;

- Keep immigrant children who are in custody in the "least restrictive conditions" possible.

Download and read the pdf of JENNY LISETTE FLORES, et al., Plaintiffs v JANET RENO, Attorney General of the United States, et al., Defendants. Case No. CV 85-4544-RJK(Px) STIPULATED SETTLEMENT AGREEMENT

Trump's administration site the Flores v. Reno, or the "Flores Settlement," as the reason the government is "forced" to separate parents from their children to prosecute them.

Recently under Trump's direction, ICE has relaunched raids across the U.S. targeting undocumented migrant parents of the DREAM'ers and children who are not eligible to stay.

Though millions of undocumented immigrants live in the U.S., it should be noted that the targets of the most recent raids by ICE are primarily from the Violent Northern Triangle of Central America.

Also, Trump is trying to send a message to El Salvador, Guatemala, and Honduras to deter asylum seekers from coming. His psychological message is simple, to remove all hope of asylum.

President Obama was faced with the "surge," a genuine increase in children and families coming to the US. Trump, on the other hand, decided that the decreasing numbers of apprehensions at the Southwest border were unacceptable. The evidence is clear the U.S. Customs and Border Protection, 2019 statistics show a decline in "Immigrant Apprehensions / Inadmissible FY2014- FY2018" under Trump. Trump has waged a war of "Zero Tolerance" attrition on immigrants. Trumps iron fist has hit immigrants harder than Obama.

The "Surge" 2012- 2014 - America's Child-Migrant Crisis

The Child-Migration "surge" began statistically in 2012 and coincided with the Los Zetas Cartel establishment of an iron grip with "Los Kaibiles," deserters from the Guatemalan special forces in northern triangle and Mexico.

The "Surge" of unaccompanied minors had to travel 2,400 miles from the vicious Northern Triangle to the Southwest border.

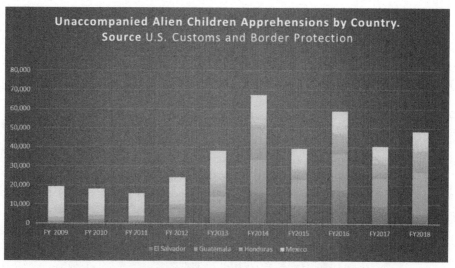

Data: (DHS D. o., 2016) + (DHS, 2018) Graphic: © Peter Lucking | ContentBrandingSolutions.com

When the U.S. Citizenship and Immigration Services (USCIS), began accepting applications for the program on under the Deferred Action for Childhood Arrivals (DACA) program August 15, 2012, many children in the Northern Triangle decided to make the journey to escape, poverty, the gang violence, and political upheaval.

We know the circumstances leading up to the surge of migrants, In August of 2014, more than 60,000 children from three countries: El Salvador, Honduras, and Guatemala, Central America's Violent Northern Triangle, arrived at the Southern Border of the United States fleeing criminal "drug gangs," violence, corruption, kidnapping, rape, rampant crime, human trafficking, and other unimaginable human rights abuses.

The U.S. Merida/CARSI Initiative

The U.S. Merida/CARSI Initiative began 2008 to fight the war on drugs in Mexico and Central America countries of Belize, Costa Rica, El Salvador, Guatemala, Honduras, Nicaragua, and Panama.

The initiative aimed at combating drug trafficking at its source, and all its associated business from child pornography to trafficking and prostitution. The retaliatory violence from the "gangs," in 2009 that the war on drugs caused and displaced many of the people of those regions.

By 2012 the U.S. Merida/CARSI Initiative was a disaster, government forces clashed violently with drug cartels leaving innocent families dead in the wake of gunfire.

In Mexico, the government forces and the cartels clashed. Two cartels particularly affect people's lives in the period leading up to the Child-Migration "surge." *La Familia* and the *Gulf Cartel* retaliation impacts many communities in Mexico.

La Familia Michoacán labeled as "the most violent criminal organization in Mexico" by former Mexican Attorney General Eduardo Medina Moracatches, operates in the region of Guerrero, Guanajuato, and Mexico states to the west of Mexico City. (Posey, 2009)

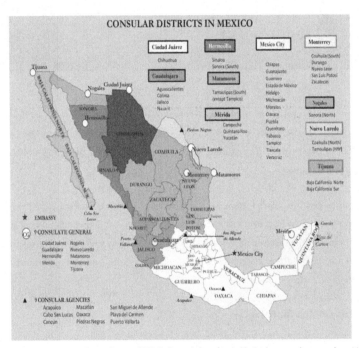

The Gulf Cartel was considered to be the most powerful Cartel in Mexico at this time with strong ties to *Los Zetas* to the south and was trying to extend its presence south into the Northern Triangle of Central America with violence that catches the reeling war-torn population of Guatemala off guard.

The Los Zetas Cartel established an iron grip with "Los Kaibiles," deserters from the Guatemalan special forces who were previously trained by the U.S. military (Morris, 2017). With this criminal muscle, they force their way South controlling Mexico's eastern coast down to the Yucatan Peninsula with a firm foothold in Guatemala.

The cartel spearheads this infiltration from a training camp in Guatemala at Ixican just south of the Mexican state of Chiapas.

Guatemala Zeta Camp Raid

"Military and law enforcement authorities in Guatemala conducted a raid on March 27 on a suspected Zeta camp near the Mexican Border, seizing an assortment of firearms, ammunition and more than 500 40 mm grenades." (Stratfor, 2009)

In 2009 Latin America Became the Murder Capital of The World and a War Zone!

By 2010 Guatemalan people were starving, on the verge of social, economic collapse where aid was flowing into the country from various nations, including the U.S.

The U.S. Merida/CARSI Initiative unleashed the dogs of war on the cartels as innocent bystanders were caught in the crossfire.

By 2011 Los Zetas was the largest drug cartel in Mexico, operating in more than half of the country's thirty-two states, recruiting across the Latin Nations and from gangs in U.S. prisons. The Washington Times article Ruthless Mexican drug cartel recruiting in the U.S.; Los Zetas looks to prisons; street gangs makes an interesting read.

Los Zetas is well organized, utilizing extorsion, kidnapping and an illicit underground railroad for the movement of drugs and migrant smuggling. With the trained logistical knowledge to turn the dribble of migrants into a cloud of diesel-belching big-rig truckloads who pay as much as $30,000 per head.

The Los Zetas prey on migrant families, children, and mothers from the violent nations of Central America, Guatemala, El Salvador, and Honduras, the "Northern Triangle." Migrants who try to operate outside of this system are often held for ransom or worse, put into the sex-slave trade.

Many immigrants ride on the roof of the trains from Central America through Mexico on the dangerous journey to the "La Jaula de Oro," or the golden cage, the United States.

The cartel extorts payment; failure to pay often results in unconscionable actions of violence, rape, sodomy, and unmentionable inhumane actions. The lifeless bodies of children and mothers are unceremoniously dumped in mass graves on the side of the railroad.

Men are often more fortunate, ordered to pay a bribe for passing. These cartel actions are still going on today according to a 2018 article by Jeff Burbank.

MEXICAN CARTELS PREY ON MIGRANTS FROM CENTRAL AMERICA

THE UNIVERSITY OF TEXAS REPORT SUGGESTS FEDERAL POLICE ADOPT 'INTERNATIONAL BEST PRACTICES' TO PROTECT MIGRANTS.

"Female migrants, who are subject to sexual assault by cartel criminals, may also end up victimized by "coerced survival sex" whereby "they are forced by, a smuggler, a police officer, migration official or another migrant to exchange sex for shelter, protection, food or the ability to proceed."

<u>Read the Full article</u>

Nothing Has Changed!

In 2011 the Guatemalan government declared a state of emergency after discovering that most of the country was under the control of Zetas!

How did the Guatemalan politicians not notice the murder and mayhem in their own country unless some politicians and law enforcement agencies turned a blind eye and were bribed?

U.S. television news at the time was captivated with the spin. Fox News covered the Guatemala massacre that left twenty-seven (27) people dead. However, few reports linked the massacre with the immigration "Surge" at the border.

Read the Article <u>Guatemala Attributes Massacre to Zetas, Declares State of Emergency</u>

Miguel Angel Treviño Morales codenamed Z-40 was the head of Los Zetas Cartel's military-style hierarchy. He was arrested on July 16, 2013. He claimed to have personally killed 2,000 people, in addition to ordering and supervising thousands of other murders, his preferred method of killing was *"el guiso" (the stew)"* (Strange, 2013). Stuffing human beings in oil barrels and set them ablaze. This method of killing makes his rival gang, MS-13, look quite tame!

The Homeland Security act of 2002 passed by Congress under President George W. Bush with additional protections provided by the *William Wilberforce Trafficking Victims Protection Reauthorization Act of 2008* set the rules.

The laws tasked Health and Human Services (HHS) with either finding a suitable relative to whom the child can be released or putting the child in long-term foster care.

This administrative limbo can take years as the system is overloaded with visa backlogs and a dam of applications and blocked courts.

You can imagine that the stress the "surge" placed on the HHS, its associated services from advocates to border services.

By 2014 the laws passed in 2002 that tasked Health and Human Services (HHS) with either finding a suitable relative to whom the child can be released or putting the child in long-term foster care were straining at the seams. The crisis had begun.

Obama's Story

In 2014 under President Obama, the "surge" of unaccompanied migrant children became a crisis, and removals and returns began to hit the jackpot.

Obama's administration needed more flexible rules on immigration and deportation; they asked Congress for an extra $1.4 billion to handle the rise in child migrants.

Obama also announced that the Federal Emergency Management Agency (FEMA) would coordinate a new multi-agency response.

Policymakers started bickering, first blaming the Obama administration for its immigration policies for the DACA DREAM'ers and giving hope to the stalled Development, Relief, and Education for Alien Minors Act (DREAM Act) proposed by a partisan effort from United States Senators Dick Durbin (D- Illinois) and Orrin Hatch (R- Utah).

Arturo Jiménez

The House decided to take the plunge by setting up two Republican-led committees to hold hearings on the topic!

Both Committees did what most inept committees do in the Washington swamp. Nothing. Nothing of any benefit or value. The committees talked, reminding me of a centipede aimlessly wandering with no head!

The House Homeland Security Committee spent months trying to decide what is the cause of the influx of children! Any of the 63,339 apprehended, unaccompanied alien children from that year could have told them.

The House Judiciary Committee looked to lay blame, not solve the problem. What has changed?

Megan McKenna of Kids in Need of Defense (KIND) stated in an interview with Jasmine Spearing Bowen of Cronkite News in November 2017 *"In about 90 percent of cases, officials can place the child with a parent, relative, or family friend."*

Back in 2013 before the "surge," in many cases, the remaining children were placed in foster care, but during and after the surge, is another story. The current story is the story about family separations and deportations.

Under the Surge, Immigrant Child Care Agencies were Bursting at the Seams

The humanitarian child immigration crisis came to a head in 2014; there were more kids than beds. The HSS - Office of Refugee Resettlement and other the agencies responsible for long-term care were dealing with over six times as many children as they have beds! Children were sleeping on cold, concrete floors!

"We need beds now," said Elaine Kelley of the HHS Office of Refugee Resettlement (ORR), which oversees the Unaccompanied Alien Children (UAC) program, on a call with child welfare leaders and providers in California. (Kelly, 2014)

The department of Health and Human Services (HHS) had several options under UAC from shelter care. Therapeutic foster and group homes, structured residential programs to juvenile detention facilities. But the real issue was money and the speed at which the system can move.

Juvenile detention facilities were only used as a last resort if the child is a danger to themselves. Judging by the U.S. history in Latin America, the United States of America is most likely to be the biggest danger to these Latinx children!

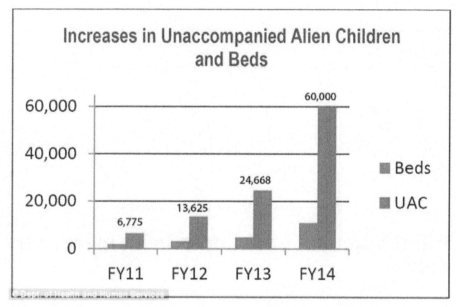

Image Source: © Department of Human Services | hhs.gov

Children Are Sleeping on Cold Concrete Floors!

If you would like to read more on Unaccompanied Alien Children are Sleeping on the Floor!

The system was at a crisis point; the Obama administration needed an immediate stopgap solution until funds could be appropriated. How simple is it to sweep the issue under the carpet and start deporting the problem?

The administration asked Congress for $1.8 billion for HHS to provide long-term housing for children.

Unaccompanied Alien Children (UAC) Removal by Obama and Department of Homeland Security DHS Increased to record levels.

Under Obama, Deportations Increased

Many immigrant advocates were angry with the Democrats due to their failure to pass comprehensive immigration reform.

- The Presidency of Barack Obama -2009 and 2016, 3,094,208 people were removed from the United States

- Work backward, data appears to show around 1,400 children were deported back to Central America in the fiscal year 2013.

https://www.acf.hhs.gov/orr/resource/unaccompanied-alien-children-released-to-sponsors-by-state

What happens to children in immigration court?

■ Removal order   ■ Voluntary departure order   Allowed to stay in US

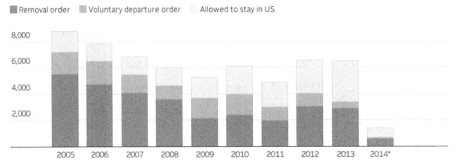

Graphic Source: Transactional Records Access Clearinghouse (TRAC)

These numbers are very arbitrary and are the statistics you see banded around by many politicians. When you dig deeper into the issue as the Migration Policy Institute (MPI) has the statistics. They are the same as the U.S. Department of Health and Human Services but a lot easier to read at-a-glance. They are horrific.

Obama is "The Deporter In Chief" - Read How He Deported Children and Families!

Obama stated in his Address to the Nation on Immigration, Nov 20, 2014, that his focus was deporting felons, not families, criminals, not children, gang members, not a mom," why were so many minor crimes the cause for deportation?

How Many Children Did the Obama Administration Deport?

More Deportations Follow Minor Crimes, Records Show (Cohen, 2014)

"New York Times analysis of internal government records shows that since President Obama took office, two-thirds of the nearly two million deportation cases involve people who had committed minor infractions, including traffic violations or had no criminal record at all. Twenty percent — or about 394,000 — of the cases involved people convicted of serious crimes, including drug-related offenses, the records show."

For years the Obama Administrations spin was that they were deporting 'criminal aliens,' but the truth is they were deporting Latinx, DREAM'ers, and many minor offenders splitting many Latino families apart.

How Many Minors Did the U.S. Send Home Under the Obama Administration?

The Pew Research Center released data in 2014 with a stunning headline, Children 12 and under are the fastest-growing group of unaccompanied minors at U.S. border. (LOPEZ J. M.-B., 2014).

The 2014 data showed a 117% increase in the number of unaccompanied children ages 12 and younger caught at the U.S.-Mexico border for the 2014 fiscal year compared with the 2013 fiscal year.

Teenagers swell the numbers creating a critical situation.

The administration was struggling to keep up with the "surge." Federal and state officials were scrambling to address the record number of unaccompanied minors apprehended at the border.

Kids sleeping under thermal banks on cold concrete floors in makeshift tent cities and warehouses had become the norm.

Crossing the U.S.-Mexico Border, Without Parents, at Increasingly Younger Ages

Total apprehensions of unaccompanied minors at the border

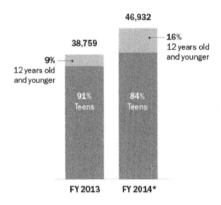

Apprehensions of unaccompanied minors at the border, by age

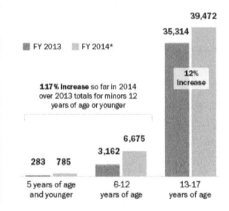

Note: Fiscal Year 2013 is Oct. 1, 2012 - Sept. 30, 2013. *Fiscal Year 2014 data is Oct. 1, 2013 - May 31, 2014.
Source: Pew Research Center analysis of U.S. Customs and Border Protection, Enforcement Integrated Database records

PEW RESEARCH CENTER

Graphic Source: Pew Research Center pewresearch.org

The Pew report confirms the government DHS numbers and identifies the violent, impoverished Northern Triangle, El Salvador, Guatemala, and Honduras as a source of the increase.

Honduras Sends Largest Number of Unaccompanied Young Children to U.S.

Apprehensions of unaccompanied minors on the U.S.-Mexico border, by country of origin

Note: Fiscal Year 2013 is Oct. 1, 2012 - Sept. 30, 2013.
*Fiscal Year 2014 data is Oct. 1, 2013 - May 31, 2014.
Source: Pew Research Center analysis of U.S. Customs and Border Protection, Enforcement Integrated Database records

PEW RESEARCH CENTER

Graphic Source: Pew Research Center pewresearch.org

The Bipartisan Policy Brief for 2014 an Outline of Immigration Issues

The Following key observations are from the Bipartisan Policy Brief of June 2014 (Immigration Task Force, 2014) in 2013 under Obama:

- Most children were trying to reach their families,

- That violence in their homelands and society from crime, gang threats forced the migration.

- They are not coming because of the Deferred Action for Childhood Arrivals (DACA).

- Children arriving at the border today are younger than in years past. In FY 2013, 24 percent of arriving children were 14 or younger, compared with 10 to 15 percent in FY 2007 and FY 2008.

- In FY 2011, a government-sponsored Legal Access Project, implemented in partnership with the Vera Institute of Justice, estimated that about 42 percent of unaccompanied children in government custody could be eligible to remain in the United States in some legal status.

Download the Bipartisan Policy Brief for 2014 pdf "Child Migration by the Numbers." You may have to sign up or read it. Or at The Bipartisan Policy Brief for 2014

So Why Did These Children, Unaccompanied Minors, and Toddlers Come?

(handwritten margin note: Statistics are worthless when they're not asking the right questions)

Table 1. Self-reported reasons for migration in 2014 surveys.

UNITED NATIONS *		ELIZABETH KENNEDY **	
Sample: 404 children migrating from El Salvador, Guatemala, Honduras, and Mexico.		Sample: 315 children migrating from El Salvador.	
Reason	Frequency	Reason	Frequency
Family or opportunity	329 (81.4%)	Crime, gang threats, & violence	188 (59.7%)
Violence in society	192 (47.5%)	Family reunification	113 (35.9%)
Abuse in home	85 (21.0%)	Study	100 (31.7%)
Deprivation	64 (15.8%)	Work	84 (26.7%)
Other	143 (35.4%)	Poverty	17 (5.4%)
		Abuse †	10 (3.2%)
		Adventure	10 (3.2%)

Note: both surveys used open-ended interviews and allowed multiple responses.
* Based on author's public comments; not reported in published results.
† Kennedy usually conducted interviews with parents present and believes the true rate is higher.

Source: Graphic from (Immigration Task Force, 2014)

We can see a common theme most children were trying to reach their families, that violence in their homelands and society from crime, gang threats forced the migration.

They are not coming because of the Deferred Action for Childhood Arrivals (DACA).

Table A-1. Compiled statistics on unaccompanied children.

Fiscal Year	2001	2002	2003	2004	2005	2006	2007	2008	2009	2010	2011	2012	2013	2014	2014*
All Children	97,954	86,433	86,606	109,285	114,222	101,778	77,778	59,578	40,461	31,291	23,089	31,029	47,397	-	-
Unaccompanied	-	-	-	-	-	-	-	-	19,668	18,634	16,056	24,481	38,833	51,279	72,394
El Salvador	-	-	-	-	-	-	-	-	1,221	1,910	1,394	3,314	5,990	11,436	16,145
Guatemala	-	-	-	-	-	-	-	-	1,115	1,517	1,565	3,835	8,068	12,670	17,887
Honduras	-	-	-	-	-	-	-	-	968	1,017	974	2,997	6,747	15,027	21,215
Mexico	-	-	-	-	-	-	-	-	16,114	13,724	11,768	13,974	17,240	12,146	17,147
Other	-	-	-	-	-	-	-	-	250	466	355	361	788	-	-
ORR custody	-	-	-	4,792	6,471	8,015	8,160	8,227	7,211	6,644	8,287	7,120	13,625	24,668	-
El Salvador	-	-	-	26%	24%	31%	27%	-	-	26%	22%	27%	26%	-	-
Guatemala	-	-	-	20%	23%	26%	29%	-	-	24%	29%	34%	37%	-	-
Honduras	-	-	-	30%	35%	28%	29%	-	-	16%	17%	27%	30%	-	-
Mexico	-	-	-	10%	6%	7%	9%	-	-	18%	22%	8%	3%	-	-
Other	-	-	-	14%	12%	7%	6%	-	-	16%	10%	4%	4%	-	-
Female	-	-	-	26%	27%	26%	24%	23%	-	29%	23%	23%	27%	-	-
Under age 14	-	-	-	-	-	-	15%	10%	-	-	17%	17%	24%	-	-

* Annualized based on first 8.5 months of FY 2014 (October 1, 2013—June 15, 2014). Does not include UACs from "other" countries.

Children (0-17)—*2001-2002:* Chad C. Haddal (2009), "Unaccompanied Alien Children: Policies and Issues," Congressional Research Service, available at http://assets.opencrs.com/rpts/RL33896_20080131.pdf. *2003-2004:* Office of Inspector General (2005), "A Review of DHS' Responsibilities for Juvenile Aliens," Department of Homeland Security, available at http://www.oig.dhs.gov/assets/Mgmt/OIG_05-45_Sep05.pdf. *2005-2010:* Lesley Sapp (2011), "Apprehensions by the U.S. Border Patrol: 2005-2010," Department of Homeland Security, available at http://www.dhs.gov/library/assets/statistics/publications/ois-apprehensions-fs-2005-2010.pdf. *2011-2013:* CBP (2011-2013), "Juvenile and Adult Apprehensions," FY 2011-FY 2013 editions, available at https://www.hsdl.org/?view&did=734591, https://www.hsdl.org/?view&did=734434, and http://www.cbp.gov/sites/default/files/documents/U.S.%20Border%20Patrol%20Fiscal%20Year%202013%20Profile.pdf.

Unaccompanied—*By country:* CBP (2014), "Southwest Border Unaccompanied Alien Children," available at http://www.cbp.gov/newsroom/stats/southwest-border-unaccompanied-children. *Other:* Calculated. *Total:* U.S. Border Patrol (2013), "Unaccompanied Children (Age 0-17) Apprehensions – Fiscal Years 2008-2012," available at http://www.rcusa.org/uploads/pdfs/appr_uac.pdf. U.S. Border Patrol (2014), "Juvenile and Adult Apprehensions – Fiscal Year 2013," available at http://www.cbp.gov/sites/default/files/documents/U.S.%20Border%20Patrol%20Fiscal%20Year%202013%20Profile.pdf.

ORR custody—*2003-2007:* Chad C. Haddal (2009), "Unaccompanied Alien Children: Policies and Issues," Congressional Research Service, available at http://assets.opencrs.com/rpts/RL33896_20080131.pdf. *2008-2011:* ORR (2008-2011), "Report to the Congress," FY 2008-2011 editions, available at http://www.acf.hhs.gov/programs/orr/resource/annual-orr-reports-to-congress. *2012-2013:* ORR, "About Unaccompanied Children's Services," available at http://www.acf.hhs.gov/programs/orr/programs/ucs/about.

Source: Graphic from (Immigration Task Force, 2014)

ICE is not forthcoming when it comes to information which they do not want the public to know. The New York Times reporter Matt Graham gained access to privy information, that is eye-opening.

The following tables based on a Freedom of Information Act (FOIA) dataset from ICE, which was obtained by The New York Times -Table 1 and Table 2 compiled in the article in the Bipartisan Policy Center by Matt Graham July 25, 2014 (Graham, Child Deportations: How Many Minors Does the U.S. Actually Send Home, 2014)

The Official Government Numbers Provided to the Governmental Affairs Hearing On "Securing the Border" On March 25, 2015 Conflict with Data provided under the Freedom of Information Act obtained by Matt Graham of the New York Times!

Table 1. Below from Graham's report shows Removals of individuals apprehended as children, FY 2009-FY 2013.

	All countries	Mexico	Northern triangle
FY 2009 **Total**	**5,762**	**2,931**	**2,117**
Minors (age 0-17) deported	4,599	2,373	1,655
18, apprehended FY 2008 or earlier	1,040	509	423
19, apprehended FY 2007 or earlier	123	49	39
FY 2010 **Total**	**5,522**	**3,514**	**1,318**
Minors (age 0-17) deported	4,170	2,657	962
18, apprehended FY 2009 or earlier	1,169	767	308
19, apprehended FY 2008 or earlier	183	90	48
FY 2011 **Total**	**3,773**	**1,938**	**1,150**
Minors (age 0-17) deported	2,777	1,409	802
18, apprehended FY 2010 or earlier	816	446	297
19, apprehended FY 2009 or earlier	180	83	51
FY 2012 **Total**	**3,277**	**1,948**	**946**
Minors (age 0-17) deported	2,517	1,548	677
18, apprehended FY 2011 or earlier	624	330	236
19, apprehended FY 2010 or earlier	136	70	33
FY 2013 **Total**	**2,418**	**1,278**	**944**
Minors (age 0-17) deported	1,669	1,022	496
18, apprehended FY 2012 or earlier	683	230	423
19, apprehended FY 2011 or earlier	66	26	25
Five-year total (FY 2009-FY 2013)	**20,752**	**11,609**	**6,475**
Minors (age 0-17) deported	15,732	9,009	4,592
18, apprehended previous FY or earlier	4,332	2,282	1,687
19, apprehended two FYs ago or earlier	688	318	196

Data Source: Calculated from ICE FOIA dataset obtained from The New York Times Graphic Source (Graham, Child Deportations: How Many Minors Does the U.S. Actually Send Home, 2014)

Between 2009 and 2013, the Obama administration Deported a total of 20,752 unaccompanied children. This number Consist of 11,609 back to Mexico and 6,475 unaccompanied minors back to the violent Northern Triangle of El Salvador, Guatemala, and Honduras.

FY 2014 Demographic Shift for ICE Removals

COUNTRY	FY 2013	FY 2014
El Salvador	21,602	27,180
Guatemala	47,749	54,423
Honduras	37,049	40,695
Mexico	241,493	176,968

Filing year	Number of cases	Outcome				
		Pending	Removal order	Voluntary departure	Stay in U.S.	Absentia*
FY 2009	4,135	331 8.0%	1,775 42.9%	1,002 24.2%	1,027 24.8%	977 23.6%
FY 2010	4,947	767 15.5%	1,857 37.5%	961 19.4%	1,362 27.5%	1,283 25.9%
FY 2011	4,430	1,067 24.1%	1,470 33.2%	646 14.6%	1,247 28.1%	1,052 23.7%
FY 2012	9,873	4,230 42.8%	2,715 27.5%	840 8.5%	2,088 21.1%	2,159 21.9%
FY 2013	19,386	13,523 69.8%	2,696 13.9%	445 2.3%	2,722 14.0%	2,286 11.8%
FY 2014	18,303	17,382 95.0%	393 2.1%	62 0.3%	466 2.5%	268 1.5%
Total	61,074	37,300 61.1%	10,906 17.9%	3,956 6.5%	8,912 14.6%	8,025 13.1%

Table 2. Immigration court outcomes for Northern Triangle juveniles, FY 2009-FY 2014. (ICE, 2014)

* About 99 percent of cases decided in absentia end in a removal order.

According to ICE data, between FY 2009 and FY 2013, about 4,600 children from Northern Triangle countries (El Salvador, Guatemala or Honduras) were removed (compulsory Removal), but wait for the 2014 and 2016 numbers in yet...

The official numbers provided by the DHS, ICE, etc., still do not add up!

How Many Male Children Grew into Men Waiting for Their Day in Court?

We need to dig deeper to find out how many children, like Carlos, a DREAM'er, whose story is told in Chapter 3. The DREAM'ers and the False Promise of DACA grew to be adults while they waited for their day in court.

We are looking at those children, minors "Unaccompanied Alien Children" (UAC) as the government derogatorily call them, at the time of their apprehension at the time of who became adults while they patiently waited for visa applications quotas and the court backlog of dockets?

- Approximately 1,700 18-year old's were removed one or more fiscal years after their apprehension
- About 200 more, 19-year old's were removed two or more fiscal years later

The data implies that the U.S. removed about a total of 6,475 migrants from El Salvador, Guatemala, or Honduras who were apprehended as children.

Overall, it appears that 20,752 "Unaccompanied Alien Children" (UAC), (individuals apprehended as children were deported in the past five fiscal years,) from all countries.

According to Transactional Records Clearinghouse (TRAC), many of the Children back in 2014 were patiently waiting for their deportation hearing.

- As of June 2014, that year about 61 percent of the immigration court cases filed for Northern Triangle juveniles since FY 2009 were still pending.

Immigration court outcomes for Northern Triangle juveniles, FY 2009-FY 2014.

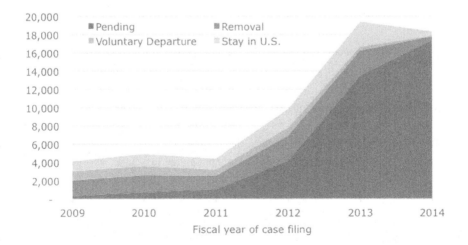

The Numbers: Removal + Returns = Deported

- **Deported:** Between October 2009 and June 2014, approximately 15,000 juvenile cases from the Northern Triangle resulted in the removal or voluntary returns.

- **Returns:** Voluntary departure order 6,500 juveniles from those countries were removed between October 2009 and September 2013, a difference of about 8,500. Several possibilities may explain this gap, including:

  Removal: Removal (5000) +6,500 = 15,000

Obama holds the record for forcefully "Removed," (Removals) of children 5,000 + the 1,900 caught up in court!

Give or take 6,900 Kids!

(And this does not include 2014-16 which mysteriously are nowhere to be found).

Seriously these are kids being sent back to a war zone!

Graham explains these differences of the numbers in his tables based on a Freedom of Information Act (FOIA) dataset from ICE, which was obtained by The New York Times -Table 1 and Table 2 and compiled in the article in the Bipartisan Policy Center by Matt Graham July 25, 2014 (Graham, Child Deportations: How Many Minors Does the U.S. Actually Send Home, 2014) as:

- **Data comparability:** The number of children deported after turning 18 is an estimate, not a precise count.

- **In absentia orders:** Children ordered removed in absentia, (or without their presence in court,) may not have been located or apprehended by ICE to enforce the removal order. About 8,000 Northern Triangle juveniles have had their cases decided in absentia since FY 2009, and about 99 percent of these cases ended with removal orders.

- **Processing removals:** Some children who have been ordered removed may not have been removed yet. Once removal is ordered, the U.S. government must coordinate with the receiving country to obtain any missing travel documents, arrange transportation, and determine who will take custody of the child upon their return.

- **Appeals.** It is unclear whether TRAC's count of removal orders includes orders that have been or could be appealed to a higher court.

More detailed data from the Department of Homeland Security would shed light on the missing data.

Based on available data, it appears that about 6,500 children from the Northern Triangle countries have been removed since FY 2009 and that most of the remainder are still awaiting their removal hearing.

Something is Hidden

In the U.S. Senate Committee on Homeland Security and Governmental Affairs Hearing on "Securing the Border: Understanding and Addressing the Root Causes of Central American Migration to the United States" March 25, 2015, William Kandel Analyst in Immigration Policy Congressional Research Service the numbers that he provides conflict with those previously made public.

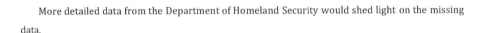

Table 3. ICE Removals of UAC by Country of Citizenship, FY2009-FY2014*

	Mexico	Guatemala	El Salvador	Honduras	All Other	Total
FY2009	350	534	96	352	29	1,361
FY2010	690	520	117	326	37	1,690
FY2011	696	515	136	297	51	1,695
FY2012	574	626	136	430	43	1,809
FY2013	548	661	159	461	39	1,868
FY2014*	335	554	146	392	30	1,457

Source: Data provided to CRS from ICE Legislative Affairs on October 20, 2014.

Notes: * FY2014 Removal data are through 07/19/2014, representing 9.5 months of FY2014. Removal counts are based on designation of UAC at time of initial book-in and may not be under the age of 18 at the time of removal. ICE data include voluntary departures in their removal.

ICE data presented in **Table 4** indicate that the number of UAC removals by that agency has remained between 1,500 and 2,000 each year between FY2009 and FY2013. CRS was unable to obtain an updated figure for FY2014 as of this writing; that shown in **Table 4** represents ICE removals of UAC for the first 9.5 months of FY2014.

The Official Government Numbers Provided to the Governmental Affairs Hearing On "Securing the Border" On March 25, 2015 Conflict with Previously Provided Data!

Considering that these numbers were provided in March of 2015, they appear rigged. The numbers conflict with previously provided data obtained under forced legal orders under the Freedom of Information Act.

(?)

Did the Obama administration want to make it seem like deportations were lower?

Image Source: © Peter Lucking | contentbrandingsolutions.com

CHAPTER 2

The DREAM'ers and the False Promise of DACA

Congress is spluttering, stalled over any policy solution for the Deferred Action for Childhood Arrivals program (DACA), leaving many DREAM'ers in limbo.

Our nation faces a shortage of skilled labor eroding the country's competitiveness in the global market.

Lawmakers fight over the opportunity to create a more skilled workforce in house, that would enable thousands of students to strive, to grow and become part of the American dream, building our economy, and contributing to our society.

So, what's wrong with this win-win picture? DREAM'ers in limbo would, according to anti-immigrant hardliners, receive "amnesty." Others point out that the DREAM Act would reward those who have earned their place in the U.S.

A Shattered Dream – The Gabriela Story

Gabriela, as a third-year high school student in Denver, skipped happily to the library to apply for a summer job cataloging books. She excitedly filled out the forms for the summer job, thinking of all the summer reading she would do.

Gabriela watched with anticipation for the postman from the porch of her classic North Denver Victorian in the hip gentrified neighborhood of Sunnyside. She was late; she started to fidget. Today the letter would come, the letter from the library.

The postman bounded up the porch steps with a pile of mail in his hand, seeing Gabriela he smiled, "Good Morning Gabby, waiting for me today?"

The postman first met Gabby and her family, at the Our Lady of Guadalupe Church, years ago when she was a little toddler; they were great community folks, attending the church; helping at the neighborhood fair every July.

"Yes." she beamed back, "I'm waiting to hear about my job application at the library."

He shuffled through the post to find her official-looking letter, smiling he handed it over.

She trembled with excitement tearing the letter open.

"Did you get the job?

Gabby was staring at the paper, tears welling up in her eyes, she seemed confused. She kept reading the words...

"Due to your illegal status, we cannot offer you the job!"

She screamed, "Mamá," and ran crying into the house.

Her parents decided it was time to reveal the truth to Gabby that they had entered the States on a temporary agricultural work visa when Gabby was three, and her sister was two. They had hitched a ride with some Mexican farmworkers coming to Colorado from Texas to pick watermelons.

They had left the horrors of Guatemala, their farm and friends, fleeing for their lives. They never looked back. They had remained without legal papers. They had worked hard since, going under the radar.

Gabriela's surname has not been used to protect her privacy. Like many of the eight hundred thousand (800,000) unauthorized immigrants on the Deferred Action for Childhood Arrivals (DACA), she fears retaliation from the U.S. immigration officials. She fears ICE will come in the night and deport her parents.

Gabriela, like many DREAM'ers, was jarred and confused. At first, she was mad at her parents; then she was just mad at the U.S. DACA gave her hope. She realized her family had stayed illegally for her, and her sister's future. It also allowed her to apply for temporary work authorization in the U.S. However, DACA is not the DREAM Act that she needs to stay in the U.S.

Without action by Congress on the actual DREAM Act, she and thousands of others will be deported. DACA has provided some relief for undocumented immigrants, but they need a long-term solution. The United States needs a long-term solution.

The DREAM'ers were mostly born in Mexico or the violent Northern Triangle of El Salvador, Guatemala, and Honduras and cocaine shoulder states of Central and South America

The DREAM'ers are left in limbo, holding on to hope as the court's fight over President Donald Trump's move to shut down DACA. What makes this worse is she followed the rules and registered. They know, ICE knows where they live

People say, "Follow your dreams, and the universe will shift the stars for you." It is time to activate the stars on the red white and blue; it is time to pass immigration reform that will allow Gabriela and the many others like her a chance to realize the American dream

Gabriela is adamant that her parents are her real heroes. After all, they took the risk; they came to find sanctuary for her and her sister from the horrors of Guatemala.

(P)

(?)

Do you think a similar biparti-zan effort would be possible in todays political climate?

◆ ◆ ◆

The DREAM Act proposal was introduced as a bill by Republican Senator Orin Hatch of Utah and Democratic Senator Dick Durbin 2001. The Bill has been passed over ten times as it has come before Congress. This has been a back and forth game of blame and excuse by both the Republicans and the

Democrats. Groups of immigrant youth who adopted the label 'DREAM'ers,' were already organized across the nation.

The Dreamers are mostly teenagers who had come to the U.S. as small children during preschool and now are high school graduates or about to graduate high school. Although they were raised in the U.S., they could only dream of continuing to college as their immigration status would undermine their financial aid and often undermine their college matriculation and graduation.

When the former President reopened his "Obama for America" offices in 2012 during his bid for reelection, the DREAM'ers organized rallies and sit-ins inside and in front of Obama's offices.

In Denver, the windows of the local Democratic Headquarters, Obama for America, were broken out by unnamed persons. The media immediately blamed the DREAM'ers who were often tearfully chanting in frustration during their rallies at Obama's unfulfilled promises.

In a last-ditch effort, then-President Obama reluctantly announced an executive action to provide relief to the DREAM'ers. Unfortunately, Obama's executive action fell far short of the bipartisan DREAM Act that Congress failed to pass many times.

"Individuals who receive deferred action will not be placed into deportation proceedings or removed from the United States for a specified period unless DHS chooses to terminate the deferral." (Department of Homeland Security, 2012)

The implication is seen by many immigrants that are hiding in the shadows as "sign here so that we can deport you when we want. So you can stay...for a while."

Many ask, "Why don't they just follow the law and get in line like everyone else?"

Truthfully, there often is no legal way to be here, and there is no "line" to get into. Notably, children who are brought here by their parents through no choice of their own or who find their way to the U.S. without their parents are at a severe disadvantage.

It never ceases to amaze me how many people are convinced that these children are somehow guilty of their circumstance of an inconvenient truth. Consider the untimely situation of my former client Carlos.

"They didn't commit a crime but their parents did"

My heart still hurts to recount the story of how Carlos came to the United States at the age of 10 with his parents and siblings in the 1990s. Carlos' uncle is a United States Citizen, and he applied for Carlos and his parents and sibling's legalization a very long time ago.

There is a category for legal immigration that allows a U.S. citizen over the age of 21 to apply for their sibling, along with that sibling's spouse and their minor children. Immigrants from Mexico in this category called the "4th Preference Family Category" must wait in an imaginary "line" which has taken anywhere from twelve to twenty years for them to arrive at the front of the "line"—which is called an available visa number.

Carlos Story- The "Line" to Deportation

I first met Carlos, his wife Claudia, and their baby daughter Sofia, along with his parents in 2002. They showed up at my office for a legal consultation. The couple were young, vibrant, a loving pair, who adored their little bundle of joy. Carlos's parents, in contrast, were aging, browbeaten, and worried with concern.

This is Carlos' story told on that fateful day. We would become more than business associates, but friends.

Carlos' family could not make ends meet in Mexico, so they applied to visit the U.S. to visit family while they pondered their situation in Mexico.

They were lucky to be approved and entered the U.S. with their tourist visas. Like most of the so-called "illegals," they came legally and then overstayed their visas and quickly became absorbed into the construction, food service, hospitality, and agriculture industries where many natural-born U.S. citizens refuse to work long-term. The employers in these and many other industries could not survive without the immigrant labor that sustains them and our economy.

Our elderly collect Social Security checks while an immigrant's paycheck is deducted for payroll taxes to provide a large surplus in Social Security that most of them will never see.

On average, the Nation's Estimated 11 million Undocumented Immigrants Pay Approximately $11.74 Billion In State and Local Taxes. (ITEP, 2017)

We enjoy our parks and city services while "illegal" immigrant families pay the same local sales taxes that we all pay to sustain such amenities.

Undocumented children enter school as a growing number of long-term working immigrants purchase homes and pay property taxes which sustain the local schools—such as in Colorado where the majority of our property taxes are distributed to the local school districts by the state.

Carlos waited patiently with his family in that 4th Preference immigration "line" based upon his U.S. citizen uncle's family petition from many years before. He and his parents realized that they were the fortunate ones to have a U.S. citizen relative as they had no other way to try and immigrate legally. Their patience was not idle as they endeavored at every turn to prove their worth to their employers, co-workers, teachers, classmates, and their neighbors.

Carlos was an outstanding student who eagerly learned English at lightning speed and became a distinguished student very early in elementary and continuing to middle school. He quickly came to realize that he had an exceptional aptitude for math and science. Upon graduation with honors from high school, Carlos directly enrolled in engineering courses.

Carlos tapped into his, and his family's saving's account to pay the local university without any eligibility for state or federal financial aid. He and his family filed their income taxes and helped their community and the local church. They waited patiently as contributing members of their local community and society as the years passed.

After 11 years of waiting in "Line," their immigrant visa number became available in 2000.

Happily, Carlos' parents were able to become Legal Permanent Residents. His brothers and sisters were also able to receive their legal immigration status. However, Carlos had just turned 21.

Carlos had "aged-out," he had become an adult while the family waited in "line" for over ten years for their visa to become available.

Carlos had dreamed of becoming a legal permanent resident and finishing school to become an engineer and take care of his aging parents. His parents struggled to make ends meet working at minimum-wage jobs. They still had to support his younger siblings who were still in high school, yet his parents were aging and lacked health insurance. They had become legal, but they couldn't sustain Carlos' dream. Suddenly, Carlos was stuck in the nightmare of our immigration system.

Carlos like Gabriela had become a defining member of those millions of children that we call the "DREAM'ers"—dreaming of becoming legal, fulfilling their potential and making a difference to their de facto homeland: the United States of America. Carlos was about to receive the backhanded thank you for getting in "line."

The immigration law cut-off was 21, and even though Carlos was a 10-year-old minor when he entered the U.S. and when his family entered the "line." His patience, hard work, and accomplishments in elementary, middle, high school, and college did not matter. His value to society as a promising engineering program student did not matter. The fact that we, and our country, needed and will benefit from Carlos and many "Dreamers," is irrelevant to the law.

Carlos was pushed to the side by the zealous U.S. immigration authorities. They were never in any rush to help him, but now eager to deport him!

Carlos shouldered his disappointment and despair; it was not his fault that the system had taken years to review his case. Yes, he had "timed out" in "line," but he was a model citizen. One that any parent would be proud of. He believed that his situation would be considered favorably and tried to stay positive for his family's sake. After all, his parents and his siblings were the lucky ones.

He thought to himself that at least they had become legal contributing citizens of the U.S.

He had to thank their lucky stars that his uncle was able to file for them and that they were able to survive all those years and finally get most of the family on a pathway to become citizens in an additional five years.

Now that they were legal, they could use the safety-net of Medicaid insurance and see a few of the benefits for which they had paid sales taxes, income taxes, social security taxes, and property taxes for all those years as contributing members of the society.

Carlos moved on; he married his beautiful heartthrob high school sweetheart, Claudia. She was his lover, companion, and friend.

They shared many traits and had similar backgrounds. Claudia came from a family that had come to the U.S. when she was a child in the '90s, just like Carlos. Claudia's family was from El Salvador and had fled the violence of the civil war that had left their country in shambles. Claudia's family filed for asylum protection to remain in the United States as political refugees who had suffered threats against their lives for their perceived political opinion.

In 2001, the U.S. immigration authorities designated the "illegal" immigrants from El Salvador eligible for **T**emporary **P**rotected **S**tatus, (TPS)

The Secretary may designate a country for TPS due to the following temporary conditions in the country:

- *Ongoing armed conflict (such as civil war)*

- *An environmental disaster (such as an earthquake or hurricane), or an epidemic*

- *Other extraordinary and temporary conditions*

(DHS, 2019).

The administration of President George W. Bush recognized that many of the Salvadorans had suffered atrocities and agreed to help the Salvadoran citizens whose country had sent troops overseas to support our wars in the Middle East. Based on the unequal and inconsistent nature of our country's immigration laws, Claudia had a better situation than Carlos because she was from El Salvador and not from Mexico.

Claudia was able to apply for this Temporary Protected Status, (TPS) but had to wait for a renewal notice from the U.S. government every eighteen months. Of course, this status covered the spouses of TPS recipients. However, Claudia and Carlos had married just after the TPS status was placed into effect. Again, time played its wicked twist, Carlos' request to be added to Claudia's TPS application was denied based on the fact that they married just after TPS was enacted.

Claudia and Carlos married for love. Their relationship and their marriage were not for potential immigration benefits. They were childhood sweethearts whose relationship had blossomed.

Their marriage was very traditional as they had requested permission from each other's families to marry and did not move in together until after their wedding. Carlos once again had to take the rejection of our byzantine immigration laws and continue with his life.

A local public notary often referred to by the Spanish-speaking community as a "*notario*," encouraged Carlos and Claudia to apply, and for Carlos to add his name to Claudia's prior application for political asylum. This "*notario*" had worked with other members of their church, so he was anointed with the blessings of people that they trusted. Of course, the notary wanted a couple of hundred dollars while assuring Claudia that an immigration attorney would charge them at least double the price and all the while force them to bring a translator in a total lack of cultural competence and disrespect for their native tongue of Spanish.

At the counsel of this unlicensed, non-attorney, Carlos and Claudia decided to add Carlos to the asylum application. They figured, "what do we have to lose by trying?" By this time, they had just become the proud parents of a baby girl named Sofia. The pregnancy was difficult, and their daughter was born slightly premature. They had hospital bills, and they lacked sleep.

Sofia did not take to her feedings easily. Carlos, with his calm and consistent demeanor, was the only one who could get the baby to feed. He took on the task of giving the baby formula from the time that he arrived home from work, throughout the night and into the morning.

Carlos had become an exceptional father who could coax Sofia his little bundle of joy into a blissful slumber. This comfort was very important for Sofia's health, as well as her naps, having allowed Carlos and Claudia to get a bit of rest as well. Claudia did her best but had to relent at feedings and bedtime lest she and Carlos lose valuable rest that they both needed to get through the next day at work.

After an official interview at the government immigration office, which was more like a mini-trial, Claudia's application for Political Asylum was denied. As a family member on the application, Carlos was also officially denied and, as such the law required that she and Carlos were passed into deportation court.

The deportation court would be their last opportunity to have their applications for political asylum heard by an Immigration Judge.

Claudia's application had been based upon her family's suffering during the Salvadoran Civil War, and there was a peace accord signed by the warring factions in the '90s and recognized by the world— including the United States. Claudia's application was denied based upon a change in the conditions of her native El Salvador. Such a change in conditions of her country meant that she and Carlos had to find some other way to become legal or they could be deported.

Just like Carlos' family, Claudia's family had applied through a U.S. citizen uncle. Just like Carlos, Claudia had "aged-out" as her family waited. Likewise, Claudia had attended and graduated from

American schools, just like Carlos. She had also ironically become a "Dreamer" who was living in a similar immigration nightmare.

There was a ray of hope for Claudia. Her sister was able to become a U.S. citizen and applied for her. The wait in the 4th Preference family category was shorter for El Salvadorans than it was for Mexicans—due to another strange immigration policy that determined that there are too many Mexicans, Indians, Chinese and Filipinos which means they have to wait longer. Since Carlos was married to Claudia, he could also immigrate with Claudia and "wait" in a "shorter line" than if he had married another Mexican.

The "wait" in a "shorter line" would take about ten years for Salvadorans and their families compared to the 15-year wait for Mexicans.

Think of this "line" as the TSA line at the airport just longer and more demeaning.

The TSA strip search is nothing compared to the detailed security check, medical screening, mental health, and genitalia examination that potential "shorter liner's," and all immigrants face as part of their interview process with a State Department officer.

Claudia still could remain in the U.S. based upon her Temporary Protected Status which thankfully, kept being renewed by President Bush. Carlos, being Mexican and having married Claudia after the TPS program was initiated, fell into an "all or nothing" situation meaning that he would have to stay or go while he "waited" for his wife's visa to become available.

Carlos was a stellar father, worker, student, and a member of the community, his local church, and society.

Carlos was a person of "Good Moral Character," he had no criminal record; he had never even been stopped for speeding or any minor offense like letting his dog off-leash or jaywalking.

Carlos had become a youth group leader at his local church in Southwest Denver. He and Claudia were active members of an evangelical Christian church called "El Shaddai." Once the baby was able to find some stability at home, Carlos increased his activities and sought to help middle school-aged kids, mostly immigrant youth just as he had been at one time. He also joined the church's Christian rock band. Carlos had become a recognized leader in his community beyond being a great role model, and a great guitar player!

Carlos was shocked and devastated when Immigration authorities charged him with being in the country illegally and required that he report to deportation court with the Immigration judge.

Carlos complied and tried in vain to explain his situation to the Immigration Judge:

- His parents and siblings were Legal Residents as he barely aged-out,

- He had a baby daughter, a U.S. citizen, who needed his love and parental guidance as a minor

- His wife held TPS status, and they were waiting for a visa in the 4th Preference category that was filed by her U.S. citizen sister that would take about five years more.

The Immigration Judge, in his black flowing robe, arrogantly explained that the courts do not wait for anyone, including Carlos, to get to the front of that "line" for an immigrant visa.

Carlos felt deserted, and abused, he had followed the law, got in "line," became a contributing member of the community only to be slapped judiciously in the face.

The judge considered the case and gave Carlos a short extension telling him, "he had better get an attorney and figure out what to do next."

Carlos and Claudia with their gorgeous baby daughter Sofia and his parents showed up at my office for a legal consultation one day in 2002.

Carlos explained how he was left out in all of the prior applications and how he was "still in line" for an immigrant visa with his sister-in-law. Unfortunately, I had to confirm what the judge had told them and try to help them make sense of the senseless quandary that had befallen him.

The Travesty of Justice

Just as of today, I always plead with my clients to "not shoot the messenger." I had to explain that the immigration system doesn't appear to be fair or just but that we had to follow this illogical law and find a way through. Carlos' parents were understandably beside themselves.

Carlos' parents explained that he had just bought a house where they lived along with Claudia, his baby daughter Sofia and two of his minor siblings. They explained how he had to leave his engineering program to help support them all. They continued to sing his praises as he was an "unusually exceptional" father to this U.S. citizen baby girl. We agreed that his defense to deportation would be a difficult path and that we should apply for something called Cancellation of Removal, or "Cancellation" for short.

If an undocumented immigrant has a qualifying relative who is a U.S. citizen, or a Legal Permanent Resident, spouse, parent or child, and has been in the country 10 years or more before being caught by immigration, is a person of "Good Moral Character," has not committed certain disqualifying offenses (which includes many misdemeanors), and their qualifying relative would encounter "Exceptional and Extremely Unusual Hardship," then they could be granted this pardon in the additional discretion of the judge. Along with this pardon comes a 'green card.'

Cancellation is sometimes mischaracterized as "The Ten-Year Pardon." Part of the requirement to be eligible for this pardon is that the "illegal" immigrant had to be present in our country for ten years or more. At some point, Congress had determined that after ten years, a person had integrated into our country sufficiently to be considered, for permanent status. They have paid taxes and received little in return.

Many people to this day think that if an immigrant has ten years presence and a United States citizen spouse or child, that they are automatically pardoned and allowed to stay. If only the law were that simple.

The key to winning the so-called "Ten-year Pardon" is to convince an immigration judge in an immigration court that the U.S. citizen or Legal Resident child, spouse or parent would suffer "Exceptional and Extremely Unusual Hardship." This level of hardship is hard to explain and even harder to meet in the legal minds of most immigration judges.

It is not a case of discretion where the judge gets to hand out green cards to people whom he or she believes deserve to stay. Rather there is the law, a bunch of regulations to implement this law and a string of precedential cases--meaning controlling cases from the supreme immigration court-- that try to define in a circular and confusing fashion just who suffers "exceptional and unusual" hardship.

For example, if Carlos' daughter had a life-threatening disease or had an officially diagnosed physical, emotional, or learning disability, then he would likely meet this high standard. Carlos would still have to show that his qualifying family members (remember his wife does not count as a TPS recipient under this law!) could not survive without further detriment in the U.S. without him or that they would suffer this "exceptional and unusual hardship" if they were to accompany him to Mexico.

Altogether he had to show that they were damned if they stayed and show that they were damned if they left with him.

Carlos had three qualifying relatives: his U.S. citizen daughter and his Legal Permanent Resident parents. Carlos had been present in the U.S. for over ten years and had been a person of Good Moral Character, perhaps the highest moral character that I had ever seen—even many years and thousands of clients later. I thought that Carlos' situation would qualify to prove that the hardship to his daughter and his parents was at a level of "Exceptional an Extremely Unusual Hardship."

The Immigration Judge received the evidence by way of doctor's notes, income documents, and testimony by Carlos, his wife, and his parents. Of course, the judge agreed that Carlos met the first three requirements of *"Cancellation of Removal:"*

    1.   His parents were Legal Permanent Residents

    2.   His daughter was a United States citizen.

    3.   He had been present in the United States for well over the required ten years.

The judge even agreed that Carlos was an exceptional father and community member.

However, the judge found that Carlos' parents had other children who he arbitrarily decided on their behalf would "have to step up and take care of their parents" if Carlos could not be in the U.S.

Also, the judge ruled that although Sofia had difficulties with eating and sleeping after a difficult pregnancy and birth, now, thanks to Carlos, she was stable enough that Claudia and the grandparents who were in the U.S. legally could take care of the baby without Carlos. He failed to take into account the loving, protective bond between father and daughter.

Furthermore, the judge noted that Claudia, as a U.S. citizen, could avail herself of food stamps, welfare, Medicaid, and other social programs through taxpayer public assistance without Carlos' income and presence. Also, the judge ruled that Carlos could avoid the "minimal" hardship to his daughter without his support and take her to Mexico! What about Claudia she was from El Salvador, how would that work?

The judge cited a ridiculous case from the 1980s, stating that "very young U.S. citizen children can simply relocate to their parent's home country and learn and adapt to a new language and culture." Of course, Carlos and Claudia tearfully expressed their intention to stay together even if Carlos had to leave. The family could not imagine that this was happening.

who becomes an immigration judge and why? Is this one of the most frustrating parts of your job?

The judge refused to recognize that Claudia was not from Mexico and that she would lack rights in Mexico since she is a citizen of El Salvador.

The judge ignored that all of these factors which added up to an obvious "severe hardship" under the totality of the circumstances. The judge appeared to be looking for a way to deny his case —a regular phenomenon in most immigration cases.

The judge ordered Carlos be removed from the country unless he departed the U.S. voluntarily within two months. Carlos was shocked. His wife, his parents (and his attorney) and everyone else was dumbfounded with disbelief at the lack of empathy and compassion shown by the judge.

Let's "wait in line" and then abusively rip your family apart, all in the name of the law! Because you can always go back to Mexico!

The court was holding Carlos accountable for an action which he had no control over as a minor. Time had passed, and now as a young adult adult, he was paying the psychological, emotional, and social abusive price of the letter of the law.

Of course, we prepared and filed an appeal of his case to the Board of Immigration Appeals— known as the "Supreme Court of Immigration." That body swiftly and unceremoniously dismissed the appeal and ordered Carlos to leave by "voluntary departure," from the U.S. without any compassion for his family.

DACA Kids and the DREAM'ers

Have you ever been stuck at an airport watching your plane being delayed time after time, promises broken? Have you ever been stuck on the phone with GoDaddy or Comcast for hours going round in circles and being upsold?

Did someone ever promise you a present or a pay rise and then default on the deal? Do you remember the frustration, disappointment, the dejection the emotional depression that these actions and events gave you?

If you have, you may have felt some of the emotions that the 800,000 young undocumented immigrants, DACA kids, and DREAM'ers feel, watching President Trump trying to end DACA.

Now imagine a person breaking into your home, defiling your privacy, and restraining you.

Yes, that is what U.S. Immigration and Customs Enforcement, (ICE) can do - at any time without cause if DACA is revoked. What makes it worse is that most DACA kids are registered with the authorities!

A dreamer or DACA kid could be snatched from their home, their security, friends, and family to be sent back to a country they do not remember! Imagine how scared DACA kids and DREAM'ers feel.

For years the Democrats and Republicans on the hill have been squabbling over the DREAM Act and DACA Act.

Meanwhile, many children have become adults hoping in vain for recognition. *I wonder if ICE officers and others have developed hatred of immigrants believing*

Many Kids have been deported, stolen in the night by ICE officers carrying out their tasks. *that the laws wouldn't be this harsh if immigrants were in danger ous*

For over eighteen years the Democrats and Republicans have been teasing illegal child immigrants with the DREAM Act. The Democrats have tried unsuccessfully to pass the "DREAM Act," an acronym for "Development, Relief, and Education for Alien Minors Act." Multiple times.

The last time on July 26, 2017. The DREAM Act of 2017 sponsored by Senator Lindsey Graham provides that, "Notwithstanding any other provision of law, the (DHS) Secretary shall" grant lawful permanent resident status on a conditional basis to an undocumented alien who:

Has been continuously physically present in the United States for four years preceding the bill's enactment;

- Was younger than 18 years of age on the initial date of U.S. entry

- Is not inadmissible on specified criminal, security, terrorism, or other grounds

- Has not participated in the persecution

- Has not been convicted of specified federal or state offenses

- Has fulfilled specified educational requirements

Source: (S.1615 - Dream Act of 2017, 2017)

In the simplest of terms, this act would provide permanent residency and a path to citizenship for all those that met its requirements.

We cannot underestimate the value of conditional permanent resident status (valid for up to eight years) for young undocumented immigrants. It stops the DREAM'ers from worrying by protecting them from deportation, allowing them to work legally in the U.S., and permitting them to travel outside the country. Most importantly, it places them on a path to permanent status and eventually, citizenship.

DACA

The Deferred Action for Childhood Arrivals (DACA) program established on June 15, 2012, when DHS announced that aliens who had been brought to the United States illegally as children and met other criteria would be considered for temporary lawful status with work authorization.

Guidelines You May Request DACA if You:

- Were under the age of 31 as of June 15, 2012;

- Came to the United States before reaching your 16th birthday;

- Have continuously resided in the United States since June 15, 2007, up to the present time;

- Were physically present in the United States on June 15, 2012, and at the time of making your request for consideration of deferred action with USCIS;

- Had no lawful status on June 15, 2012;

- Are currently in school, have graduated or obtained a certificate of completion from high school, have obtained a general education development (GED) certificate, or are an honorably discharged veteran of the Coast Guard or Armed Forces of the United States; and

- Have not been convicted of a felony, significant misdemeanor, or three or more other misdemeanors, and do not otherwise pose a threat to national security or public safety.

This is a copy of the bill that President Trump tried to rescind. Had Trump been able to rescind this law, DACA kids would have been deported.

Important information about DACA requests: Due to federal court orders, USCIS has resumed accepting requests to renew a grant of deferred action under DACA. USCIS is not accepting requests from individuals who have never before been granted deferred action under DACA. Until further notice, and unless otherwise provided in this guidance, the DACA policy will be operated on the terms in place before it was rescinded on Sept. 5, 2017. For more information, visit Deferred Action for Childhood Arrivals: Response to January 2018 Preliminary Injunction.

Source: (The U S Cittizenship and Immigration Services, 2012)

There are almost 800,000 young undocumented immigrants DACA kids and DREAM'ers we ho came to America as children, have lived here since at least 2007 and met other requirements, are recipients of Deferred Action for Childhood Arrivals (DACA), through which they qualified for temporary protection from deportation and legal work authorization for a renewable period of two years.

"Voluntary Departure." Claudia and Sofia's Detention and Repatriation to the U.S.

Sadly, Carlos and his wife and their young daughter Sofi left for Mexico with trepidation. Upon arriving in Mexico, Claudia was detained by Mexican immigration authorities! She was forced to return to the U.S. under her Temporary Protected Status for Salvadorans.

It had been a year since Republican Senator Orin Hatch, and Democratic Senator Dick Durbin first introduced the **D**evelopment, **R**elief, and **E**ducation for **A**lien **M**inors Act, famously referred to as The DREAM Act, in August of 2001. This proposed law would have provided a pathway for Carlos and other "Dreamers" who had arrived in the U.S. as children to have an earned pathway to citizenship.

That proposal failed as the Democrats in the U.S. Congress refused to support a bill that did not provide opportunities for more than those who came to the U.S. as children. The Democrats maintained that they were holding out for an immigration law that would benefit many more people than the DREAM Act—"a more comprehensive proposal."

We and the DREAM'ers, along with The Nation's Estimated 11 Million Undocumented Immigrants are Still Waiting For "A More Comprehensive Proposal!"

Carlos would have easily met the criteria for the DREAM Act bill as he came to the U.S. before the age of 16, he graduated from local schools, he enrolled and completed two years of college, he was a person of "good moral character," and he was younger than the 30-year age limit.

Carlos stuck in Mexico, a place he did not remember, where he had no family, and where he did not feel as if he was at home. He monitored the news intently as the Dream Act would be introduced many times in the following 14 years only to fail as Democrats and Republicans took turns shooting down the various versions of the Dream Act as he waited in Mexico.

The Democrats shot down the DREAM Act in 2007, again refusing to allow Republican George W. Bush the opportunity to take credit for helping DREAM'ers. In 2009 and 2010, the Democrats had their opportunity to declare a political win and pass the DREAM Act as they had won the presidency and both chambers of Congress.

Of course, Republicans held out from giving the Democrats the four votes they needed to claim the political victory. Republicans kept claiming that the Democrats failed to include enough security measures in their proposals even though Democrats were introducing bills with nearly the same requirements and language that Republicans had introduced in previous iterations of the bill.

The Democratic Party held majority votes in both the Senate and the House of Representatives during Obama's first two years. Another version of the Dream Act introduced by Democrats in 2011 was largely opposed by Republicans to prevent President Barack Obama from fulfilling another of his promises from his election campaign; however, Obama and the Democrats missed their best opportunity to help the DREAM'ers and failed to pass any significant legislation.

The False Promises of DACA—Not the DREAM ACT

In 2012, President Obama would finally do something to appease the Dreamers and break the political deadlock. The President and the Democratic Party had been embarrassed publicly as several angry, and emotional protests by DREAMERS and their supporters demanded that they deliver the actual DREAM Act first proposed in 2001.

As a last-ditch effort to maintain support for reelection, on June 15, 2012, the Obama administration invented the temporary Deferred Action for Childhood Arrivals program or "DACA." Obama employed a very strained interpretation of executive power to delay deportations to avoid having to rely on Congress to pass an actual law benefitting DREAM'ers.

Executive
Action

On June 15, 2012, President Obama announced that DREAMERS who met similar criteria to the DREAM Act would have their deportation "deferred." Applicants were granted a 2-year work permit while their deportation was put on hold.

Shocking, the actual DREAM Act was never passed by Congress. Many Dreamers and members of the public mistakenly thought that Obama's DACA and the DREAM Act were the same things. In their confusion, many immigrants and immigrant advocacy groups joined the Democratic Party in hailing Obama as a bold protectorate of the young DREAM'ers.

Interestingly, Obama's DACA program was only a band-aid for the DREAM'ers, a stopgap, reprieve that gave hope to the DREAM'ers that they could remain temporarily while waiting for Congress to pass the actual DREAM Act later.

Carlos was eagerly watching this process unfold from his forced exile in Mexico. Like many of the Dreamers, he has repeatedly expressed his support for the benefit of the DACA even though it is a temporary measure with an uncertain future.

He yearned to be home in the country he was raised in with his wife and child, taking care of his parents, continuing his education and his pursuit of the American Dream. It did not matter to him and many DREAM'ers that DACA was a false promise, a false hope created by the Democrats and President Obama that led DREAM'ers to a legal no man's land.

DACA which was implemented years after Carlos was forced to leave the U.S., did not benefit those who were outside of the U.S. Once again Carlos was left out by the law and the "line" that never materialized. He still believed and hoped for a version of the Dream Act that would allow him to reenter the U.S. and reclaim his dream.

Like many of the DREAM'ers, Carlos would have preferred to remain in legal limbo as a virtual pawn in this political game between Democrats and Republicans than to have been a victim in the immigration court system that resulted in his being "voluntarily" deported to Mexico.

On the Beach

In Mexico, Carlos survived the traumatic separation from his family. He accepted work at a Chili's restaurant in Cancun, Mexico where he served mostly U.S. Citizens who came down to drink beer, get drunk, and party at the beaches.

Carlos' education, charm, and mastery of the English language allowed him to be a waiter. His customers marveled at his English. Every day they would sit at his tables, sunburned and sandaled, as they would ask him the question: "How come your English is so good?"

Carlos would oblige them, and he would tell his sad story; he missed his daughter and that his situation had resulted in Claudia initiating a divorce. Large tables of guests were shocked by this story and sad to hear Carlos was raised in the U.S. since he was a child and now was in this situation.

This also meant that he continued to endure a long separation from his daughter--the little girl that he helped nurture through her rough start in this world. Just as the immigration judge who deported Carlos had suggested, little Sofia would have to avail herself of public assistance without Carlos to continue his economic support for her, her mom, and her grandparents.

Carlos said he felt like he was stuck in a rotating hell, performing the best work he could obtain in Mexico. He did all he could, even considering trying to come back across the border to his home in Denver, Colorado.

Instead, Carlos told his story to the partying Americans and Canadians at his tables--interrupting their mindless, alcohol-tinged vacations, including many from his home in Colorado, and sometimes he made a few extra pesos from the tips given to him out of the sympathy these tourists had for his situation.

Last we spoke, Carlos explained his bittersweet return to the U.S. in 2014 once an immigrant visa became available to him and his wife. A year after returning to the U.S., their situation had resulted in Claudia finalizing their divorce. Carlos became a single father and began his life anew. Just as the immigration judge who deported Carlos had suggested, little Sofia would have to avail herself of public assistance while Carlos had to start his life from scratch while continuing his economic support for her, her mom and her grandparents.

What Will Happen the DREAM'ers?

No matter what happens with the current DACA recipients in the courts, DACA will not likely become available to other applicants, and the DREAM Act is still further out on the horizon. It is even more obvious that the DREAM Act will be the only measure preventing millions of children who were raised here in the U.S., like Carlos and Gabby, from being deported and separated from their United States citizen children and their Legal Permanent Resident parents.

Like the millions of children who exist without legal status in the U.S., Carlos finally realized his dream because he was able to get in a "line and wait his turn" five times for over 25 years. Carlos is the lucky one; however, there are millions like Carlos who have no lines to enter because they do not happen to have U.S. citizen uncles or marry someone with TPS or political asylum.

So many of the children who grew up in the U.S., who did all that they could do to be contributing and productive members of our country, including repeated attempts to "do it the right way" have no options unless the DREAM Act is finally implemented, and they are provided a pathway to earned legal presence and the eventual privilege of becoming a U.S. citizen.

Out of the estimated 2 million DREAM'ers who were eligible to apply for the temporary benefits of DACA, over one million of them declined placement voluntarily on Obama's list for future deportation. Many of those who declined to apply for DACA verbalized their fear to me that, at worst, President Obama was unintentionally placing them in a position to be ushered out of the country and away from all that they knew. Others suspected that this as was an intentional ruse that was designed and thinly veiled to make them live permanently as the political pawns of our daily political debates.

Many DREAM'ers are reluctantly conscious that they are hostage to career politicians on both the Left and the Right of the spectrum. Thus, many of the young people eligible to request DACA refused unilaterally to give the government their addresses, the names of their families, their work and school histories, their cell phone number and their voluntary agreement to be deported in the future.

In a last-ditch effort to proffer votes by the growing Latino American voters—one million Latinos become of voting age every year—former President Obama announced an expansion of the DACA policy to include those who had been in the country even longer. The former president also announced a new program aimed at the parents of DACA recipients called the Deferred Action for Parental Responsibility or "DAPA" program to provide the same tenuous benefits to adult immigrant parents of DACA recipients.

Unfortunately, "DAPA" was challenged in the Supreme Court to the United States in 579 U.S. (2016) United States v. Texas. The 2014 executive action by President Obama to allow around five million unauthorized immigrants who were the parents of citizens and or of lawful permanent residents to apply for a program that would spare them from deportation and provide them with work permits., got a 4-4 tie in the Supreme Court. This effectively blocked the plan.

The Official Government Numbers Provided to the Governmental Affairs Hearing On "Securing the Border" On March 25, 2015 Conflict with Data provided under the Freedom of Information Act obtained by Matt Graham of the New York Times!

		All countries	Mexico	Northern triangle
FY 2009	**Total**	**5,762**	**2,931**	**2,117**
	Minors (age 0-17) deported	4,599	2,373	1,655
	18, apprehended FY 2008 or earlier	1,040	509	423
	19, apprehended FY 2007 or earlier	123	49	39
FY 2010	**Total**	**5,522**	**3,514**	**1,318**
	Minors (age 0-17) deported	4,170	2,657	962
	18, apprehended FY 2009 or earlier	1,169	767	308
	19, apprehended FY 2008 or earlier	183	90	48
FY 2011	**Total**	**3,773**	**1,938**	**1,150**
	Minors (age 0-17) deported	2,777	1,409	802
	18, apprehended FY 2010 or earlier	816	446	297
	19, apprehended FY 2009 or earlier	180	83	51
FY 2012	**Total**	**3,277**	**1,948**	**946**
	Minors (age 0-17) deported	2,517	1,548	677
	18, apprehended FY 2011 or earlier	624	330	236
	19, apprehended FY 2010 or earlier	136	70	33
FY 2013	**Total**	**2,418**	**1,278**	**944**
	Minors (age 0-17) deported	1,669	1,022	496
	18, apprehended FY 2012 or earlier	683	230	423
	19, apprehended FY 2011 or earlier	66	26	25
Five-year total (FY 2009-FY 2013)		**20,752**	**11,609**	**6,475**
	Minors (age 0-17) deported	15,732	9,009	4,592
	18, apprehended previous FY or earlier	4,332	2,282	1,687
	19, apprehended two FYs ago or earlier	688	318	196

Data Source: Calculated from ICE FOIA dataset obtained from The New York Times Graphic Source (Graham, Child Deportations: How Many Minors Does the U.S. Actually Send Home, 2014)

Between 2009 and 2013, the Obama administration deported a total of 20,752 unaccompanied children. This number consists of 11,609 back to Mexico and 6,475 unaccompanied minors back to the violent Northern Triangle of El Salvador, Guatemala, and Honduras.

Remember the official Government numbers provided to the Governmental Affairs Hearing On "Securing the Border" On March 25, 2015, they conflict with these numbers obtained under the Freedom of information act by Matt Graham of the New York Times.

Between 2009 and 2013, the Obama administration Deported a total of 20,752 unaccompanied children. This number consisting of 11,609 back to Mexico and 6,475 unaccompanied minors back to the violent Northern Triangle of El Salvador, Guatemala, and Honduras. This data conflicts with both the Mexican deportation of minors and the 5,366 to the northern triangle previously provided by the government departments.

The data implies that the U.S. removed about a total of 6,475 migrants from El Salvador, Guatemala, and Honduras who were apprehended as children.

Former President Obama's rush to deport many children who arrived in 2014 while attempting to expand the benefits of the weak DACA program and create this new policy to extend the "deferred deportation benefits" to their parents through the DAPA program has stood as a glaring example of the Democratic Party's inability to address the issue of immigrant children. All of America was watching as Latino voters refused this pandering by the Democratic Party to the fastest-growing electorate.

The political fallout from the abandonment of pro-immigrant voters to make it to the polls was imminent. Perhaps it was the arrogance of Democratic Party operatives whose assumption that DACA would turn out the same number of voters in the Latino community that had voted for President Obama in the next election for president in 2016 out of blind loyalty.

Perhaps the fallout was bolstered by then-Secretary of State Hillary Clinton's published personal memoir boasting of her role in producing a military coup in Honduras in 2009 to depose the democratically elected leader in that country.

Perhaps a contributing factor was Secretary Clinton's strong influence in the presidency of her husband Bill Clinton where the most draconian penalties in the last 50 years of immigration law were implemented.

The quick stroke of President Clinton's pen solidified the Illegal Immigration Reform and Immigrant Responsibility Act (IIRAIRA) and the Anti-terrorism and Effective Death Penalty Act (IIRAIRA) into law. Those Clinton-era bills criminalized immigrants and put in place permanent bars which did not exist before 1996. Those laws resulted in countless separations of families from their U.S. citizen spouses, children and parents, and the Democratic Party still have not recovered their past credibility as the protectorates of immigrants.

In a stunning victory in the Electoral College, Republican Donald Trump was elected as the next President of the United States in November of 2016.

DACA was terminated by President Trump leaving the DREAM'ers fate at the mercy of the federal courts

---

Needless to say, DACA was terminated by President Trump in his first year as president and the legality of President Obama's signature "that we can deport you now, but you hope that we won't until later" program has left the fate of DREAM'ers at the mercy of the federal courts, including the U.S. Supreme Court who agreed to take up the case. Decision expected by the end of 2019.

The DREAM'ers situation is compounded by the fact that since 2014, their situation has become the "line in the sand" where many U.S. citizens clearly want the Dream Act to be implemented; however, they are less sure what to do with the huge number of children who have entered from Central America during the current humanitarian crisis of Central America.

The media has intentionally or unintentionally framed the discussion into a simple choice that we either help the DACA recipients or help the recently arrived children who we have relegated to one of the ugliest foster care situations in our country's history.

Our government's inability to address this humanitarian crisis is now playing out on all media platforms. The media are breaking stories daily about children who are being forced to wait in the crime-riddled borderlands of Mexico, then being shoved into overcrowded tented cages on our side of the Southern border as youngsters in our government's hands have begun to die in custody in increasing numbers. The situation has begun to resemble the worst of our country's past policies of internment, segregation, and abuse of vulnerable minority groups.

There is an outcry from the public, but the politicians are once again brokering the discussion which now pits DACA kids against the refugee children. Who are we going to help? We are told to pick one, click one.

Many believe that the construction of the wall will solve this issue by literally shutting the door to more kids coming to the U.S. As the argument goes, once we ensure border security, then we can solve our immigration problem at home.

The "Wall" is a Symbolic Distraction from The Issues, Problems, and Solutions for Immigration.

The "wall" doesn't work and doesn't matter as it is just a symbolic distraction from the issues, problems, and solutions.

Alternatively, the public could ask for our leaders to lead and provide an approach that will address the problems and not just appeal to the lowest common denominator.

President Trump and the Republicans have already declared that immigration will be the principal issue that will define the presidential debates for the 2020 elections.

President Trump's announcement has the Democrats cowering in a corner, unable to provide an answer as only one of the declared candidates on the extensive list has provided any meaningful proposals as to how to address the underlying issues of the Dreamers and the refugee children at the border.

Former President Barack Obama promised immigrants' and immigrant rights groups sweeping changes. He made overtures to many Latino voters during his campaign in 2007.

Barack said he would; "Provide a path to citizenship for undocumented immigrants."

I will support "a system that allows undocumented immigrants who are in good standing to pay a fine, learn English, and go to the back of the line for the opportunity to become citizens." (PolitiFact, 2019)

Barack said he would "Introduce a comprehensive immigration bill in the first year."

"I cannot guarantee that it is going to be in the first 100 days. But what I can guarantee is that we will have in the first year an immigration bill that I strongly support and that I'm promoting. And I want to move that forward as quickly as possible." (Avalos, 2008)

Sources: Jorge Ramos TV clip with candidate Barack Obama, May 28, 2008, on JorgeRamos.com May 29,2008

The big shift in the Latino vote was heavily for Obama in 2008; over ten million people believed in his rhetoric, his promises to the immigrant children.

In Colorado, my home state Latino voter turnout rose from 8 percent of those who voted in 2004 to 13 percent, according to the local news at the time.

Mr. Obama carried the Latino vote in Colorado by a large majority. The Community was talking excitedly with hope.

On January 20, 2009, Barack Obama was inaugurated as the 44th President of the United States.

I believe Obama had promising ideas but failed miserably in delivering the Democrats promise of comprehensive immigration reform. They could have passed it as the Democrats controlled the majority in Congress for the first 100 days as he promised.

The Latinx community waited anxiously for the Immigration promises to be fulfilled, or even started in the legislature.

On March 26, 2009, a bipartisan team of the 111th Congress led by Senators Dick Durbin (D-IL), Richard Lugar (R-IN), Harry Reid (D-NV), Mel Martinez (R-FL), Patrick Leahy (D-VT), Joseph Lieberman (I-CT), Ted Kennedy (D-MA), and Russ Feingold (D-WI) and U.S. Representative Howard Berman (D-CA), co-sponsored the 2009 version of the DREAM Act.

March 26, 2009, the Bipartisan DREAM Act was Introduced to Both Chambers of Congress.

Immigrants Could Qualify in Part, By Meeting the Following Requirements:
- Be between the ages of 12 and 35 at the time the Law is enacted
- Arrived in the United States before the age of 16
- Resided continuously in the United States for at least five consecutive years since the date of their arrival

- Graduated from a US high school or obtained a General Education Diploma

- Be a person of Good moral character

Source: (Congress, 2009-2010)

There were other stipulations, but the bill failed, leaving DREAM'ers dejected holding placards on the steps of Congress.

Obama dithered for a year verbally promising "Comprehensive Immigration Reform" and guess what happened?

On December 15, 2009, Democratic Rep. Luis Gutierrez championing immigrants and workers' rights introduced a bill of his own! The "Comprehensive Immigration Reform," as it is known by supporters, was highlighted in the acronym of Mr. Gutierrez's bill: "C.I.R. A.S.A.P." Perhaps a bit poignant, his dig at Obama is clear. His actions echoed the needs and thoughts of the DREAM'ers on the steps of Congress.

Luis Gutierrez' advocacy for immigrant rights is a story of challenges, passion, and joy, in his memoirs, *Still Dreaming: My Journey from the Barrio to Capitol Hill*, he inspires us all to stand up for our rights and those of others.

High on the hill in the swamp of sweaty politics, Luis Gutierrez' bill was declared dead on arrival by jostling Republicans and Democrats trying to be in the limelight. The very thought of providing an earned pathway to citizenship to children who had arrived through no fault of their own was absurd in the eyes of Congress! The bill did not get President Obama's support.

While the Obama Administration floundered, with false promises and inaction. The voices of the DREAM'ers strengthened frustrated by the ineptitude they marched to shame and tell Congress and Obama it was time to act.

To placate the marchers and Latino community, President Obama kept spouting forth support of "comprehensive immigration reform." Obama had no solidified plan, so frustrated State and Federal lawmakers got to work.

Governor Schwarzenegger's Administration Pumped Iron and Blocked the California DREAM Act from 2006 – 2007. But as The Saying goes, "I'll be back."

In 2010 as the sizzling summer sun beat down on surfers in California, the independent, forward-thinking state saw the quandary and passed the California DREAM Act, on August 31, 2010, other states followed to protect children under sixteen years of age and allow them to attend school and receive student aid.

On December 8, 2010, Republican members in the House of Representatives passed the version of the DREAM Act., a legislative proposal for a multi-phase process for qualifying children in the United States; children who were not American citizens who have resided in the U.S., that would initially grant conditional residency status and, upon meeting further qualifications, permanent residency.

The **D**evelopment, **R**elief, and **E**ducation for **A**lien **M**inors Act - DREAM Act was reintroduced in the Senate on August 1, 2001, S. 1291 by United States Senators Dick Durbin (D- Illinois) and Orrin Hatch (R- Utah).

DREAM Act-To Meet the Conditional Resident Status, the Individual Must:

- have proof that they entered the United States before the age of 16 and must have continuously lived in the country for at least five years

- have graduated from a United States high school or obtained a GED in the US.

- demonstrate good moral character

- pass criminal background checks and reviews

After having obtained and held conditional resident status, permanent residency may be granted if the following requirements have been met within six years' timeframe.

DREAM Act-For Permanent Residency, the Individual Must:

- Have attended an institution of higher learning or served in the United States military for at least two years and if discharged, have received an honorable discharge

- Pass a series of background checks

- Continue to demonstrate good moral character

If these requirements are not fulfilled the 'conditional resident' will lose their legal status and be subject to deportation.

The debate in the Senate began, and like Obama, floundered flapping like a fish out of water. The bill was dead before Christmas.

The gift of a path to residency gone like a leaf blown by the cold winter wind.

2011 and a fresh Spring start saw Senate Majority Leader Harry Reid reintroduce the DREAM Act again with Obama's support; only to fail again! However, the Republicans fought hard to make The Democrats include the requirement for every U.S. employer to use E-Verify to confirm a person's nationality and immigration status.

Another Year passed! DREAM'ers were becoming disenfranchised; an election was coming.

On June 15, 2012, From the white house, Rose Garden President Obama announced the Administration would stop deporting undocumented immigrants who match certain criteria included in the proposed DREAM Act.

Watch The historic CNN Video Clip

The Republicans were outraged. Why? Because they had cosponsored the DREAM Act and the political thunder and kudos had been stolen from under their feet.

On August 15, 2012, the U.S. Citizenship, and Immigration Services (USCIS) began accepting applications under the Obama administration's new *Deferred Action for Childhood Arrivals* (DACA) program.

The innocent immigrants followed the Pied Piper giving the government all the information that Trump would need and any President to get ICE to deport them.

Thousands upon thousands applied for the new program, gathering in jovial elated lines in front of Immigrant Rights offices from Los Angeles to New York.

The application costs $495. DACA leads to temporary work authorization, which is good for two years. DREAM'ers with the work authorization card can get a social security number, allowing them to pay taxes, and many states receive a driver's license.

DACA was crafted and penned to help address the immigration status of the same people as the DREAM Act.

Often, DACA and the DREAM Act are debated together, with little distinction between them. Many people focus attention on the methodology of the implementation between the DREAM Act's legislation through Congress in contrast to the implementation of DACA through the president's executive implementation.

I believe the Democrats did not want Republicans to receive credit for the DREAM Act.

Do you think the DREAM'ers and DACA recipients care who receives credit? NO! They need action.

The Democratic Party-controlled Congress, hold majorities in both the Senate and the House of Representatives during Obama's first two years.

The DREAM Act proposal, which had been first introduced as a bill by Republican Senator Orin Hatch and Democratic Senator Dick Durbin of Utah, has been tabled over ten times since 2001. The bill was passed over by the Democrats who promised their own more comprehensive bill. The Democrat's bill never emerged, and advocacy groups were livid.

In June of 2013, the Republicans in the house tried to halt DACA by defunding it. However, one thing that the Obama Administration did well was to ensure the DACA program was self-funded through the applications, and not Congress.

Daring to Dream?

Who are these people who dare to DREAM? To hope for a better-legalized future?

The Migration Policy Institute (MPI) estimates as of August 2018, 699,350 people signed up for DACA. The federal government estimates 1.326 million are likely eligible.

DACA Recipients & Program Participation Rate, by State

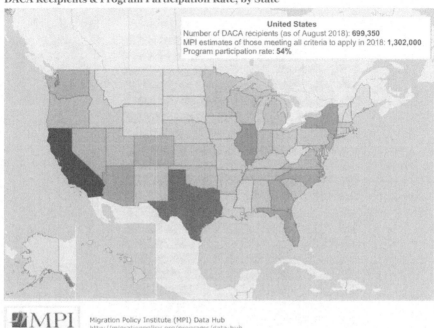

United States
Number of DACA recipients (as of August 2018): **699,350**
MPI estimates of those meeting all criteria to apply in 2018: **1,302,000**
Program participation rate: **54%**

Migration Policy Institute (MPI) Data Hub
http://migrationpolicy.org/programs/data-hub

Image Source: The Migration Policy Institute MPI - The darker the blue, the more DACA people are eligible

The map above is interactive on the MPI site. **Hover over each state to see the number of DACA people per state.**

DACA Recipients & Program Participation Rate, by Country of Origin

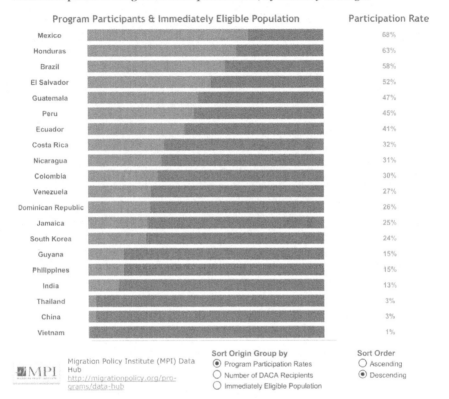

The Fading Promise Of DACA

A climate of intensifying fear surrounds Trump's "Zero Tolerance" storm trooper tactics. His immigration policies and the fear of potential deportation has led many illegal immigrant families around the country, to prepare for the worst.

Many communities and immigrant families are planning for ICE to strike like lightning in the night. Securing a future for their children with long term plans that include coordinating a legal guardian, in case they are separated.

Today a fight is going on in the courts of the U.S. to save DACA recipients. The U.S. supreme court is expected to rule on the issue by the end of 2019.

Meanwhile, many DACA recipients are processing passports for their U.S. born children as a last resort so that the entire family can leave the country in the event of deportation.

The problem is many of these families have members who are regarded as U.S. citizens by the countries they will flee to. The result may be that they will be separated by the very government of the country they flee!

The DREAM'ers are Left in Limbo "winding down," to Nowhere

In September 2017, President Donald Trump's administration announced the program was "winding down," as tens of thousands of refugees began fleeing the violent Northern Triangle of Guatemala, El Salvador, and Honduras.

Image Source: © Peter Lucking | contentbrandingsolutions.com

CHAPTER 3

Hillary Clinton: Sowing the Seeds of a Military Coup in Honduras

How did we arrive at this precarious juncture? Why are children flocking to the U.S. in the thousands?

Some Americans have visions of parents from Central America, sending their children packing with a knapsack from their porch swings amid cornfields in Guatemala. They believe that the humanitarian crisis of children at our Southern border is the result of a simple choice by tens of thousands of parents to send their children to the U.S. This would require us to believe that Central American parents are less than good parents—we would have to believe that they are lesser human beings.

Those of us who are parents should know that this is not true and ask ourselves: "Why would parents send their children?" There must be more complicated reasons. Others blame former President Obama for the false promise of DACA and have alleged that the implementation of DACA without Congressional approval is tantamount to inviting every teenager with a dream to the United States.

U.S. Interference: Drugs, Gangs and Ruining Presidents

The truth is so much further, and it requires one to look at our recent history to understand that we have created this situation for ourselves by interfering with Central American governments. About twenty-one years ago, I decided to see what was happening in Central America; however, the problems started long before that.

U.S.-Based Money, Guns, Gangs and Hillary Clinton Effect on Honduras

Our government has created this crisis, which has led to mass migration by children from Honduras, Guatemala, and El Salvador into the United States.

To understand the situation requires a quick review of the U.S. government's intervention in Central America. Over a hundred years ago, our government began to directly shape and control the countries of Central America to align them with private U.S. companies.

For example, Honduras was transformed into a one-crop "Banana Republic" where U.S. companies controlled the agricultural fields along with the country's banking and mining sectors.

The American government has used direct military action along the way and was successful in propping up the Honduran military as the foundation of the ruling elite to protect private interests from the U.S. Particularly in the '80s under former President Ronald Reagan, Honduras was used as the base for U.S. military intervention in neighboring Nicaragua.

Our government solidified decades of rule by military elites in Honduras as hundreds of U.S. military troops were stationed in bases that coordinated with the CIA to train the "Contra" rebels to topple Nicaragua's leftist regime in the '80s. Twenty years later, de facto military rule was disrupted as the democratically elected Manuel Zelaya became president of Honduras in 2006.

Manuel Zelaya was a liberal-capitalist reformer, however his well-intentioned efforts to convene a constitutional assembly to rewrite his government's military-controlled laws alarmed our government and the military elite in Honduras. Also, Zelaya was open to dialogue from left-leaning Venezuela and wished to strengthen the Organization of American States beyond their traditional subservience to the United States on all matters.

Once former President Obama had been elected in 2007, he tasked then-Secretary of State Hillary Clinton to coordinate with U.S. interests to ensure that Honduras and Manuel Zelaya would stay in line with our countries foreign policy and economic interests.

Hillary Clinton and the U.S. Department of State were more than just aware the military elite in Honduras was initiating a Coup d'état to oust Zelaya from his democratically elected position. They were a party to the intrigue, aiding and abetting the coordinated installation of a military-controlled government. Once the coup was completed, Hillary Clinton and the U.S. Department of State helped organize a special election and then arranged for international recognition of the newly installed dictator Juan Orlando Hernandez in 2009.

The number of political assassinations, illegal arrests, and kidnappings attributed to the Honduran government's collusion with criminal gangs increased to alarming numbers. The chaos that ensued in Honduran society was then amplified by the Obama administration's decision to reduce funds that sustained education, health, and environmental controls. (Bader, 2009)

By 2010, this provided the perfect storm for U.S. based, criminal syndicates the Mara Salvatrucha's to seize the opportunity and expand the illegal drug trade and human trafficking from the prisons in the Los Angeles, California area while providing "contract services" to those who wished to repress political expression in Honduras.

While U.S. journalists and academics, downplayed the U.S. role in Honduras, academics and the world community are now pointing to U.S. intervention as the cause of the current mass migration by Hondurans, particularly Honduran children to the U.S.

Hillary Clinton even removed reference to her role in the Honduran coup during the Obama years in her the later versions of her published memoir.

Today, President Trump has cut economic aid as he lays blame on Honduras and the other two Central American countries for the migrant caravans that have formed to seek refuge in the United States.

The Story of Guatemala's and El Salvador's Widows and Children

I have long been interested in the issue of our government's destabilization of Central America. Even in Greeley, Colorado, where I lived off-and-for a few years as a child, there was always a sense of solidarity with the refugees fleeing violence from Central America.

My mother worked in the local meat-packing plant. Often, she was the only English-speaker to work on the "line" cutting meat all day as it came down a conveyor belt. She worked shoulder to shoulder with immigrant workers with whom she could barely communicate.

As a child in the '80s, I accompanied my mom and step-dad, Guillermo Garibay, to meetings at churches and community centers where Salvadoran refugees were pleading for help in the form of humanitarian and legal aid for those fleeing the violence caused by civil war.

In the case of El Salvador, the U.S. government was supporting the government against leftist rebels during the sunset of the Cold War between the U.S. and the former Soviet Union. We heard from Salvadoran and U.S. community advocates who wished to inform the public through the organization Communities in Support of The People of El Salvador (CiSPES).

I cherish the memories of such meetings. Even as a child, I *felt* the despair and urgency of their pleas for help to end our government's sponsorship of bloodshed and widow-making.

Today I feel that there is a disconnect due to the artificial interface of a smartphone and the somehow all-too-safe distance of live images since the advent of the internet, Facebook, Twitter, and Instagram. That experience has stayed with me into adolescence through college and into law school so much that I decided to travel to Central America in 1998 to better understand what was happening.

In the early evening of March 31, 1998, I along with three other law students from the University of Colorado School of Law in Boulder, Colorado flew to Guatemala City to meet with human rights organizations. Sean McAllister, Don Zettler, Katherine Hall, and I took a red-eye flight to Los Angeles for a connecting flight to Guatemala.

Our goal was to bring back news regarding the success and challenges of the peace accords signed on December 26, 1996, by the Guatemalan Government and the Guatemalan National Revolutionary Unity (URNG). Our friend, Will Harrell, coordinated the trip.

Both the Government and the guerrilla rebel coalition began a massive dismantling of their armed forces that had conflicted for three decades. Both sides agreed to provide posts in the more inclusive government to end the bloodshed that had resulted in human rights abuses, including mass killings, ethnic cleansing, and genocide.

Despite the hope brought by the new accords, Guatemala was ranked 4th in the world in kidnappings per capita and ranked 2nd for the highest number of kidnappings at 900 per year—this was only second to Colombia which had the highest number of kidnappings in the world in 1997.

Arriving about 6 a.m. to Guatemala City via Los Angeles, California, the three law students and I woke up with the sun in the industrial and highly polluted capital of Guatemala.

We took a taxi to the home of a U.N. worker who had agreed to house us for our 3-day whirlwind stay. We happily accepted the offer of a shower, coffee, and *plátanos*, sweet fried plantains before meeting the other two members of our delegation and our first meeting that same morning at 8:30 a.m.

My head was spinning filled with information from relentless meetings in a whirlwind schedule. We met with human rights groups hour after hour around-the-clock for two days.

We met with a worker's union called *UNSITRAGUA*, which stands for **the Syndicated Union of Guatemalan Workers**. This umbrella organization integrated different unions of workers throughout Guatemala that were organized by workers in various branches of Industry, Services, Agricultural, self-employed, and independent contractors.

Next, we shuttled by taxi to the Human Rights Office for the Catholic Archbishop of Guatemala, Juan José Gerardi Conedera, who helped broker the Peace Accords between the government and opposition groups.

Their reception for us was very upbeat, politely formal. Of course, the religious representatives were among the best dressed and had relatively nice offices—almost stereotypically the picture of Catholic powerbrokers in a Third World country. They welcomed us in their pressed black suits with priest collars. A significant percentage of the country, including government and opposition groups alike, respected the church and looked to them for invaluable guidance for reconciliation for the sins of the civil war.

Ironically, the Archbishop, Juan José Gerardi Conedera was murdered a month after we returned from our trip. On April 26, 1998, two days after the release of the REMHI project in a report entitled

Page | 67

"Nunca Más," (Never Again), Bishop Gerardi was bludgeoned to death with a cinder block in his home in Guatemala City.

The Bishop was one of the dissenters that effectively damned the Guatemalan military for the atrocities committed during the internal armed conflict. Recovery of Historical Memory (REMHI) Project report found that the military was responsible for 85% of the human rights violations committed during the 36-years of civil war and that the guerrilla groups were responsible for 9%. The Report named those responsible, making its authors a target.

Some statistics from the REMHI project report

- 6,500 collective and individual interviews: 92% with victims and 8% with those responsible for the events.

- Direct victims of the war, approximately: 150,000 people killed; 50,000 missing; 1 million refugees; 200,000 children orphaned; 40,000 women widowed. Total: 1,440,000 victims.

- Of the 55,021 victims registered in the period 1960-96 (80% in the period 1980- 83), 25,123 were killed (45.7%); 3,893 missing (7.1%); 5,516 tortured (10.0%); 723 held hostage (1.3%); 5,079 detained irregularly (9.2%); 152 victims of sexual violations (0.3%); 10,157 victims of different types of attacks (18.5%); and 323 of other violations (0.6%).

Source: (Beristain, 1998)

Everyone was so positive during our trip that it later turned my stomach to learn of his assassination.

The Death of Archbishop Juan José Gerardi Conedera was such a setback to many of the efforts that we witnessed on our trip. It happened so quickly that we were not able to publish all of the details our student delegation report in the journal of the National Lawyers Guild.

After an hour, we were whisked off to our 11 o'clock meeting with The Guatemalan Association of Jurists (ACJ). I remember meeting with Marlene Grajeda from the ACJ. This valiant group of attorneys regularly held educational forums for urban workers and rural villagers alike concerning their human and constitutional rights. During these forums, the ACJ would identify cases where Guatemalan citizens were detained, jailed, or "disappeared" for demanding their rights. The ACJ would then provide legal advocacy for those recognized as "political prisoners." It would be an understatement to call their work dangerous in a land where the murders of lawyers had become commonplace during the civil war.

I do not remember that we even had time to eat lunch. I vaguely remember buying some food off the street on our way into one of these meetings.

Next up was a meeting with Vitalino Similox the Secretary of the Conference of Evangelical Churches. As Secretary, we were with the head of a national religious organization of non-Catholic churches. He explained that one-third of the population of Guatemala had turned to the Evangelical Christian religion.

Vitalino Similox' organization, which went by the Acronym CIEDEG had actively implemented educational and technical, agricultural, and various social assistance to one hundred and thirty communities. Like the ACJ and the other groups, many of their workers were in danger. Two of their evangelical pastors had been murdered in the three years before our delegation visit. Mr. Similox analogized the experience of his activist pastors to the African American church organizers in the South of the United States during the heyday of the Klu Klux Klan.

Amidst the whirlwind of these afternoon meetings with indigenous rights groups such as CERJ and CPR, I will never forget the organization of mostly Mayan indigenous women who welcomed us to their central office at 3 pm that day. There I witnessed dozens of women with an even larger group of young children engaged in a massive mutual help organization housed in a building that had a combination of mixed, temporary roofing and open-air "rooms."

Mayan women welcomed our student delegation with small gifts that were hand-made by their members who all wore bright hand embroidered dresses.

Their Mayan blouses were full of colorful and intricate flowers and animals of orange, white, black, red, green, and yellow threads worn from head to toe. I remember feeling like a giant at my entire five-foot, six inches as I towered over the women, none of whom were taller than four-foot, ten inches, many of them shorter.

The widows of *CONAVIGUA* were women whose husbands, sons and daughters had been either killed or had "disappeared" during the three decades of Guatemala's civil war. Since 1988 they have organized daily to alleviate and solve the most immediate and urgent needs of their members, including a lack of food, medicine, housing, and clothing.

The widows explained that on a local level, they work by developing projects for Guatemalan women that allow them to build work skills, learn entrepreneurial strategies, produce products that they can sell and grow their food.

In the larger political arena and their rural countryside villages, these widows advocate to create laws for the protection of widows and mothers, to stop the abuses of exploitation and sexual violence by soldiers, military commissioners, chiefs of civil patrols, and others.

Every woman at *CONAVIGUA* had two or more children when I visited back in 1998. Of course, they continued to engage in lobbying the Guatemalan government for more education programs and health initiatives for children who rarely are offered more than a third-grade education before working in the plantations to plant, care and harvest food marked for the United States.

The brave and dynamic women I met such as Marta Mendoza, and Carmen Gomez toiled in exhumations of mass graves of victims of the armed conflicts to first, help identify loved ones who had been "disappeared" and then, second, to offer dignified burials to allow family and friends to honor those who have passed. The widows were kind and decent in their insistence to us that women, in general, must be respected and receive equal treatment by their government.

They noted that the Peace Accords, while positive, had largely failed to include women in the government posts that were opened to former government opposition groups and human rights advocates. Appropriately, Marta and the others turned their heads slightly in the direction of the children and pointed with their eyes to all the children in attendance who represented a small fraction, a drop-in-the-ocean, of fatherless children strewn across Guatemala in the wake of a brutal and still smoldering civil war.

Caravan of Mothers and Widows are searching for the lost children some the U.S. sent back, dumped unceremoniously across the border. Others are buried in nameless graves.

Every year for the past thirteen years a Caravan of Mothers, with many from the widows of *CONAVIGUA* from Guatemala travel the 2,500 miles from the violent Northern Triangle joining with widows, and mothers from El Salvador, Honduras and Nicaragua to the United States across Mexico searching for their children who went missing while migrating through the country from the violence and rampant crime of Central America.

Many widows and mothers are searching for the children the U.S. sent back, dumped unceremoniously across the border. Lost in limbo in a hostile foreign land, never to return to their mothers.

Photojournalist Encarni Pindado covered their heart-wrenching journey in search of the lost children in a BBC article *The caravan of mothers looking for their lost children*, December 17, 2017.

The stories are emotional, gut-wrenching, and tragic. Rosa Nelly Santos, who heads a committee for disappeared migrants in Honduras spoke words that are quoted in the article that made me cry.

"Before migrants died of thirst or were bitten by a snake while crossing the desert. Today they die at the hands of organized crime, and our girls, are raped by people linked to organized crime."

We need to add our voices to the cry for help. We need to encourage our politicians to do more. We need to Act.

As the sun was setting on Guatemala City that day, we trekked to our next encounter with CPR an indigenous rights group. Little did I know that 16 years later, some of these children would find their way to the United States, and into my office to seek shelter from the proliferation of violent criminals who steadily took control of Guatemala, El Salvador, and Honduras at the beginning of the 21st Century.

The Secretary of State Hillary Clintons stance on Iraq and Libya are well known, but what often gets left out of the fog of war is her staunch support behind the 2009 Honduran coup that ousted an elected President Manuel Zelaya. Then-Secretary Clinton, personally strategized with dissidents, people in business, and the Honduran military, to remove Zelaya and install a military dictator

"We strategized on a plan to restore order in Honduras and ensure that free and fair elections could be held quickly and legitimately, which would render the question of Zelaya moot and give the Honduran people a chance to choose their future," Hillary Clinton wrote in her hardcover autobiography, Hard Choices, published in 2014.

It is interesting to note that that quote and its associated discussion disappeared from paperback addition, during editing!

The omission was first noted in a scathing essay by Belén Fernández in the book *False Choices: The Faux Feminism of Hillary Rodham Clinton* that was cited in The Nation. (Grandin, Before Her Murder, Berta Cáceres Singled Out Hillary Clinton for Criticism, 2016).

In the hardcover edition of *Hard Choices,* Clinton promotes the coup and new elections as a triumph of regional diplomacy. Clinton pushed for elections as she states in *Hard Choices* for a *"unity government."*

Unfortunately, the legacy of American political interference and clandestine operations in both central and south America has laid a treacherous foundation that has encouraged the suppression of the freedom of speech, caused political, economic, and social upheaval and led to humanitarian atrocities. Consequently, the migration of displaced people from these zones should be no surprise.

The cartels have thrived and exploited the region's instability, using the confusion of political violence as they solidified their control over trafficking routes.

The U.S. Embassy Dispatches from Honduras

In 2009 The U.S. Embassy in Honduras sent classified diplomatic dispatches to Washington. Analysis of the dispatches from Honduras shows the forced removal of the Honduran president, Manuel Zelaya. The dispatches address the much-debated question of whether it was an illegal coup.

Read the leaked confidential cable provided to the New York Times by WikiLeaks and published by the New York Times: A Selection From the Cache of Diplomatic Dispatches (Diplomatic Dispatches, 2011), or at The U.S. Embassy Dispatches from Honduras.

The leak of a cache of over a quarter of a million confidential diplomatic cables by WikiLeaks to multiple news agencies around the world sent shudders through the diplomatic establishment worldwide.

Secretary Hillary Clinton and the Obama Administration have been scrambling to limit the fallout from the disclosure of American diplomatic protectionist actions.

The White House issued a press release on November 28, 2010

"...these cables could compromise private discussions with foreign governments and opposition leaders, and when the substance of private conversations is printed on the front pages of newspapers across the world, it can deeply impact not only US foreign policy interests, but those of our allies and

friends around the world. To be clear -- such disclosures put at risk our diplomats, intelligence professionals, and people around the world who come to the United States for assistance in promoting democracy and open government...

...Wikileaks has put at risk not only the cause of human rights but also the lives and work of these individuals. We condemn in the strongest terms the unauthorized disclosure of classified documents and sensitive national security information." The White House · 1600 Pennsylvania Avenue, NW · Washington DC 20500 · 202-456-1111."

These White House leaks illustrate the depth that the Obama Administration, Secretary of State Hillary Clinton, and Rahm Emanuel the former White House chief of staff will go to, to continue the *Clintonism* policies.

Based on the U.S. Embassy Dispatches from Honduras, President Manuel Zelaya never resigned.

As the Dispatches state: "Zelaya had to be removed from the country to prevent a bloodbath..."

The Diplomatic cables reveal a U.S. policy that instigated a revolution, favored unchecked capitalism, that benefited the U.S. trade, and militarization without balancing the economic, political, and social consequences to the impoverished Hondurans.

In Honduras, the fall out of these actions was felt for years.

The Coup d'état in Honduras

The leader of the Coup d'état was Honduran General Romeo Vásquez Velásquez, a graduate of the notorious School of the Americas, a U.S. Army training program nicknamed the "School of Assassins."

Today that school is located at Fort Benning near Columbus, Georgia and is known as the Western Hemisphere Institute for Security Cooperation (WHINSEC) it is a United States Department of Defense Institute.

The school's torrid history is legendary in Latin America for the sizable number of graduates who have engaged in or led coups. The school's graduates are renowned for their scorched earth policies, cruelty, torture, and murder of political opponents and dissenters.

Berta Cáceres was a dissenter, a voice for the indigenous people and the environment she opposed the 2009 Honduran Coup. She opposed General Romeo Vásquez Velásquez and the economic, environmental, and social-economic changes that *Clintonism* brought.

Berta Cáceres saw through *Clintonism* and politics. She lambasted North American corporations and the U.S. governments for supporting the 2009 military coup. She talked passionately sharing her viewpoint, opposing the Honduran elite who at that time were promoting development projects that the Council of Popular and Indigenous Organizations of Honduras (COPINH) and Berta considered threats to their very existence.

It is believed that Berta Cáceres was assassinated on March 2, 2016, by the orders of a private dam-building company.

Why were these projects that in the eyes of many U.S. citizens appeared on the surface to be beneficial to the Economy opposed locally?

These dam projects were opposed locally because they eliminated access to the rivers, forests, and mountain environments critical for agriculture. Most importantly, these projects ignored community-based agro-development.

The Consequences of American Intervention

Following the *"unity government,"* rise to power, Honduras became the murder capital of the world, with 90.4 homicides per 100,000 people in 2012, according to the 2011 Global Study on Homicide from the U.N. Office of Drugs and Crime. (United Nations Office on Drugs and Crime, 2012)

"Organized crime -- especially drug trafficking -- accounted for a quarter of deaths caused by firearms in the Americas, compared to only 5% of homicides in Asia and Europe," the report says. "That does not mean, however, that organized crime groups are not active in those two regions, but rather that they may be operating in ways that do not employ lethal violence to the same extent."

The findings of the U.N. study are stunning.

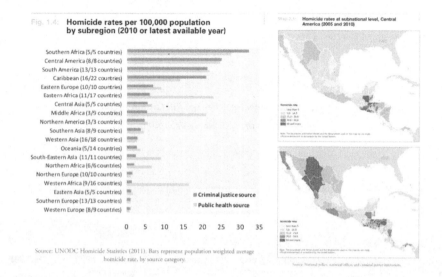

Fig. 1.4: **Homicide rates per 100,000 population by subregion (2010 or latest available year)**

Southern Africa (5/5 countries)
Central America (8/8 countries)
South America (13/13 countries)
Caribbean (16/22 countries)
Eastern Europe (10/10 countries)
Eastern Africa (11/17 countries)
Central Asia (5/5 countries)
Middle Africa (3/9 countries)
Northern America (3/3 countries)
Southern Asia (8/9 countries)
Western Asia (16/18 countries)
Oceania (5/14 countries)
South-Eastern Asia (11/11 countries)
Northern Africa (6/6 countries)
Northern Europe (10/10 countries)
Western Africa (9/16 countries)
Eastern Asia (5/5 countries)
Southern Europe (13/13 countries)
Western Europe (8/9 countries)

Criminal justice source
Public health source

0   5   10   15   20   25   30   35

Source: UNODC Homicide Statistics (2011). Bars represent population weighted average homicide rate, by source category.

Map 2.1: Homicide rates at subnational level, Central America (2005 and 2010)

Source: National police, statistical office, and criminal justice institutions.

Central America's Violent Northern Triangle, El Salvador, Guatemala, and Honduras and the southern bordering state of Nicaragua is the second most dangerous place in the world. No wonder people are fleeing the area.

Clintonism encourages corruption through unfettered capitalism and in many ways, encourages military-style rule versus democracy.

In 1982 under President Ronald Reagan U.S. Military aid for Guatemala continued despite official curbs, and as we all know The Iran Contra affair reached epic proportions in the violent Central Triangle and shoulder nations of South America.

CNN and the New York Times both reported and confirmed that financial aid, in the form of weapons often documented and disguised as "aircraft parts" was flowing into Guatemala. Adding to the mass genocide and homicide rates. (Meislin, 1982)

"Homicide rates in Central America and the Caribbean are nearing a "crisis point," according to a United Nations report.

Across Central America, homicide rates have increased in five out of eight countries over the past five years, with Honduras seeing homicide rates more than double between 2005 and 2010.

Mexico saw a 65% increase over the same period."

Source: (Report: Americas and Caribbean top global murder rates, 2011)

Hillary Clinton's plan for Central America Mirrored Bill Clinton's Plan Colombia. The Implications are Extremely Troubling.

- Jun 2009: A military coup ousted Honduran president Manuel Zelaya, and Parliament elects Porfirio Lobo to replace him

Bill Clinton's Plan Colombia continued Kissinger's diplomatic and philosophical philosophies in Latin America protecting American interests by creating the para- militarization of society. The Land-grab that followed left impoverished rural farmers with no choice but to work for the corporations.

Military death squads ruled tyrannically, torturing dissenters, massacring indigenous people, and mysteriously removing all political dissenters. The disappearances and killing of non-combatants, from politicians, environmentalist like Berta Cáceres to religious leaders like Archbishop, Juan José Gerardi Conedera were routine under Plan Colombia.

Berta Cáceres opposed the Obama's Administrations 2009 Honduran coup that Hillary Clinton, as secretary of state, made possible by destabilizing and then by deposing president Manuel Zelaya and undercutting the opposition movement demanding his restoration. In so doing, Hillary Clinton and the U.S. administration allied with the worst sectors of Honduran society.

Manuel Zelaya had supported Berta Cáceres fight against land dispossession, water rights, and mining. As a president, Zelaya was not perfect, but he was using his elected democratic power for the good of the people of Honduras.

You may say that Manuel Zelaya policies were "socialistic" and not in the U.S. interests. But his policies were in the interests of the people of Honduras and the sovereign state of Honduras.

Manuel Zelaya Removal led to:

- The "social cleansing" of the LGBT community and the suppression of transgender rights.

- The rise of paramilitary security forces.

- The Land-grab of the country's land and resources to transnational corporations.

- The murder and disappearance of street children and gang members.

- The rising of paramilitary security forces aligned with criminal drug cartels and syndicates.

- Explosive Environmental destruction.

- The privatization of rivers and consequent dam projects.

Source (Grandin, The Clinton-Backed Honduran Regime Is Picking Off Indigenous Leaders, 2016)

By 2009: Latin America is the murder capital of the world, it is the only region in the world where murder rates increased in the first decade of the 21st century

---

- Nov 2010: Gangsters kill 14 people in Honduras

- 2011: Honduras has the highest murder rate in the world

- The US role in the Honduras coup and subsequent violence

"Secretary of State Hillary Clinton -- played an important role in preventing Zelaya's return to office and the junta consolidating its power in the face of massive nonviolent protests." (Zunes, 2016)

Honduras was not the only Latin American country in the Triangle to suffer a "constitutional coup," of an elected leader through formally legal mechanisms under Hillary Clinton's State Department manipulation.

El Salvador

To make matters worse in Central Americas Violent Northern Triangle in 2012 Hillary Clinton's State Department, directed ambassador, Mari Carmen Aponte, to threaten El Salvador's leftist FMLN government with the withholding of aid.

The threat to withhold critical development aid unless El Salvador passed a major privatization law.

Ambassador Aponte went on to warn Salvadorans about the need to buy corporate manufactured genetically modified organism (GMO) seeds, insisting that the FMLN's seed-cooperative program violated the terms of the Central American Free Trade Agreement (CAFTA).

Clinton and Obama's reach touched South America.

Paraguay

Far to the South in Paraguay, a leftist former Catholic priest, and bishop of the Diocese of San Pedro del Paraná, Fernando Armando Lugo Méndez the Paraguayan president 2008- 20012, was removed from office for his anti-capitalist views by his powerful agro-industry opponents. Many Latin American nations called it a coup.

Hillary Clinton's State Department followed typical *Clintonism* doctrine, quickly recognizing the new government.

It appears that at this time, Bill Clinton's multibillion-dollar aid program became one of the worst human-rights violators in the world, with Plan Colombia.

Clintonism policies fed off each other; Hillary Clinton recommended its adoption for Central America!

The result was devastating violence and corruption rampant to the cocaine trade, that spread from the Cocaine States of Columbia in the northern shoulder of South America across the bridge to Central America affecting Panama and Costa Rica sandwiching the violent Northern Triangle of El Salvador, Guatemala, and Honduras between the Central American and Mexican cartels, and military regimes that were taking over the lucrative export of the drugs to the United States.

To make matters worse the collapse of Mexico's and Central America's agricultural sector caused by NAFTA and CAFTA, bolstered the cycle of criminal and gang violence that engulfs the region today.

The opening of national markets to US agro-industry destroyed many local agricultural-based economies. Human migration to find work created a pool of humanity for the gangs to prey on.

The violence has been accelerated by the privatization of the economy leading to the rapid spread of mining, hydroelectric, biofuel, and petroleum industry monoliths, which can dictate wages that create inhuman living conditions. Thus, the protests.

The lack of environmental laws in frontier town economies has devastated local ecosystems, poisoning the land, and water.

The old ways of the "Gaucho," or the cowboys who lived off the land, are gone replaced by sprawling environmental scars that will take decades to heal.

The displacement of humanity from the land along with social change has created a cycle of criminal threats that justify harsher government and Militarized Industry security counterinsurgency measures that in hand with starvation and atrocious living and working conditions provokes protest.

Militia Murder Squads Deal out Death indiscriminately.

Militia death squads deal with protesters, trade unionists, and dissenters like Berta Cáceres, an environmental activist and indigenous leader with swift, lethal action.

Berta Cáceres leader of the Council of Popular and Indigenous Organizations of Honduras (COPINH) and hundreds of others in Honduras were murdered because they opposed projects like the Agua Zarca Dam at the Río Gualcarque which painted the Indigenous Communities as violent criminals because they protected their land from land invasions and usurping of their land by the government.

This tyranny is why many start the long nearly three-thousand-mile trek across three nations to seek asylum in the U.S. This living hell and degradation of the environment is directly related to greed and corruption that was created through "Clintonism" that encourages unchecked capitalism and profit over human rights.

Berta Cáceres blasted Canadian and U.S. corporations and governments for supporting the 2009 military coup and working alongside the Honduran elite to promote development projects that

COPINH and Berta considered threats to their very existence because they eliminated access to the rivers, forests and mountain environments critical for agriculture and food and water access. Most importantly, these projects ignored community-based development, defined, and carried out by the Lenca themselves.

Clintonism and its politics encouraged corporate projects like the Agua Zarca Dam, throughout Latin America, displacing many indigenous people whose voices were silenced by the sounds of progress.

There are no "Environmental Impact Studies" or humanitarian rights for the indigenous people. There are two choices fight or migrate to seek asylum.

If you would like to read more on this there is a white paper, *The Agua Zarca Dam and Lenca Communities in Honduras: Transnational Investment Leads to Violence against and Criminalization of Indigenous Communities* by Annie Bird, Co-Director, Rights Action. October 3, 2013, that outlines the issues clearly and precisely.

Clintonism did protect the United States' national interests overseas but at a cost to local, and indigenous people and their livelihoods. This policy did not start with the Clintons but was developed around the Realpolitik of former president Richard Nixon's Secretary of State Henry Kissinger.

"Kissinger and the Clintons go back a ways, to when Bill in the early 1990s sought out Kissinger's support to pass NAFTA and to, in the words of the economist Jeff Faux, serve as "the perfect tutor for a new Democratic president trying to convince Republicans and their business allies that they could count on him to champion Reagan's vision."

Hillary has continued the apprenticeship, soliciting Kissinger's advice, and calling him "friend." *(Grandin, Hillary Clinton's Embrace of Kissinger Is Inexcusable, 2016)*

Henry Kissinger was a believer in the classic Realpolitik. For Kissinger, moral value came in securing national interests, not abstract principles of justice and rights.

The American Foreign Policy developed between 1969 – 1977 under Kissinger, was based on an ideological bias against negotiations with the so-called socialist and "communist" regimes in Latin America.

Kissinger had great détente but showed incredible ignorance and racist judgment when dealing with Latin America, whose people he believed were "more susceptible to communist propaganda and less capable of ruling themselves." (Gilder Lehrman, 2018)

Kissinger's policies and those of the Clintons to pursue American national interests often blinded U.S. policy to the very negative effects of foreign imperialism in so-called "third world" Nations.

The similarities in approach between Kissinger's classic Realpolitik and Clintonism is hardly surprising as Kissinger mentored the Clintons.

The militarization of the U.S. border wall began with President Bill Clinton, guided by the Senior Adviser to the President for policy and strategy, Rahm Emanuel.

In 2008 President Obama appointed Rahm Emanuel to serve as White House chief of staff continuing the *Clintonism* policies.

"So I think we need to do more of a Colombian plan for Central America, because remember what was going in Colombia when first my husband and then President Bush had Plan Colombia, which was to try to use our leverage to rein in the government in their actions against the FARC and the guerillas, but also to help the government stop the advance of the FARC and guerillas. And now we're in the middle of peace talks. It didn't happen overnight. It took several years.

But I want to see a much more comprehensive approach towards Central America because it's not just Honduras. The highest murder rate is in El Salvador, and we've got Guatemala with all the problems you know so well." - From the TRANSCRIPT: Hillary Clinton meets with the Daily News Editorial Board, April 9, 2016. (Clinton, 2016)

Death Squads, Torture, Massacres, 'Disappearances,' And Killing of Non-Combatants, Became Routinized Under Plan Colombia.

The record of *Clintonism* in Latin America reveals the failure of U.S. policy that favors capitalism, free trade, and militarization without balancing the economic change to the impoverished classes.

Let us take Columbia staggering Internally displaced (IDP) numbers from the Central Intelligence Agency, (CIA) World Factbook.

"Between 1985 and September 2017, nearly 7.6 million persons have been internally displaced, the highest total in the world... Colombia also has one of the world's highest levels of forced disappearances. About 30,000 cases have been recorded over the last four decades." - (CIA, 2018)

The Clintonist plan Columbia provided billions of dollars in assistance programs to Columbia, leading to a land grab by the powerful Military, elite, and major conglomerates. Then secretary Hillary Clinton played it forward into Central America.

Image Source: © Peter Lucking | contentbrandingsolutions.com

CHAPTER 4

The River of Humanity

My clients, Elaizer, and Susana are the lucky ones, who endured so much pain and trauma enough to flee their homes, even leave their extended families, suffer abuses as they travel thousands of miles with little more than the clothes on their backs, going hungry for an endless number of nights.

Joining the river of migrant humanity fleeing Central Americas violent Northern Triangle of El Salvador, Guatemala, and Honduras to the United States; they come to seek asylum.

Thousands of children suffer again as they enter our country in huddled masses into camps at the border, and then frigid camps inside our border.

Daring to Dream the Elaizer and Aunt Susana's Story

Susana Vicente is from the Chiquita neighborhood, in the village of San Vicente, municipality of Momostenango, in the state of Totonicapán, Guatemala. She came to the U.S. at the age of 16. In our discussions and interviews, Susana lived the life of the widows, I met during my trip to Guatemala in the '90s.

She describes how her life was very difficult because most of the citizens of Guatemala are indigenous Mayans who primarily speak one of 23 indigenous dialects. Before coming to the United States, Susana spoke the language of Quiché her entire life. Life was very difficult for Susana as she was orphaned by her mother, who died of an unknown disease when she was 13. As a result, she had to take care of her eight younger siblings, including a baby with special needs.

Like so many of the indigenous Mayans who comprise over 90% of Guatemala, she and her family were stuck between the rebel guerrillas and the government army who were fighting a civil war of nearly four decades (36 years) in that country. Susana explains that they had always lacked support from the government because her family lived in the rural areas of their "Third World Nation."

There were schools for young elementary-aged children. However, they did not attend out of fear that they would not return alive in such village centers due to the conflict. To make matters worse, they were often pulled from their homes by the army who would accuse them of helping the guerrillas.

At the same time, the rebels would threaten her family. For example, when Susana was about 13 years old, she remembers the rebels forcing them at gunpoint out of their home.

Susana's family did not have a big house; it was a one-room hut, a very simple house, where the whole family of 10 would sleep in one room. These visits, which included accusations of helping the other side and severe physical and sexual abuse—including the forcible inscription of the men and raping of the girls and women—became a regular occurrence in Guatemala.

Susana was powerless, like many others, she was unable to plead for help because the government labeled her and other Mayans in the countryside as part of the rebel guerrillas.

The guerrillas, on the other hand, tried to force Susana's family to help them, but they did not want to involve themselves in the civil war.

The army told them that they were involved in the rebel's cause simply because Susana and her family "allowed" them to be close to their homes—even though there was little the villagers could do to keep the armed rebellion as a distance. It was a constant struggle between the guerrillas and the army. Susana yearned to live her life in peace.

After enduring this vicious cycle of abuse by the armed forces for four years, Susana fled Guatemala in 1995 due to the violence of the civil war. She had never been outside of her village and found two other teenagers who had worked in the big city and motivated her to make the journey with them.

After crossing into Mexico, they experienced many hardships, from gangs to starvation including walking for days without food and water. They had to keep moving since Central Americans were not very welcome in Mexico where the severe poverty made them very vulnerable to the criminal elements looking to convert young refugee women into prostitutes or to simply take advantage of their desperate situation.

Fortunately, Susana and the other two young women made it to the border of the United States. Sadly, they were caught and turned away back into Mexico, where they were detained by government officials and then became victims of sexual abuse that Susana still wishes to avoid discussing.

The sex trafficking and maquiladoras across the border in Ciudad Juárez, Mexico, for example, have led to the violent deaths of hundreds of women and girls since 1993. Gang wars, robbery, rape, and assault await many female and children waiting in the immigration line. The issue is so bad that it even has its own name, *feminicidio,* which means the murder of women in Spanish.

I cannot blame her for wanting to leave these horrible experiences behind. After suffering rape in the Mexican detention, the girls were released and renewed their trek to the United States. Eventually, they crossed to the United States successfully.

As Susana likes to say, quoting the song by the Mexican supergroup *Los Tigres Del Norte*, she and her companions were "*Tres Veces Mojados*" which means three times wet by crossing both of the rivers, first between Guatemala and Mexico, then crossing the river between Mexico and the United States, and then after she was sent back and "getting wet" a third time before arriving to live in the U.S.

Arriving in the U.S. Susana realized that here in the United States, there are many opportunities that one does not have in her own country; however, Susana wishes to be clear that her decision to come here was not out of economic necessity. They were very poor but lived a simple and happy life, when the civil war, drug cartels, and gangs were not tearing them apart.

Susana only fled her home to save her life. She feared that she would be killed like many of the people around her. Susana, like many teenagers in the vicious Northern Triangle of Central American nations rocked by civil wars, caught up in the aftermath of the Cold War between the United States and the former Soviet Union, dreamed of tranquility and peace.

In 1996, a year after Susana left Guatemala, the government signed a peace agreement with the coalition of resistance groups, including the rebel guerrillas, but unfortunately, peace never came to Guatemala.

Susana arrived in the state of Georgia and quickly moved to Colorado. She found work, met her husband and began raising her three children in Greeley, Colorado, which is about an hour north of Denver.

Susana started learning English, which was a great challenge since she only spoke the Mayan dialect *Quiche*. Ironically, Susana learned Spanish first in the U.S. as it provided her the transition, she needed to become an English speaker. There are already many classes, textbooks, and multimedia sources that have been developed to help Spanish speakers learn English, so Susana decided to study for the GED in Spanish. She continues to study English at the local community college.

There are entire communities from Guatemala that live near Susana in Greeley. Many of them speak other dialects of the Mayan language and have had to learn Spanish, in order to learn English, to become English speakers. Also, like Susana, many of them were able to become legal permanent residents after a long-protracted process to receive political asylum here as refugees of the civil war.

At this time, Susana's sister Rutilia and her four children continued to live in post-civil war, Guatemala. Her sister Rutilia had married in 1996. Rutilia's husband had come to the US as a teenager for the same reasons as Susana back in 1991. About five years later, He returned to his family in the same village where Susana was born with hopes that the Peace Accords formally ending the Guatemalan Civil War would provide him and the community a fresh start.

The cycle of abuse from the government and the growing criminal element, drug cartels, gangs, and ex-guerrilla groups that were not successfully integrated into the coalition government continued almost unfettered.

Soon after the birth of their children, Susana's brother-in-law was quickly run out of town due to the persecution by the government and the ex-guerrillas in the smoldering aftermath of the civil war. Staying in the village brought more difficulty for the family. At the same time, work in Guatemala did not pay much. According to Susana, a day's work was only compensated with one or two pounds of sugar. Susana explained that this forced the men that had not been killed in the Civil War to leave Guatemala. Many of them came to the U.S. to try and provide for their families, to give their children something better.

In 2006, Susana went back to Guatemala to the family home with her children so that they could know her family. Many of Susana's friends, families, and relations along with good memories from when she lived in Guatemala were still present.

They still lived in the same small adobe house with a thatched roof. Their home was one room with a separate small structure for the kitchen for which they had to go outside of the house in order to enter the house. There were the same outhouse and a *temescal* to bathe, which is more like a sauna where rocks are heated with small branches which then heats water treated with boiling minerals and herbs. They had chickens and sheep, pigs, ducks, and a dog named Naron.

Susana found that the government had changed very little and that the rebel guerrillas were replaced with gangs rooted in U.S. prison gangs called the *Maras*. The local *"Maras"* gang is an offshoot of a criminal syndicate that has been traced to Los Angeles area prisons called the Mara Salvatruchas.

The *"Maras"* spread directly to El Salvador as the result of our government deporting ex-convicts from Los Angeles and the California area prisons to El Salvador.

According to the Department of Homeland Security, our government deported over 40,000 ex-convicts to El Salvador alone. A high percentage of those convicts were forced to join the Mara Salvatrucha gang while in U.S. prisons.

To have "protection" from the other gangs in prison, Central American youth banded together for mutual protection. In the 1980s these groups were taken under the control of ex-soldiers and ex-military vigilantes who were expelled from El Salvador's civil war. Into the 1990s the gang became known by their initials "MS-13" and became entrenched in the illegal weapons and the drug trade in Los Angeles.

In the 2000s, the gang was duplicated into a twin syndicate known as "Barrio 18," which has at times been referred to as "MS-18" by journalist and the public. The 21st Century witnessed the spread of the *Maras* influence into the countries neighboring El Salvador which are Guatemala and Honduras.

The *Maras* have grown with such influence that they now pervade the governments of Central America's violent Northern Triangle. Violence and rampant crime are commonplace and continue to drive asylum seekers from El Salvador, Guatemala, and Honduras. There are countless movies that have chronicled these gangs and their growing influence across international borders.

Susana's return with her children was a bittersweet reunion for her and a harsh lesson for her U.S. citizen children.

Susana's nephew Elaizer was there, along with the other two children. Just as Susana had done before her, Rutilia served roles as both mom and dad. Unsurprisingly, Susana recounts how in 2006 she only found single mothers in her and the neighboring villages the men were gone killed or taken by the gangs or the government.

It was as if the Guatemalan Civil War had never gone away, Susana explains. "My sister had to take care of the children, then go to work, plant the land, raise the animals, go to the mountain to get firewood to cook. At that moment, I realized that she was a father and mother to them. Their dad was far away. They were suffering without their father's love, his support when they needed it most."

Susana recounted sadly. "That was the saddest and hardest thing for my children and me when we went to visit."

Susana's nephew, her sister Rutilia's oldest child, Elaizer, was only eight years old during Susana's visit in 2006. He had grown up in the same environment where the men were forcibly, taken from their homes, where the guerrillas and government both raped all the women and took all the male children that were ten years or older. They witnessed and suffered these abuses even after Elaizer was born.

Despite their hard times, Elaizer still misses home and remembers his life in Guatemala. In an interview, he told me about these memories.

Elaizer recalls that just before his aunt Susana left for the U.S. when he was seven years old. He had to work as the man of the house because poverty forced him to go to work, to meet the needs of both the house and for his mother.

Elaizer expresses sadness his body slumps when he recounts how hard it was to live without the love of his father. On the other hand, Elaizer would have liked to believe that his father never totally abandoned them as he continued to send money, gifts, and messages over time.

Elaizer remembers that his mother was responsible for the activities that a man usually does, such as carrying out agricultural activities, planting corn, gathering firewood to be able to cook.

He remembers being so poor that they could not even buy corn. Instead, they grew their corn and other vegetables because they did not have money to buy ingredients.

Elaizer still recalls the dilapidated small shack. Their one-room house where everyone slept on the floor. He still remembers how his backs hurt in the morning because he did not sleep comfortably or calmly as he does today.

As time passed and at age ten (10), Elaizer began to help her collect wood in the forest. Everything was very difficult, for Elaizer as he remembers how they would walk for two to three hours to the forest carrying a gallon of water for their thirst. They carried wood on their backs and sometimes it was very heavy, so they had to rest halfway because their aching bodies asked for it; then they continued until they had enough to take home since there was no money to buy firewood.

Livestock helped them survive. They raised a few sheep, chickens and a dog named Neron (pronounced "nay-rone.") Neron was short and long with sinewy legs and short white hair that drooped along his snout and a brown spot on his back. Elaizer's description made me think of a version of Snoopy's brother Spike from the beloved Peanuts cartoon strip.

Elaizer remembers his dog Naron fondly, he was very obedient and never entered the kitchen, never ate the chickens, and did not run after the neighbors. Naron always barked at strangers only if they entered their yard. Naron would accompany his mom, his brother Randy and his little sister Araceli to help shepherd the chickens who would wander away from the house. They were not allowed to fetch their chickens on another person's property.

When they would leave the house, for example, to collect twigs and branches to heat their home and kitchen, they would also collect plants to feed their chickens for about 2 to 3 hours, three times a week. Naron would stay home and guard the house until they returned.

Elaizer reports that his father left at such an early age that he does not even remember his father being present. Elaizer remembers that his mom had to be both mom and dad for Elaizer. They lived with their grandmother, his father's mom, Seferina, and cared for her along with his two siblings.

Since her trip back to Guatemala in 2006, Susana maintained contact with her family, including her nephew Elaizer, through letters, photos and sometimes by phone because they did not have a telephone, there were just three phones in the whole village. To communicate, they had to walk a good distance to the village and then wait up to three hours for their turn to use the phone.

The best way to communicate was to record cassette tapes and send them by mail. Susana explained that by communicating this way kept them connected, and they were able to avoid feeling so lonely. Of course, this manner of communication was not ideal, and Susana was completely unaware of what happened next—eight years after she last had personal contact with her family in Guatemala.

Despite their poverty, Rutilia tried to take Elaizer to and from school every day so that the thieves, gang members, and the constant street violence would not prevent him from his education. Rutilia feared that the "*Maras*" gangs would kidnap Elaizer, so she accompanied him to and from school.

Kidnapping by the *Maras* was common in their area of Guatemala as it had become in El Salvador and Honduras. By the time that Elaizer was 13, he left school to help his mother; however, he began to receive threats from the Mara's who controlled the illegal drugs and paid off the police in the area. Rutilia could not protect Elaizer every day from the growing presence of the *Maras*. They told Elaizer that he would join them one way or another.

Elaizer's Journey

On December 10th, 2014, Susana received a strange phone call at her home in Greeley, Colorado. The voice at the other end of the telephone told Susana, "I am an Immigration agent. Elaizer is here, his mother is Rutilia, and we want to make sure that it is true that he is your nephew and that you will take responsibility for him?" Susana blurted out, "Yes!"

Susana was stunned as this was something completely unexpected because she did not know that her nephew, Elaizer had come to the United States until she received the call. Susana could only react with surprise. She could not imagine that her 16-year-old nephew would traverse through Mexico all the way to the United States. Images of the hardships she suffered, leaving Guatemala at 16 years of age began to flood her mind. She was able to focus quickly, as she felt her motherly instinct activated.

"I'm going to take care of him, just tell me what I should do to have him as soon as possible with me," she told the agent.

Susana was then told that Elaizer would be sent to a place for minor detainees called Casa Hogar in South Texas while the paperwork was processed to send Elaizer on an airplane to Denver, Colorado which is about 40 minutes from where Susana lived in Greeley.

Christmas was near, so Susana contacted Casa Hogar, and begged them to do the paperwork as soon as possible so that Elaizer could be with her at Christmas. She shuddered at the thought of Elaizer spending Christmas alone in the youth detention in Texas. Fortunately, the detention center, which contracted with the U.S. Department of Health and Human Services (HHS) rushed the paperwork.

Shortly after that, Susana was given some sad news, that the HHS was not able to secure a flight for Elaizer until after the New Year, sometime in January.

Fortunately for Elaizer, the officials suggested to Susana that she could come to Texas and take him back personally. Susana and her husband did not hesitate and booked the next flight to Texas to pick up Elaizer from the detention center in Texas. Susana explained that she believed that he had already risked his life coming from Guatemala to the United States. She was not going to allow him to risk his life again and feared that he might be "lost" or abused by the immigration agents based upon the rumors that were circulating within the immigrant community in Greeley.

Later Susana's fear was validated by our Governments admission that more than 1,400 children were lost after being in their custody and there were reports of thousands of instances of physical and sexual abuse mostly by private foster agencies hired by HHS and sometimes, by Border Patrol agents.

After flying with her husband and children down to Texas. Susana told her family that she still could not believe that Elaizer was in the U.S. She could not wait to see him. Susana remembers that she and her family were received kindly by the foster home. After all, not many people traveled on short notice with their children over 1,000 miles to pick up an unaccompanied minor.

Susana recounted the joyful moment when the officials presented Elaizer. She recalls that he appeared, "much taller, thinner but with the same kind eyes, mahogany brown skin, and strong cheekbones that she remembered seeing eight years previously."

After she and family members hugged Elaizer, the first thing Susana did was ask was if Elaizer was okay and if he had suffered any abuse. Because in that case, Susana, the "mama bear" was prepared to roar.

Elaizer reassured her that, "he had been treated well."

Triumphantly, Susana brought Elaizer home to Greeley for Christmas. He was surrounded by his cousins and loving aunt and uncle. Elaizer describes it as the most beautiful Christmas gift that he has ever received. After he was finally settled, Elaizer recounted how his journey and how he had arrived in the U.S. as an unaccompanied child.

Elaizer describes the road in Mexico as very long and lonely. Just like his aunt Susana, he had to walk many hours across many states in Mexico, which left him feeling like he would never arrive. Every day, he thought that he was coming closer, but every day, he was reminded that Mexico is a massive nation with 31 states.

He walked day and night and sometimes was able to hitch a ride on a bus. Likewise, he suffered from hunger and cold. He ran out of all the savings after two weeks of walking. When he asked people along the way "How far is the North?" and people would always respond that the North was just a few hours away although he continued for weeks.

Finally, Elaizer and his companions arrived exhausted, penniless, and without strength to continue. His companions made them rest one day and one more night under the trees.

The following day, Elaizer saw the United States border. He explains that in his mind, he built up the resolve to cross: "I thought *there* is the North, there is little distance left. I must fight through the hunger and tiredness, do it for myself and my family, I thought." When sunset came around 6 p.m., he decided to cross to this side of the border, to the USA. But it did not go as he had planned.

As soon as he entered the US, he was caught by the Border Patrol. They took Elaizer by surprise—which wasn't that difficult in his exhausted and malnourished state. He wanted to flee, but he could not. They handcuffed him with his hands behind his back.

The officers kindly told him, "Quiet; everything will be fine; you are already in the USA."

When Elaizer heard that, he cried, remembering the tortuous journey that took days of walking in the hot baking sun and under the cool night skies to finally arrive.

The officers thought that his tears were out of fear and told him, "Everything will be fine; nothing will happen to you; we will take you to a safe, quiet place."

Elaizer reports that he was scared because he did not know these officers, and was afraid of what they might do to him, but the tears were pure emotion for having made it to the U.S., to safety and a new life.

The border officers took him to the immigration station where he was interrogated. They asked him where he was from and his age. Elaizer told them that he was from Guatemala and was 16 years old.

They asked him, "Why did you leave your country so young, why did you come?" He told them that violence and poverty forced him to make the journey.

They asked: - "Do you have a relative here to contact?" He gave them his Aunt Susana's name, and he did not even have her telephone number. Luckily, a caring worker in the HHS office at the group detention center/foster care found Susana's telephone number.

Elaizer estimates that it was about two weeks until all the papers they needed from his aunt Susana were processed. He felt lonely, but calmer when the foster home allowed him to talk to his aunt.

Susana reassured Elaizer over the telephone, "I'm going to do everything possible so that you can get out and be with us before Christmas."

Susana sent Elaizer immediately to the local high school and proudly watched him graduate four years later in May of 2018 despite having to learn every single word of English. Elaizer expresses his gratitude to Susana for constantly motivating him in his studies.

She encouraged Elaizer, "Here you have better opportunities if you go to school. That will serve you enough to learn English, that's the first thing you'll need." As time passed and he learned words in English, the most basic; the colors, the small objects of the house, etc.

Elaizer talks about his "dreams" to continue his studies, to play professional soccer, and to help his mother and siblings in Guatemala. Even the local newspaper, The Greeley Tribune printed a photograph of Elaizer in his white jersey sprinting down the field, guiding the soccer ball past a player on a rival high school.

I believe that Susana summed it up best when she said. *"I would love for people to understand, for young people to have the opportunity to have a better life and future, to be good young people. It's what*

I want most in life. That they do not take away the opportunity; we all deserve it, understanding the situation of each person. I would love that this boy is an example for the whole of humanity."

Elaizer enthusiastically chimed in. *"I also want to send the message that we Latinos who come to this country, we come in search of opportunities, looking for a better life. We are not criminals or coming to harm the country. We are just looking for better opportunities, a better life, and to get ahead. We are all the same; we must not ignore each other."*

Susana continued. *"I would like you to realize all that what Latin American workers are doing to take this country forward--it is not to destroy it. We are moving it forward because without us, where do the taxes come from, where does all the money being invested come from? If it is not for the Hispanics, for the Latino workers? We are paying taxes, we are living here, in my case, the government has never helped me--no Medicare, not any help for my children. Thank God I am legal here. I've been working, so my children have insurance and don't take anything away from the government."*

Fortunately for Elaizer, Susana had sought out qualified legal assistance. She first contacted my mentor Jim Salvator. Jim was highly regarded in Northern Colorado for his continuing advocacy for children, indigenous Mayan children from Guatemala in particular. However, Jim had recently retired from immigration law shortly after Elaizer's arrival. Jim provided my telephone and another colleague's contact number to Susana.

Susana called me that same day. At my office, we laid out a strategy to obtain Special Immigrant Juvenile Status for Elaizer and avoid his possible deportation. First, we had to get Susana named as his legal guardian by the local county court. I had never appeared in a guardianship court proceeding before, so I knew that we had to find some help. We contacted a family law attorney in the Greeley area named Jeri Shepherd, who I had met during my earlier days volunteering at First Amendment rallies.

Elaizer and the Special Immigrant Juvenile (SIJ) classification

"If you are in the United States and need the protection of a juvenile court because you have been abused, abandoned, or neglected by a parent, you may be eligible for Special Immigrant Juvenile (SIJ) classification. If SIJ classification is granted, you may qualify for lawful permanent residency (also known as getting a Green Card)." (Official Website of the Department of Homeland Security, 2018).

Special Immigrant Juvenile (SIJ) classification. Petition by law and regulation states that it is supposed to be adjudicated within 180 days. However, my personal experience is it can take another six (6) months just to get to court.

Then over one year to adjudicate, and wait endlessly for an available visa, which is limited in number. There is a three-year backlog for visas as of the spring of 2019 and growing.

"Elaizer went through all these stages. They filed, for his Visa, it became available. Before his Permeant residence green card could go through, his Visa retrogressed before he could get his green card.

Elaizer is now in limbo. Administrative limbo, waiting for Visas to come back and they keep retrogressing. It is a troublesome process - once the visa comes back, gets adjudicate, it could be years.

Five years later, in 2019, Elaizer turned 19 years old. He presently lives in Greeley. He goes to high school like any other child. He worries he could be deported any day."

Every Cloud Has a Silver Lining

Jeri had shown me long ago how to become a Legal Observer at these rallies, and I had worked under her and another attorneys' guidance. She took Elaizer's case and quickly initiated a guardianship proceeding so that Susana could become the legal advocate for Elaizer since he was a minor present in the county without his parents. Jeri had never done this type of legal work to later use the guardianship process to obtain legal status for a child with federal immigration authorities.

With the guidance of a veteran immigrant child advocate from North Carolina named Claudia Hurtado Meyers, Jeri and was able to craft an order for the county judge to sign as part of his written legal findings declaring that Elaizer had been *abandoned by one or both of his parents*, that he *would reside permanently as a minor with Susana in the United States*, that he had been subjected to dangerous conditions in Guatemala at work and was subjected to danger by the local gangs trying to recruit him, and thus, *that it was not in his best interest as a child not to return to Guatemala*. The local county judge took testimony from Susana and Elaizer. The judge also received letters from Elaizer's teachers and coaches at school.

That same day the judge signed the proposed order for guardianship. With this order in hand, we were able to file the Special Immigrant Juvenile Status petition to the federal immigration authorities under the U.S. Citizenship and Immigration Authorities in Vermont, which if approved by the feds, would eventually allow Elaizer to become a Permanent Resident.

We worked quickly to make this happen before Elaizer was set to appear before an Immigration Judge. We were able to show the judge that this was done and in process. The Federal Immigration Judge in Denver, through the U.S. Department of Justice, had the power to decide if she would wait for the other branch of the federal government to approve the petition.

We had to work with urgency and move quickly for Elaizer, and the other thirty clients who are all Unaccompanied Alien Minors or UAC's as our government derogatorily refer to them.

The Immigration Judge was given the "Children's" docket, and former President Obama had decreed that most prior cases consisting of adults on all Immigration Court dockets would be rescheduled five years into the future so that the courts could quickly resolve the cases of these recently arrived children. President Obama's administration coldly implemented this "rocket docket," as we immigration attorneys called it, to send this message to Central America: "Don't send your children to our country."

Every cloud has a silver lining.' Luckily everything worked out for Elaizer in his journey to the United States as his petition for Special Immigrant Juvenile Status was approved by USCIS.

The Immigration Judge also let Elaizer wait for the decision, and once it arrived, she terminated deportation proceedings so that Elaizer could next apply for Permanent Residence. Elaizer was one of the lucky ones. However, Elaizer arrived during the first "surge" of 60,000 children that arrived in the latter half of 2014.

Arturo Jiménez

Image Source: © Peter Lucking | contentbrandingsolutions.com

CHAPTER 5

Obama Gets Rid of The Children Flooding the Border

There is a common misbelief that President Obama's 2012 immigration policy created the crisis at the border, encouraging Latinx migrant children to flood over the wall from Latin American countries.

As a lawyer, we are trained to look at the timeline and connect the pieces.

The DACA policy allowed certain young people without legal status to apply for a two-year deferral of any removal proceedings.

Republican politicians from Pennsylvania Senator, Rick Santorum, Texas Senator Ted Cruz, have touted the executive order of 2012 in some form or another as responsible for children flooding over the border.

They have made statements to the effect that. "The Obama administration knew what was happening with the issuance of the executive order in 2012, which created floods of these children coming across."

The problem is the timeline does not line up.

On June 15, 2012, about four months before the presidential election, the Obama administration issued a memo the memo contained certain stipulations that directly pertained to the DREAM'ers.

"The following criteria should be satisfied before an individual is considered for an exercise of prosecutorial discretion pursuant to this memorandum:

■ *came to the United States under the age of sixteen;*

- *has continuously resided in the United States for a least five years preceding the date of*
- *this memorandum and is present in the United States on the date of this memorandum;*
- *is currently in school, has graduated from high school, has obtained a general education*
- *development certificate, or is an honorably discharged veteran of the Coast Guard or*
- *Armed Forces of the United States;*
- *has not been convicted of a felony offense, a significant misdemeanor offense, multiple*
- *misdemeanor offenses, or otherwise poses a threat to national security or public safety;*
- *and*
- *is not above the age of thirty."*

Read the Obama Memo Here

Obama's memo targeted people that were already in the U.S. who had lived or were brought here as children for giving them a path to Citizenship.

The memo came after Republicans first rejected the bill, introduced in 2001 the Development, Relief, and Education for Alien Minors, (DREAM) Act, a bipartisan legislation from Senator Orin Hatch (R-UT) and Senator Richard Durbin (D-IL) that would have put these immigrants on a path to citizenship. The DREAM Act never came into law but hovered encouragingly close to being passing for nine years.

In 2010 the DREAM Act was passed in the House of Representatives but fell short of the 60 Senators by five votes that are needed to proceed to vote on the bill.

The decade of teasing migrants and illegal immigrants living in the U.S. by the potential of the (DREAM) Act, a bipartisan legislation from Senator Orin Hatch (R-UT) and Senator Richard Durbin (D-IL) did nothing to encourage migrants.

Misguided Senators may point to the memo and say, "Yes I told you so, it was Obama's Fault."

Research, however, shows a different picture when we look at the government numbers for the FY2014 in a Congressional Research paper, *Unaccompanied Alien Children: An Overview* by William A. Kandel, Analyst in Immigration Policy. January 18, 2017

Figure 2. UACs in ORR Custody, October 2008 through May 2014
Monthy Referrals

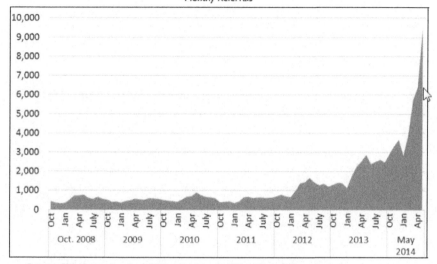

Source: CRS presentation of unpublished data from the Office of Refugee Resettlement.

Unaccompanied Alien Children UAC's as the government derogatorily calls them increased dramatically in January of 2012 months *before* the June 15 Obama memo.

Based on this chart, arrivals doubled before Obama announced his memo outlining the new policy.

Download the Congressional Research paper, Unaccompanied Alien Children: An Overview by William A. Kandel, Analyst in Immigration Policy, January 18, 2017, here.

Therefore, we should look elsewhere to find the source of the migration from the violent Northern Triangle of El Salvador, Guatemala, and Honduras to the United States as it was not related to the Obama Administration memo.

The cause comes from the political, economic, and social upheaval in countries affected by the violence caused by U.S. policies in Latin America.

The Next Wave of Dreamers

Just as Carlos was returning to the U.S. from his long exile in Mexico in August of 2014, more than 60,000 children from three countries: El Salvador, Honduras, and Guatemala arrived at the Southern border of the United States during the Presidency of Barak Obama.

Obama's administration swiftly but quietly enacted a deliberate policy to deport many of these children back to their countries of origin. The policy was intended to send a message to the region now known as the Golden Triangle.

That message was to tell the parents and government officials simply "not to send your kids to the United States and to take care of your problems in your own country."

The policy did not work. Even though all three Central American countries continued to send what the Obama administration labeled as the "Unaccompanied Alien Children" (officially referred to as the "UAC's"). Also, a growing number of single-parent and two-parent families began to flee to the United States to escape burgeoning criminal "gangs" that are uncontrolled by or, as some allege are in collusion with, the governments of those countries.

Obama's successor President Donald Trump simply continued the policy, albeit in a more celebratory manner. President Trump's personally making the situation a centerpiece to his policy. What has come to light during the Trump administration are the detention camps implemented by Obama, many of these camps furnishings featuring canopy tents draped over cages of children. President Trump upped the ante on detained families and openly separated parents and children into different sections of these camps and in many instances, into completely different facilities.

Most recently, Trump's focus has been to prevent caravans of tens of thousands of migrants from the Golden Triangle from entering the U.S. border completely. His administration as ordered troops to the border and issued orders to use lethal force on men, women, and children "if necessary" harkening back to the *Wild West* when territorial governors ordered troops with bayonets to police elderly and children of the so-called *Indians* of the plains.

While both Democrats and Republicans engage in a media war to blame the other party and demonize either side, approximately 14,000 children remain in camps and institutions that now are spread across the United States. At the same time, the President has threatened to cut off funds to the countries in the Northern Triangle to place blame on them for an estimated 1% of their total population fleeing to the U.S. border to seek protection from rampant crime.

In the summer of 2014, the "border kids" tens of thousands of unaccompanied minors fled from the Violent Northern Triangle of El Salvador, Guatemala, and Honduras.

The Obama Administration was overwhelmed, congress held yet another immigration hearing and Vice President Joe Biden passionately told immigration Lawyers, "These are our children." Biden urged lawyers to offer children free legal advice!

If they were charged with a crime, then, they would have the right to a free lawyer. But Kids, innocent minors who have no clue what is happening do not have that right.

Immigrant children don't have the right to a free lawyer or any other type of lawyer!

Immigrant children are not entitled to attorneys paid for by the government when facing deportation, a federal appeals court ruled on January 29, 2018, continuing the inhumane treatment of children migrants fleeing from atrocities.

This is like putting children in a cage with a hungry lion, the lion being the experienced government attorneys, who will eat them alive.

The three-judge panel of the 9th U.S. Circuit Court of Appeals said in 2018, **"requiring the government to provide free attorneys would be an expense that would "strain an already overextended immigration system."**

It is important to note that in January of 2018, the government FY2017 number of Unaccompanied Alien Children Apprehensions by Country. (Source U.S. Customs and Border Protection) crossing the Southern border was a meager 40,631 compared to the astronomical number of FY2014 67,339 under the Obama Administration.

Therefore, if the system is straining in 2018 as it is today what was it doing back in 2014?

In 2014, the immigration system was strained, overextended under the combined weight of children migrants.

Advocates, mostly churches and associated immigration attorneys learned that the Department of Homeland Security had set up a detention camp for children and families in Artesia, New Mexico.

President Obama's horrific immigration policies of 2014 combined with a legislative impasse on the DREAM Act, and Obama's announcement to expand DACA to cover additional illegal immigrants did little to stem the flow of "border kids" tens of thousands of unaccompanied minors continued to flee from the Violent Northern Triangle of El Salvador, Guatemala, and Honduras.

Secretary of State Hillary Clinton led the Obama Administrations charge to deter migrants; she favored deportation. The Deportation of thousands of Central American migrants back to the Violent Northern Triangle.

Contrary to the U.N. Declaration of Human Rights, "Recognition of the inherent dignity and the equal and inalienable rights of all members of the human family is the foundation of freedom, justice, and peace in the world."

In a town hall meeting, June 2014, Hillary Clinton stated. "We have to send a clear message that just because your child gets across the border doesn't mean your child gets to stay. We don't want to send a message contrary to our laws or encourage more to come."

In response to the *"Tent Cities"* for the *"border kids'"* legal teams were assembled paid for by charitable contributions and aid groups. The fear of another 2009, notorious T. Don Hutto facility near Austin, Texas, reoccurring urged advocates for immigrant rights lawyers to rush to the camps. The Bush-era allegations still echoing in many of stark conditions and sexual abuse.

The teams, including members of the local Colorado Chapter of the American Immigration Lawyers Association (AILA), rushed to visit the camps and provide direct legal representation to the detainees. Why the rush you ask? You would have thought that our government would have the migrant children's rights at heart. Because the government doesn't recognize children's rights to an attorney, choosing to treat them like lambs to the slaughter of expert government lawyers with no legal representation.

Meanwhile, organizations prepared to file suit and challenge the horrid and substandard conditions. As a result, Artesia was ordered closed by the Federal Courts, who referenced the inadequate detention conditions. Undeterred the DHS/ICE simply moved the detainees to other camps such as the one near Dilley, Texas.

What followed was a policy to disperse large numbers of immigrant children across the nation. States such as New York, Pennsylvania, and Michigan received large numbers of children.

Obama's Illegal Immigration Plan Alarms Migrant Children's' Advocates

---

"News that President Obama is seeking more than $2 billion to deal with the flood of unaccompanied children coming across the southern border is widely seen as a welcome sign for the overburdened border patrol agents and workers tasked with caring for the children once they come into U.S. custody.

But the president's plan to ask Congress to grant more authority to the Department of Homeland Security (DHS) to speed up the removal of unaccompanied minors who might not be eligible to remain in the U.S. has spread alarm among advocates for the children." (KAPLAN, 2014)

I was extremely concerned by the news. The estimated stream of 52,000 children crossing the border implied that speeding up this process would deny unaccompanied minors the traditional child-friendly welfare policies, and due process protections. Instead, it would aid in returning these children to dangerous, violent Northern Triangle of Central America.

My thoughts were strengthened when Mike McCaul, R-Texas, Chairman of the House Homeland Security Committee, commended Obama's move in an interview on CBS News' *"Face the Nation."*

"I don't think the flow will stop until a message of deterrence is sent back to Central America," he stated. *"I think a message of deterrence. I know the president came out with a strong statement today. I applaud that. But I think, you know, we have to be humanitarian at the same time, let them know that if they do come, they cannot stay here; otherwise, we'll never stop the flow."*

It appeared that the government was looking to treat children coming from the Northern Triangle of Central America in the same way as children from Mexico! Mexico is just next door, so they dump children across the border.

The fate of a child or family is determined by a border patrol agent initial *"drive-by screening,"* that may or may not identify that child as a refugee and allow them to speak to an asylum officer.

This subjective view of the situation by the agent can mean detention or deportation through the courts. The Agent determines whether the child or family have a fear of returning to their homeland, and are at risk of human trafficking to prostitution, or cannot be sent home alone for other reasons, etc., they are detained. If not, they are dumped across the border.

The initial *"drive-by screening"* as some agent's call can be fundamentally unfair to children, depriving them of due process, that we should as humanitarians and Americans provide them.

The *"drive-by screening,"* relies on the political bias, experience, and training the officer receives, not to mention whether they are in the club.

At the "CLUB" agents posted inappropriate jokes about migrant deaths, along with racist and sexist content.

Carla Provost, chief of U.S. Border Patrol, and many other officers were in a secret Facebook club which was exposed in 2019. The *"CLUB"* was a place where agents posted inappropriate jokes about migrant deaths, with racist and sexist content.

This is inappropriate behavior for a professional border agent and should not be condoned.

U.S. Government Response—Administration's and Congress' Actions

The following summary is from the Bipartisan Policy Brief for 2014, "Child Migration by the Numbers**"** (Immigration Task Force, 2014) *in 2013 under Obama:*

- *"24 percent of children in government custody were under 14*

- *An unprecedented number of apprehended children are from Central America... In FY 2004, about 83 percent of apprehended children were Mexican; in FY 2014, just 24 percent of UAC was from Mexico. The DHS numbers confirm this for 2014 and the years following.*

- *Children from Mexico can usually be returned home quickly, but children from Central America must go through formal removal proceedings. As a result, the number of migrant children in* government custody more than tripled between FY 2011 and FY 2013 and is expected to double again in FY 2014.

- Most UAC apprehensions are occurring in the Rio Grande, Texas border sector, which has accounted for 93 percent of the increase in UAC apprehensions between FY 2013 and FY 2014.

The increase in Child apprehensions overwhelmed the government's capacity to screen children promptly.

- Children arriving at the border today are younger than in years past. In FY 2013, 24 percent of arriving children were 14 or younger, compared with 10 to 15 percent in FY 2007 and FY 2008.
- In FY 2011, a government-sponsored Legal Access Project, implemented in partnership with the Vera Institute of Justice, estimated that about 42 percent of unaccompanied children in government custody could be eligible to remain in the United States in some legal status."

The Pew Research Center, confirms, *"Children 12 and under are a fastest growing group of unaccompanied minors at U.S. border..."* (The Pew Research Center, 2014)

These were the children in detention camps under the Obama Administration.

Crisis at the Border? Overall the numbers were down, but New Migrant Flows Are Testing the System and would prove overwhelming.

FY 2014 Demographic Shift for ICE Removals

COUNTRY	FY 2013	FY 2014
El Salvador	21,602	27,180
Guatemala	47,749	54,423
Honduras	37,049	40,695
Mexico	241,493	176,968

Source: (ICE, 2014) and the Bipartisan.org

For a chronological history of the <u>Obama Administrations Actions on Immigration</u> provided by the (American Immigration Council, 2015), please follow the link.

Image Source: © Peter Lucking | contentbrandingsolutions.com

CHAPTER 6

Swimming with the Whales

It is very difficult for me to write about this. I am a veteran immigration attorney. I have represented many people who have suffered persecution ranging from those forced to undergo female genital mutilation, people who endured extreme torture with electric shocks directly to their sexual organs, victims of repeated rapes while they were still children, to those who have had their homes demolished, and their family members "disappeared" and never returned.

I have never accompanied my clients on their journey to the U.S. I have never stood in their shoes to find their way to this country. I write this story, with a heavy heart, detailing my recent journey to the Southern Border to see with my eyes what people endure to try to achieve a better life.

In 2018, in response to the migrant caravans, President Trump and his administration characterized this as an affront to our immigration laws that amounted to a hostile "invasion." In an extreme act, the President ordered troops to the border, ordering them to prepare for a showdown with the migrant caravans. Furthermore, the President authorized the use of guns to defend the troops.

Trump is repeating President George W. Bush words and actions.

Bush wanted to build the border "wall." He ended the "catch and release" policy.

President Trump ordered troops to the Southern Border with Mexico grandstanding in the media and shutting down the government until Congress would give him money for a wall.

Trump's Caravan of Exaggeration

From President Trump's Twitter accusations that "The Democrats are Organizing the Caravans," to Vice President Mike Pence's ludicrous statements at a Washington Post event:

"In the last fiscal year, we apprehended more than ten terrorists or suspected terrorists per day at our Southern border from countries that are referred to in the lexicon as "other than Mexico" – that means from the Middle East region."

Trump's Twitter accusations that Gangs of MS-13 people are supposedly hopping on the caravan bandwagon is unfounded. There has been no proof given to back up the alternate facts and misguided statements from the administration.

But as Trump twittered, it must be so...

And yes, Trump believes his own "bull roar!" After a month-long obsessive attack against the caravan warning in speeches of the looming invasion of criminals, gang members and "Middle Easterners." He believed that he had rewritten history enough to allow his administration to change the law!

Unconcerned for the legality, President Trump has begun to resemble a dictator, an American oligarch, or a king who believes that he can do anything he wants.

Unfortunately for Trump, the Law is the Law. As USA TODAY put it in a great article by Allen Gomez on Nov 20, 2018, entitled:

Federal Judge Blocks Trump's New Asylum Rules: 'He may not rewrite the immigration laws.'

"U.S. District Judge Jon Tigar ruled late Monday that the administration's new policy of cutting off asylum to immigrants who enter the country illegally appears to run afoul of U.S. law that specifically allows them to do so...

The Court's ruling makes clear that the President cannot override Congress, and will save lives," said Lee Gelernt, the ACLU attorney who brought the suit."

Read the Article at USA TODAY

For some unknown reason, his legal advisers and administration were upset by Judge Jon Tigar's ruling.

It should be noted, however, that Trump's game of chess with the children stuck at the border as pawns in his immigration game worked in his favor.

Thousands of migrants were stranded at the south of the border in Tijuana, Mexico at the San Ysidro Port of Entry, trying to request their asylum. Unfortunately, San Ysidro Port of Entry can process approximately 100 requests a day, or can it?

Meanwhile, many stranded asylum seekers who believed they were free of life-threatening situations and had reached the finish line have been turned back from San Ysidro Port of Entry, raped, beaten, and kidnapped and held for ransom by cartel members.

It should come as no surprise that people whose lives are at risk would try to enter the United States of America to escape persecution and the violence from cartel members on the Mexican side of the border.

The Unrest at the Border

I watch the news reports with tears in my eyes, the nation that I should love is run by a government that disgusts and angers me.

Peaceful protests on the Mexican U.S. Southern border by thousands of Latinx migrants from Central America and the violent Northern Triangle of El Salvador, Guatemala, and Honduras turn into riots as patience terns into frustration.

US Border Agents Fire Tear Gas across the Border at Migrants Protesting the Slow Asylum Process.

Source Photo: David Guzmán/EPA-EFE via AP - USA today

The U.S. fires tear gas across the border into Mexico to prevent people crossing at Tijuana on November 25, 2018

🖤 2012 Oct. 10, 2012, a U.S. border patrol Agent Swartz shot 16-year-old Jose Antonio, Elena Rodriguez.

In to 2012 Agent Swartz fired through a border fence, striking Jose Antonio Elena Rodriguez about ten times as he walked innocently down a street in Nogales, Mexico.

Let us hope that this does not happen again.

Thousands of immigrants from Central America and the Northern Triangle are waiting, sleeping in tents and on the bare sidewalk. Migrant children and families are confused, tired, and hungry.

Image Source: Dreamstime © Viorel Dudau

They wait for an opportunity to apply for asylum in the U.S. The wait will be a long one.

Long before the Caravans of "criminals and rapists" arrived, President Trump had initiated a change, the change that is being challenged in the courts.

A change to the asylum rules which forced the refugees, families, women, and children, to stay indefinitely south of the border in Mexico. Every day they must get in line, a line of thousands and make an appointment to speak to a border officer at designated ports of entry.

Asylum seekers whose patience ran out may and did try to cross the border, but they will be shot with rubber bullets and tear gas canisters.

President announces plans to open more child and family detention centers on military bases to avoid scrutiny by legal groups

---

At this time, the President also announced plans to open more child and family detention centers on military bases to avoid scrutiny by legal groups and the press by limiting access. Besides, the President openly called for detention policies at the border and in these camps that would serve to separate children from their parents.

Many of these policies had already been tried by former President Obama in a much quieter fashion—including the reopening of former Japanese internment camps from World War II to house immigrant families and children.

Migrant Protection Protocol or MPP – Take a number and Wait in Mexico!

In November of 2018, President Trump upped the ante from President Obama's quiet policies and announced his plans for a so-called Migrant Protection Protocol (MPP), that would require all asylum seekers who presented themselves or were caught trying to enter at the Southern Border, to be "metered" which meant to take a number and wait in Mexico. This new policy was directed at the refugees, mostly children from Central America who were not from Mexico. Immediately I thought about how Susana had been turned back by the U.S. Border Patrol to Mexico and suffering sexual abuse by officials in Mexico as a teenage girl.

By January of 2019, the Border Patrol and the U.S. Asylum officers began implementing this program. I and many others have volunteered to go down to the border first to witness first-hand how this new program is affecting those children fleeing persecution and violence in Central America.

It has surprised me at how very difficult it was for me to write about this trip to the border. After all, I am a veteran immigration attorney who has represented many people who have suffered terrible persecution.

Horror at the Border: The Migrant Protection Protocols

On February 28th, 2019, I boarded an airplane from Denver to San Diego, California, along with a friend, amateur photographer, and videographer, Rob Coca. Although we had registered as volunteers and contacted the now-famous non-profit organization *Al Otro Lado* (translation TO THE OTHER SIDE), we had not received a confirmation back from their staff.

We were determined to see with our own eyes what was happening to immigrants arriving at the Southern border of the United States. A difficult time for refugees and those seeking protection because President Trump declared in November 2018 that all applicants for political asylum would have to wait in Mexico under the so-called Migrant Protection Protocols (MPP). We, like many citizens in the U.S., had heard the news reports of U.S. Military personnel and the U.S. Customs and Border Protection ("Border Patrol") using rubber bullets and tear-gassing families and children.

We had also seen the reports of Border Patrol separating children and even heard the reports of deaths once children came into the hands of the Border Patrol.

Rob and I boarded the plane without a clear idea of where our journey would lead us. After a two and a half (2 ½) hour flight, we took a bus directly from the airport in San Diego, we then boarded a train which took us directly to the Southern border at the city of San Ysidro on the U.S. side and the Mexican city of Tijuana on the other.

Michael Cordova, an old friend from college, met us at our stop and shuttled us across the border in his car. He pointed out many spirals of sharp razor wire; recently placed along the fencing at the border crossing into Tijuana, Mexico. The rolls of shiny razor wire were more decorative and reminded me of an industrial, punk-rock club called, Rock Island, where I used to frequent as a teenager.

Interestingly, none of the rolls of razor wire was connected, leaving large gaps, and anyone, including me, could easily climb over every twenty feet.

Obviously, "Building the wall" is more of a symbolic political statement by President Trump than a realistic solution.

Thousands of people drive across the border at that point every day into Mexico--many of them retired Americans on their way to a second home at the beachside city of Rosarito or the manicured golf courses and vineyards of Ensenada on the Mexican side.

The rolls of prickling razor-sharp barbed wire announce the tenor of Trump's presidency; open hate for immigrants and ugly nationalism harkening back to Nazi Germany during the Second World War.

I recalled watching the celebration on television in the late 1980s as the Berlin Wall of the former Soviet Union was being demolished. It made me wonder what décor, what symbols awaited the refugees begging for protection as they entered a country whose elected leader publicly declared that he wanted them to suffer.

As we arrived in Tijuana that evening, we avoided the throngs of teenagers, mostly white kids from Orange County who came across to Mexico to take advantage of lower drinking age laws and attend seedy nightclubs that boasted young sex workers for hire, many of these prostitutes were teenage girls and boys from Mexico and other parts of Latin America.

The crowds of American kids coming to party in Tijuana had diminished somewhat in recent years due to the violence and crime initiated by the drug cartels on the Mexican side of the U.S.-Mexico border. The heavy bass speakers of a nearby nightclub reminded me that the danger of street crime did not stop American kids from coming to this nearby outpost of alcohol and sin.

The drunken American revelers and reverberating thump of the pounding deep bass sound combined with my concern for the situation made it difficult to sleep that night.

The next morning, we took a taxi to the offices of Al Otro Lado on the outskirts of Tijuana. We walked around the block, through the alley three times, but we could not locate the office.

Finally, we noticed a small 8 x 11 paper that indicated the door was on the alley side. By this time another immigration attorney from Denver, Joy Athanasiou had joined us. The three of us rounded the corner to look for the door.

We were starting to look out of place, and the locals were starting to give us that look that dumb tourists receive when they can't find the bathroom at an archeological site that doesn't have one. Luckily, a broad-faced woman with a big smile and a black baseball cap with white letters "STAR" printed across the front rescued us.

"That door there!" She called out pointing from across the alley. "You are looking to help the migrants--yes?" She asked in Spanglish, half Spanish, and half English.

"Buenos Dias," Good morning, I replied in Spanish. "Yes, we are, thank you."

Joy, Rob and I came up to the nondescript door, magically it appeared to open as if we were Aladdin, and we had suddenly come upon the Cave of Wonders. We collectively sighed relief, followed by a spike in our heart rate at the excitement to have finally made it.

Up to this point, we were checking our email responses on all three of our telephones to no avail. The organization that we had contacted never replied, so we were not sure whether we would be able to volunteer.

Later I found out that both the U.S. and Mexican governments were keeping a list of the organizers and volunteers of these organizations, so their caution and safeguards made all the sense in the world.

"Are you here for medical or legal?" A voice asked from inside the door.

Just then it became apparent that the door had not opened magically at all but that a volunteer who spoke American English was holding it open for us as we walked up. My eyes had to adjust from the brightness of the Mexican sun before I could make out a twenty-something freckled White guy with glasses and short-cropped curly hair at the entrance.

"Yes... Legal." I replied with the dumb pause of the tourist that I had become due to circling the building for the last hour.

"Go back to the third room," he ordered. We marched in and shifted into business mode.

Together Joy, Rob and I found the third room down a dimly lit hallway with fliers in English and Spanish pointing to childcare, medical attention, and legal help. We entered a big bright room that looked like a classroom and was ready with white plastic chairs, matching tables, a copier, and a whiteboard.

No one was there. I felt the anxious despair once again of the dumb tourist as we sat and waited for another half hour wondering what was going on. Finally, someone wandered in. They looked busy and did not greet us.

"Are we in the right place for legal orientation?" I asked.

"Yes. This is the place. Go into the next room," the woman ordered.

We passed through a small hallway into the next room and found about ten people working in a very focused tone as if they were in an air traffic control room. Right behind us, about 20 more people from the U.S. walked in on our heels speaking in a very cordial but business-like chatter with each other. The air traffic controllers that is how I recall them put down their tasks and turned to shepherd us into order and told us to have a seat around a large conference table. By the seriousness of their voices, it was clear that we were in the right place. Once the orientation began, all my worries melted away with what happened next.

First, we were asked to close our eyes and imagine that we were swimming in the ocean with a group of whales. We were asked to surface to the top of the waves and breath in deeply so that we could fill our lungs to submerge and breath underwater. We were asked to surface again and blow our air out so that we could take another breath and resubmerge, holding our breath for a moment as we did our work for a time and then return to the surface again.

We breathed together and asked to imagine that we were swimming with a family of whales. We imagined we were surfacing, expelling our used-up air and taking another deep breath along with baby whales, mother whales, and father whales. We were submerging to do our work with these families but only to resurface and recharge.

We were asked to imagine that this family of whales swam and breathed together for a lifetime and that we were joining alongside them in their migration. We needed to breathe and take care of ourselves alongside the people that we were about to serve. We also needed to match the pace and complement our group during this journey. As I drew in a long breath along with the 30 other "whales" in the room, I could hear them uniting with the determination towards the collective goal of assisting the refugees at the border as fellow human beings.

This exercise also reminded all of us of the dignity of our human condition, that the emotional health of the volunteers and the people we came to serve was just as important as addressing their physical and legal needs. At the same time, this seemingly simple exercise illuminated the fact that migration is a manifestation of our natural, timeless, and cyclical human life. I felt enlightened and ready to get to work!

The dedication, thoughtfulness, and organization of the air traffic controllers turned them into immediate wise gurus of the borderlands. They made the complex task of assigning thirty total strangers specific duties appear to be an almost seamless process.

Next, we were shuttled into orientation with two other people where our credentials were checked, and we were assigned volunteer work immediately. The staff organized us based on our professional and language abilities into various groups to serve the refugees. The group leaders generated updates from committee leaders like generals, dished out assignments to all of us volunteers like trauma surgeons in an operating room and elicited opinions on what needed to be tweaked for the day like rocket engineers preparing for a launch.

Soon after that, refugees from Guatemala, Honduras, El Salvador, Cameroon, Ghana, Africa and other parts of the world diligently started streaming in to prepare for their interviews with U.S. asylum officers.

I soon learned that many of them were invited to Al Otro Lado after U.S. officials had caught them and their children on the border and turned them back to Mexico to take a number and wait with for an "appointment."

Many others heard through the streets that they could seek medical attention, receive help to find a place to live temporarily, and seek legal help during their forced four to six-week wait in Mexico.

As we all hear in the news each day, everyone at the border is worried that U.S. immigration officials will continue to separate children from their families.

It is well documented that our country deported over 2,000 people while their children, including some babies just a few months old, remained in the United States in various stages of foster care.

As I have documented earlier many children waited in camps, mostly in Texas but now spread across the U.S. Due to overcrowding with inhumane conditions many children were being spread across the U.S. to private foster homes in Tennessee, Florida, Michigan, Pennsylvania, New Jersey, Maryland, Indiana, and California, just to name a few.

News of the Trump Administration's family separation policy has spread across the world. After Al Otro Lado, the American Civil Liberties Union (ACLU) and other organizations had brought successful lawsuits against the government to halt such family separations; the Trump Administration made an official retreat from the practice. Unfortunately, the practice was much more widespread than our government admitted which cast doubts in everyone's mind that the practice would end.

Every family arriving at the border is worried that our government will separate them and their children. Thus, all of them wanted to know how they could stay together and avoid the nightmare of losing their children. For most, this would be worse for them than the persecution back in their home country. They all understood that having a signed declaration stating that "I do not consent to have my children separated from me" was an essential element of their first interaction with our border officials.

Just as important as finding shelter for them and their children. Many had camped out on the streets. Others found shelters run by the Mexican Government in sports stadiums or abandoned nightclubs near the border.

Many of the migrant population seeking protection in the U.S. had even more special considerations that made them much more vulnerable to the forced homelessness of the new Trump policy.

I have to recognize and compliment the great hearts of many Mexican citizens near the border who have collaborated with humanitarian activists from the United States and other countries to form various shelters for single mothers with small children, children as young as five years old traveling alone, gay, lesbian and transgender refugees.

One fact that surprised me was the many African families who had made it to our Southern Border. Even more surprising was the ability of many African individuals to learn Spanish quickly enough to advocate for themselves while they traveled across the Atlantic Ocean through South America, Central American, and Mexico. Many of the Africans, despite language barriers, pulled together and brought other Africans to shelters where they could hope to find other families with similar languages.

We were exhausted from our first day at the border. The "Stay in Mexico" policy is inflicting further trauma on these families and children.

The volunteer work that I did that day was the same legal counseling that I provide to immigrants in my office in Denver. The difference is the desperate situation of being forced to sink or swim on the Mexican side for up to six weeks while waiting for an "appointment" to turn yourself into the Border Patrol. This policy has created such profound desperation for those who had struggled to travel so far that it was difficult to provide legal advice and separate myself from the tragic situation of this unnecessary human suffering.

The stories that some refugees shared with me about their trip to the U.S. are shocking and sad.

It is a reality that many refugees endure armed assaults, rape, and even death along their tumultuous journey through mountains, deserts, jungles, and third-world urban jungles along the route to the United States.

One young gentleman stared into my eyes and seemed to beg for a sympathetic ear as he recounted how he lost his close friend in the jungle of one Central American country after an armed assault by criminals. This cordial young man just needed someone to care, to have empathy with his sadness and loss.

As I looked into the back of his large black pupils, I saw his eyes quiver like someone about to cry, but there were no tears and no words from his lips for a couple of minutes. He did not cry but stared into my eyes like someone who had cried too much already.

I assured him with a hand on his shoulder and told him that I was sorry for his loss. I did my best to show that I cared, and I spent extra time with him to ask more about his situation.

I must admit that it brings tears to my eyes every time that I recall this conversation and others that I had at the border.

I finally learned after 20 years, just how mentally exhausting it is to work with refugees outside of the United States. As my head hit the pillow at my room that night, I wasn't prepared mentally for the next day. Perhaps it was a premonition that the next day would kick my butt and I kept waking up almost every hour of the night.

The next morning, we were running late. I met our team from Colorado in the shallow lobby of our hotel. Rob, Joy and I jogged down the street to find an Oxxo, the equivalent of a 7-Eleven convenience store, to buy a quick cup of coffee before reporting to the border.

Hastily we jumped into a taxi to speed us to the border. The driver, who like all the Mexican citizens we encountered in Tijuana, was encouraged and supportive of our trip to help the refugees along their way.

I felt fortunate to be able to use my Spanish language skills to explain our story and where he needed to take us. Many of the refugees, including many indigenous families from Guatemala, only spoke their local dialects and rudimentary Spanish that made it that much more difficult to communicate and survive Trump's "Wait in Mexico" policy.

I couldn't imagine how Susana and Elaizer my Guatemalan clients had faired with their Mayan accents and their broken Spanish in Mexico. Memories of their stories flooded through my mind.

I recalled my visit to Guatemala over 20 years ago and meeting the representatives of over twenty different indigenous populations that all spoke a different dialect of the Mayan language.

When we arrived, we saw a line of about a hundred people winding underneath a highway overpass as the grey morning sky poured rain over our heads. Everyone, including me, had on multiple layers of clothes as the humidity stuck its cold hands onto our skin, chilling us to the bone. It was bad enough that so many people were living in temporary shelters or living homeless on the streets of a foreign land, but the pouring rain seemed to be dumping salt into the wounds of a truly chilling situation.

It was there at our Southern border that I first caught sight of the Mexican Immigration Officials or "Grupo Beta" as they are known. They looked like the ultimate school crossing guards in their bright orange sweaters and coats. I had been warned about them by my friend Chucho in Mexico City years before. It should not come as a surprise that even some of the government officials in the countries along the migrant route engaged in abusive behavior. In fact, throughout Mexico, there exist routes, including safe houses where Mexican families will hide refugee families during their journey to the United States, to protect them from government abuse.

The Mexican officials have a reputation for being corrupt and many times brutal to the migrants trekking through Mexico.

I visited Chucho in 2005 in his hometown, which happened to be the largest city on the planet at the time. He shared with me that Mexican immigration officials often come into his neighborhood to hunt down Central American refugees to take their money, sexually violate them and sometimes to send adolescents into the sex trade.

Chucho's family would take the refugees into his family's home, feed them, give them a change of clothes and, sometimes, give them a ride as far away as the next state. He and his parents were proud to be a part of an "underground railroad" similar to the one that used to exist in the United States during the time of slavery in the 1800s to help slaves along their routes to escape the abuses by their slave masters and arrive in the free states of the Northern United States.

Chucho's family even had a room in their home with a secret door that could be covered with a blanket to hide refugees until the Mexican immigration officials would abandon their searches.

Visiting Chucho's family and hearing their stories made me remember the plight of Jewish children hiding from the Nazis that I first read about as a teenager in the book The Diary of Anne Frank. Chucho's eyewitness accounts served to further validate my client Susana's report of being sexually abused while in a Mexican government detention center.

Community members from far outskirts on the Southeastern edges of the Mexican metropolis would find refugee families marooned on the street and send them on to trusted members of the underground railroad like Chucho and his family on the Northwestern edge of Mexico City.

Now, in 2019, I wondered if the international attention and the national pride of Mexico were enough to keep "Grupo Beta" in check. I prayed that this group working the border was different from the officials that Chucho and his family encountered.

Ironically, the Mexican migration police called the Grupo Beta now was placed in charge by the U.S. Border Patrol under the Immigration and Customs Enforcement (ICE) to keep the refugees safe during their four to six-week wait. Also, ICE had placed the Mexican government immigration officials in charge of taking the refugees into custody when their number became available after about five weeks and tasked them with driving them over to the U.S. Border patrol.

That cold rainy day at the border in March of 2019, I witnessed "Grupo Beta" calling the numbers of those who had waited their turn.

The U.S. Border Patrol only takes an average of 40 people per day out of thousands waiting at this particular port of entry at the border. They created another line ad hoc, right next to a gushing downspout from the overhead bridge that was partially in the pouring rain for those being turned over the ICE.

The Betas were in charge of loading the people into vans and their belongings into trucks to drive them to the *Hieleras* or "iceboxes" which is the name of the detention cells where the Immigration and Customs Enforcement (coincidentally also referred to as "ICE") of the United States would then detain them for three to ten days in an underground holding facility.

The U.S. immigration officials also call them the "iceboxes" because the temperature inside has been registered at about 48 degrees—just slightly warmer than our home refrigerators.

In 2018, Human Rights Watch reported that besides being overcrowded, these concrete holding cells featured no more than foil blankets, lacked soap, beds and other basics generally required of a detention center on American soil.

Detainees are forced to sleep, crowded in these frigid cells without mattresses or shoes.

One of our jobs at the border that day was to prepare refugees for this cold as they transferred to the *Hieleras* of ICE. There were large supplies of wool socks that we gave out to all the families to help minimize the cold concrete as much as possible. Also, we had wool sweaters.

There was another policy in the "icebox" for which we had to prepare the detainees, the removal of their outer layer of clothes. We had to explain that people should change into their warmest base layer as ICE would not only take their belongings and paperwork but all their outer layers of clothing. As many of the refugees had only a tank top or a thin t-shirt as their base layer, they had to change theirs and their children's clothes quickly right there in the street.

We held up blankets on three sides to provide makeshift triangular changing stations to shield the mothers and children as they quickly disrobed and redressed into a warm layer.

The most shocking image in my mind was assisting many of the refugees as they were frantically writing the important telephone numbers that they would need for the one phone call that they would be permitted to make by ICE on their arms with Sharpie pens. Furthermore, all the parents were writing their full names in permanent ink on the arms of their children to ensure that their kids could be united with them in case of separation.

Horror ran down my spine, chilling my hands, shaking my body uncontrollably as scenes of concentration camps and tattooed numbers flashed past my eyes, a waking nightmare. The frantic desperation and cruelty reminded me that humans could be so cruel when their humanity is cast aside.

Many of the small children were confused, crying they truly did not know their parents' full legal names, so this branding appeared to be an intelligent and necessary practice.

Even more cautious frightened parents were writing their children's names and dates of birth on their children's arms as their children were too young to know how to spell their full names and many did not know their exact birth year.

When I described this scene to a friend Dave Stalls who founded *Street Fraternity* a drop-in center for refugee youth in Denver, he said what came to my mind, "Auschwitz"—referring to the concentration camps in Nazi Germany circa World War II.

After I returned to the U.S., I recalled a conversation with Nicole Ramos, one of the three women directors of Al Otro Lado and Director of the Border Rights Project.

She told me that she was preparing for a speaking tour in the U.S. to bring to light the injustices inflicted upon asylum seekers at our borders. Unfortunately, Nicole had to prepare a legal team for fear of detention by our government upon her return.

The local San Diego news outlets broke a story almost at the same time that I was on my trip to Mexico in March of 2019. The story is revealing in that the U.S. and Mexico had labeled many journalists and one lawyer—Nicole Ramos, as instigators and collaborators because of their assistance to individual asylum seekers who arrive at our Southern border as part of the migrant caravans from Central America.

Nicole, a heroic American, was now blacklisted. Worse, she has been treated like a criminal by both governments as she sought to raise more money for diapers and socks for refugees entering "the icebox."

Another arm of this valiant organization, Al Otro Lado (alotrolado.org) based in Los Angeles, California also recently won a lawsuit to allow twenty-nine parents who had been deported without their children to reenter the U.S. to await the asylum process for their children. At the same time, the American Immigration Lawyers Association, the American Immigration Council and the Catholic Legal Immigration Network, were successful in forcing our government to release fifteen infants from ICE custody.

Nicole and her team in Tijuana are doing what is right, and I am incensed that both the Mexican and United States governments would label them as instigators when they are truly doing God's work.

I am a very good listener, and I have heard thousands of stories of traumatic events from my clients over the years, however standing with refugees at our border have shaken me to tears now that I am back in the States.

Death and Politics at The Border

In remembrance of the two children who died in U.S. border custody in December of 2018

♥ Jakelin Caal, 7, from Guatemala, died Dec. 8, at an El Paso children's hospital.

♥ Felipe Gomez Alonzo, 8, from Guatemala, died Dec 24. in U.S. custody at a New Mexico hospital.

All of this was preceded by a handful of refugee caravans making their way from Central America through Mexico to request political asylum.

We do not need a "wall" we need help for the U.S. officials at the processing centers on the border.

For example, at the San Ysidro Port of Entry, the U.S.' largest land entry point, on the Southern Border is presently only processing 20 people a day according to the CBS news report By Kate Smith on January 25, 2019

The country's busiest border crossing will allow 20 people to claim asylum a day. They used to take up to 100 - (Smith, 2019)

"The capacity reduction — known in immigration circles as "metering" — came the same day that the Trump administration implemented its "Migrant Protection Protocol," a sweeping policy change that forces asylum seekers to stay in Mexico while they await their U.S. immigration court hearings. Prior to the policy change, asylum seekers waited in the United States, either behind bars or non-detained but monitored."

At the 20 people per day rate, it will take the 47,986 people the U.S. Customs, and Border Protection agency has captured in FY 2019 February a mere twelve and a half years to get processed!

U.S. Border Patrol Southwest Border Apprehensions FY 2019

USBP	Demographic	OCT	NOV	DEC	JAN	FEB	MAR	APR	MAY	JUN	JUL	AUG	SEP	Total
Southwest Border	UAC	4,968	5,262	4,763	5,119	6,825								26,937
	Family Units	23,116	25,164	27,507	24,189	36,174								136,150
Southwest Border Total Apprehensions		51,002	51,857	50,749	47,986	66,450								268,044

Source: U.S. Customs and Border Protection

It is not surprising that the migrants get impatient, they have walked, ridden trains slept like vagrants on the cold dirt and gone hungry for over 2,500 miles. They have been attacked and harassed along the tortuous journey from the violent Northern Triangle.

It is not surprising that they gather in caravans to gain protection by numbers on a journey that many will not complete.

Litigation on Behalf of the 10,000 Children Held In Over 1000 Detention Centers

On January 18, 2019, the Southern Poverty Law Center (SPLC) filed a class-action lawsuit, on behalf of more than 10,000 children against the Trump administration for violating due process rights of immigrant children and their sponsors.

Many notable advocates for immigration including the Catholic Legal Immigration Network, Inc., joined a class-action lawsuit, as organizational plaintiffs.

Southern Poverty Law Center (SPLC) filed a class-action lawsuit against the Trump administration on behalf of over 10,000 children currently in detention centers

---

SPLC filed today against the Trump administration on behalf of over 10,000 children currently being held in over 100 detention centers across the country.

Source: Read the Lawsuit filling Case No. 1:18-CV-903-LMB

In a News article on the SPLC website, SPLC sued the Trump administration for violating due process rights of immigrant children and their sponsors, posted January 22, 2019, the SPLC stated:

The lawsuit charges that this situation is primarily the result of the ongoing cooperation between the ORR and Immigration and Customs Enforcement (ICE) which, hand-in-hand with family separation, is a deliberate strategy to deter vulnerable migrants from traveling to the U.S.

Source *Exhibit 2 Memorandum of Agreement*

A memo drafted in late 2017 and obtained on January 17, 2019, reveals that the administration intended the very result this policy has caused: the prolonged detention of children.

Source: Read the full article

The leaked memo Exhibit 5 of the lawsuit titled *Draft Memorandum – Policy Options to Respond to Border Surge of Illegal Immigration* confirms the inhuman intent of the Trump administration to knowingly create the prolonged detention of children. It implies a deep hatred of immigrants.

Source: Read the Memo For your self

Does that remind you of anything? Is it an echo in history?

On April 26, 1938, Nazi law began down the slippery slope to the "Decree for the Reporting of Jewish-Owned Property" the vast *Konzentrationslager*, the Nazi detention camp system that had existed for several years at that point.

The *Konzentratsionslager* system did not emerge from a vacuum. It came out of a political system and society that was unconcerned and unwilling to either believe or act against oppression and acts against humanity.

"Hitler did not invent the hatred of Jews. Jews in Europe had been victims of discrimination and persecution since the Middle Ages, often for religious reasons. Christians saw the Jewish faith as an aberration that had to be quashed." - (Ann Frank House, 2019)

The derogatory antisemitism rhetoric of Hitler who blamed social injustices of the time on Jews helped to create the dehumanization of the Jews allowing their detention. This derogatory propaganda is similar to the rhetoric and tweets that President Trump uses in his hostility against immigrants!

If Presidents Trump's misleading <u>tweet</u> that the U.S. is "on track to APPREHEND more than one million people coming across the Southern Border this year," is to be believed we do not need a wall but a welcoming committee.

Apart from the fact that this statement is a LIE, or as his administration would say an alternate truth, it shows the low level of deceit and political propaganda that Trump will stoop to.

Through the first five months of FY 2019, U.S. Customs and Border Protection reports there have been 268,044 apprehensions on the Southwest Border, nothing near the one million apprehensions reported by the President.

Southwest Border Migration FY 2019

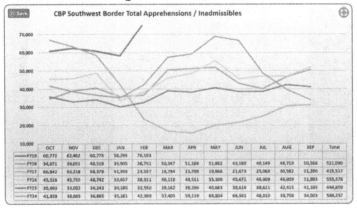

U.S. Border Patrol Southwest Border Apprehensions FY 2019

USBP	Demographic	OCT	NOV	DEC	JAN	FEB	MAR	APR	MAY	JUN	JUL	AUG	SEP	Total
Southwest Border	UAC	4,968	5,262	4,763	5,119	6,825								26,937
	Family Units	23,116	25,164	27,507	24,189	36,174								136,150
Southwest Border Total Apprehensions		51,002	51,857	50,749	47,986	66,450								268,044

This equates to a monthly average of 53,609, which would put the U.S. on track for 643,306 this fiscal year up till February 2020.

The U.S. Customs and Border Protection Agency (CBP) tracks apprehensions by fiscal year, and 643,306 would be 62 percent higher than the last fiscal year.

What is sad to see in these numbers are the rising number of Unaccompanied Alien Children, (UAC) crossing and the number of family units which under Trump's executive orders will be split up and sent to different detention camps in the U.S.

It is obvious by the FY2019 numbers that his despotism and rhetoric are not working.

We will see more families separated and children detained before it gets better.

Trump's Slogan, "Build the Wall and Crime Will Fall," Is A Propaganda Stunt.

Trump's slogan, "Build the Wall, and Crime Will Fall" is another propaganda stunt of a misguided vision of the U.S., where we all should watch as millions of malicious immigrants, families, and children are flooding across the border.

The sad truth is that anyone believes this contrived nonsense.

Migrants are trying to escape oppression. They are trying to reach the safety of the most powerful nation in the world.

"Instead of Demonizing undocumented immigrants in this country, pass comprehensive immigration reform, provide a legal path to citizenship." - Bernie Sanders.

Presently in 2019, our country is experiencing a humanitarian crisis of children at the border that we have never witnessed before. The U.S. Border Patrol Southwest Border Apprehensions FY2019 show alarming numbers of apprehensions and inadmissible migrants for March 92,835 - 10,888, April 99,290 - 10,172, May 132,880 - 11,393 and June 94,897 - 9,447. Two-thirds of these apprehensions are Unaccompanied Alien children or family units. (Department of Homeland Security, 2019).

The American Immigration Lawyers Association (AILA) points out in their June 13, 2019 policy paper on Effective Border Management that according to the Border Patrol's own numbers available at www.cbp.gov/newsroom/stats/sw-border-migration that while almost 100% of arrests at the Southern Border were made on Mexican citizens in the year 2000 that number has flipped in 2019 where almost 75% are from Honduras, Guatemala and El Salvador.

Even more alarming, the Migration Policy Institute reports that the percentage of families and children being apprehended at our border with Mexico has risen from 10 percent in 2012 to about 72 percent in May of 2019.

The lucky ones like Elaizer, and Susana whose story is told *in CHAPTER 5 The River of Humanity* found someone, an uncle, a family friend or even a relative in the U.S. who could take them to a faraway state such as Colorado, Kansas, Utah or Wyoming and then come to my office with a legal retainer to hire my services and apply for Political Asylum or Special Immigrant Juvenile Status.

There are a handful of people working in my profession who believe that they are "saving these people" however that is the furthest from the truth.

The families fleeing persecution that they have suffered in their home countries are the real heroes who have endured more than we can imagine. I feel fortunate and honored to assist them in requesting the protection of our great nation.

The United States is the beacon of hope for many in the world because our nation was formed by those who had fled persecution in their own countries. We take for granted the principle of E Pluribus Unum that our country has broadcast to the far reaches of the planet.

I believe that most of the people of the world love their homes, their culture, their family but when that is removed, we have given an invitation even if it is in the form of our arrogant boasting of how we have forged a nation of many into one under the rule of law.

One of my fears is that every day, people like my heroic friend Chucho and his family in Mexico will suffer unbearable trauma in their country and feel that they will have to flee to the United States. What a shame it is to force someone like him and the others who love their home country so much and who work tirelessly to make their communities better to have to leave their homes behind and embark on a tragic journey.

I share my friend's desire for him to be able to stay in his own country for the rest of his life. Much the same for all the immigrants that I have met over my lifetime, they have lived a heroic life that many in this country do not know.

Perhaps we can recognize our privileged lives and "Make America Great Again." We are lucky to have such strong and determined people come to remind us of the roots of our nation and humanity.

The immigration problem and the obsession with a wall did not begin with President Trump. Families, women, and children did not just appear at the foot of the towering wall without reason.

The immorality of brutal bipartisan U.S. policy in Central America's violent Northern Triangle of El Salvador, Guatemala, and Honduras, which have some of the highest homicide rates in the world, has a root cause.

That cause is U.S. action and foreign policy that looks like the typical classical colonialist empire-building of Great Britain and the Soviet Union. *Clintonism* politics have stoked this desperate situation.

President Trump is not innocent and continues these policies though his Administration's interference in Venezuela.

From his 2018 budget plan that sees a gain of 14% ($73.9 billion) in Defense Department outlays to total $597.1 billion in military spending to his slogan, "Make America Great Again" we see a continuous trend from the White House to find military solutions to the world's ills.

President Trump's is not innocent of crimes against humanity. His obsessive need for a "wall" combined with his failure to address the humanitarian crisis that confronts the children at our border is a crime against humanity.

Heartbreaking cries of children reverberate off the cold grey concrete, chain-link fences groan, and space blankets crackle to the body racking sobs of desperation.

The pitiful heart-rendering cries, "Dad... I no, Papa... I no Pap-aa... I no Papa" tear at your soul, children lie shivering on the hard-cold concrete, red frightened dust lined eyes search for a familiar face.

This is not Somalia or Syria; this is the U.S. detention center in the Rio Grande Valley along the Texas border with Mexico. We are supposed to be civilized, the greatest nation in the world, yet we treat children like cattle.

Don't believe me? Listen to the Audio recording obtained from ProPublica by the Guardian Newspaper Children separated from parents cry at U.S. detention center – audio (Guardian News, 2018)

Children are being processed inhumanely, lambs to the slaughter, forcefully separated from their parents and family, ripped from their fathers and mothers by U.S. officials at the Customs and Border Protection detention facilities along the border, following President Donald Trump's cold-hearted "Zero Tolerance" immigration policy directives.

News Headlines from across the world describe a disturbing picture, outlined by Senator Elizabeth Warren in her CNN interview after visiting an Immigration Center in McAllen Texas.

Transcript: CNN breaking news, McAllen, TX, Senator Elizabeth Warren (D) Massachusetts Speaks About Immigration Facility in TX

"I just came from the center. It is a disturbing picture. There are children by themselves. I saw a six-month-old baby, little girls, little boys.

There are mothers with their babies and small children. Family units are together if it is a very small child. I saw little girls that are twelve years old are taken away from their families separately and little boys.

They're all on concrete floors in cages. There is just no other way to describe it. They are big chain-link cages on cold concrete floors, and metal blankets handed out to people. People are all just waiting and frightened. I was very lucky to have someone with me that speaks Spanish.

We were able to ask people individually about their stories, about what brought them here. Where they came from. Those, particularly from El Salvador, talked about the violence. Talked about how the gangs had threatened them individually. One woman explained she that had given a drink of water to the police and now the gangs believe she is helping the police. So, she sold everything she had, and she and her four-year-old son fled the country. She believes that she would not survive if she went back.

We talked to others, mothers from Honduras in particular who said there is nothing there for us. We have no jobs; we have no money; we have no food for our children, and America is our last hope.

The question we asked many of them where they sat in this cage; were they glad they came? And for all of them, it brought smiles, and they said 'Yes, I am here in America.'

This is not over; this only the processing center on the front end. I've finished here, I'm going from here to Catholic Charities, and then I will go on to the detention centers which will be the next place many of these people will go. I've got more work to do. Forgive me if I can't stay long." - Senator Elizabeth Warren

Source: Watch the CNN Video

Minors like Eddy, age seventeen and Lilian, age nine are Guatemalan fleeing from violence with their mother. Ripped away from their mother, dejected, alone with no knowledge of where their mother was taken. Abruptly they were flown to foster care in Grand Rapids, Michigan separated again, and placed in separate homes.

Imagine that these are your children or your neighbor's children, would it be acceptable? Humane? Does this really happen in a first world country? The greatest country on earth. YES!

Minors Separated from Parents and Detained At US Border Tell Of Anguish.

Many Americans will say something along the lines, "The United States people voted Trump as president to be tough on immigration, they will forcefully stress the fact the parents of these children are illegally entering the States."

It is not true that the majority of U.S. citizens voted for Trump. These people may indeed be entering the U.S. without permission, and many are asking for asylum and sanctuary.

The truth is that there are humane ways of treating children and people. For us as a nation to stoop to the levels of forcible deportation and separation of families makes us in my humble opinion no better than the German Nazis with their concentration camps and detention centers where you could be detained or confined without trial. Some of the early German detention camps make our tent cities look like slums. It was inhuman then and is inhuman and despicable now.

The conditions I found on my visit to the border on February 28, 2019, made me wonder, what type of person would treat humanity, children, and families in this brutal manner and allow these atrocities to happen.

In July of 2018 U.S. Department of Health and Human Services, the Office of Refugee Resettlement, that administers children and families, increased the number of shelter beds from about 6,500 to about 13,000 beds.

Great article to read https://www.acf.hhs.gov/orr/resource/unaccompanied-alien-https://www.hhs.gov/sites/default/files/Unaccompanied-Alien-Children-Sheltered-at-Homestead.pdfchildren-frequently-asked-questions

The temporary influx shelter established at Homestead will increase from the current capacity 1,350 beds to 2,350 beds in increments of 250... Unaccompanied migrant children at Homestead Temporary Shelter:

Read the PDF https://www.hhs.gov/sites/default/files/Unaccompanied-Alien-Children-Sheltered-at-Homestead.pdf

NEWS HEADLINES READ LIKE BILLBOARDS OF OPPRESSION

Family Separation May Have Hit Thousands More Migrant Children Than Reported - (Jordan, The New Your Times, 2019)

The Lost Children of Trump's administration - (The New York Times Editorial Board, 2019)

Trump Administration to Nearly Double Size of Detention Center for Migrant Teenagers - (Jordan, Trump Administration to Nearly Double Size of Detention Center for Migrant Teenagers, 2019)

The House Homeland Security Committee interviewed Homeland Security Secretary Kirstjen Nielsen March 6, 2019. CNN broadcast much of the hearing live.

It was apparent that Security Secretary Kirstjen Nielsen was playing dumb failing to provide the documentation that Bennie Thompson head of the House Homeland Security Committee had asked for. Why do I say this? Because much of the requested information is available on the Department of Homeland Securities web site. The information is tainted by Presidents Trump's Shutdown of the government in early 2019.

Question That We All Want to Know The Answer To

How many children have been separated from their parents?

Based on Attorney General Jeff Session vow on May 7, 2018, to prosecute all illegal border crossers and separate children from their parents.

"If you cross the border unlawfully…. then we will prosecute you," Sessions said. "If you smuggle an illegal alien across the border, then we'll prosecute you… If you're smuggling a child, then we're going to prosecute you, and that child will be separated from you, probably, as required by law. If you don't want your child separated, then don't bring them across the border illegally. It's not our fault that somebody does that." (Sacchetti, 2018)

*Always the caring humanitarian Sessions continued, "no doubt" people illegally crossing the border are fleeing danger or despair, "We cannot take everyone on this planet who is in a **difficult situation**."*

In July of 2018 HHS Secretary Alex Azar stated that "under 3,000" children were still separated from their parents.

Perhaps we should take everyone from a nation that we the United States of America has a hand in creating the **'difficult situation.'**

How many children are in Detention camps?

We know that in July of 2018 U.S. Department of Health and Human Services, the Office of Refugee Resettlement, that administers children and families, increased the number of shelter beds from about 6,500 to about 13,000 beds.

We know that children are still sleeping on floors from the Elizabeth Warren interview. Therefore at least 13,000 kids + the ones on the floors put this at anywhere around on the low end 15,000 to +17,000 if there is a space between each bed like a military barracks. Whatever the number it is one too many.

MSNBC believes there are 13,000 -14,000 migrant children in detention: Inside border detention centers where thousands of children are being held.

Based on research, I believe over 15,000 children have been detained.

How long will it take a child to become a legal American Resident?

First off, undocumented immigrant children are not provided legal representation by Law! They must find their representation or argue their case and represent themselves.

Children must first secure a predicate order from a local county judge, then find a guardian or a single parent. The children must be abandoned or abused; the children must convince a judge that it is not in their best interest to go back to the home country.

Special Immigrant Juvenile Petition by law and regulation is supposed to be adjudicated within 180 days. However, I have had cases that go on another six (6) months or more.

Often it takes over one year to decide. Children wait to get an available visa, which is number limited. There is a 3-year backlog for visas as of today and growing.

My client, Elaizer, went through all these stages. The Visa category, for youth from the Northern Triangle, retrogressed before he could get his green card. Elaizer existed in limbo, administrative red tape, waiting for Visas to come back and then wait longer. It is a traumatic troubled process for any adult, let alone a child.

What is the Hidden Life of an Undocumented US Immigrant Like?

"Like millions of illegal immigrants in the US, Sylvia has spent decades building a life here - until her undocumented status was discovered by the authorities. She must now return to Mexico, leaving her children behind."

Source: Watch the video from AFP news agency https://www.youtube.com/watch?v=ZMlTmOip3ig

Instead of the focus being on the humanitarian crisis at the border, we have entered a continuous two-year election cycle!

The Democrats are squabbling vying for power and control, and lifelong Republicans are leaving the sinking ship in disgust.

Meanwhile, the 2018 *"Caravan"* of 3,000 Central American migrants' has arrived, been detained, and its size dominated the political immigration discussion for a moment in time. Today they are forgotten in the hype of the news cycle.

The 2019 "Convoy" will make the "Caravan" seem like a small drop in a bucket. This is what Trump Fears; therefore, he rushes to build a wall.

The *"Caravan"* of 3,000 Central American Migrants

Many people in the *"caravan"* of 3,000 migrants sought refuge in Mexico. Some of the U.S. media and anti-immigration politicians have screamed to shut down the boarders worried about the "Caravan."

President Trump makes derogatory references to the Caravan's people, fathers' mothers and, children as, "These aren't people-These are animals." Then continues his venting rhetoric by attacking Mexico and its administration with more uneducated rhetoric "they do nothing" to help the United States. (Gomez G. K., 2018)

Mexico has borne the brunt of the migrations from the Triangle. The UN Refugee Agency has expressed alarm over the migration and displacement of people from the Triangle and Northern tip of South America.

"According to the Mexican Commission for Aid to Refugees (COMAR), from 2013 to 2017, refugee applications were increased for citizens of Honduras, El Salvador, Guatemala, and Nicaragua, including unaccompanied children.

Thus, it went from 972 people from the Northern Triangle in 2013 to 13,997 last year, who demanded refugee status in Mexico." (Becerra, 2018)

Mexico's President of the Human Rights Commission of the Senate of the Republic, Angélica de la Peña Gómez has clearly understood the cause of the plight of people from the Northern Triangle, "the rule of law in all our countries, has to be restored based on its internal processes." This, in turn, will stem the flow.

Mexico's President of the Foreign Affairs Committee of the Chamber of Deputies, Víctor Manuel Giorgana Jiménez, recounted that Mexico has an "open-door policy for asylum seekers."

Is Mexico Doing Nothing? Not True.
Mexico is Taking on The Lion's Share of The Humanitarian Crisis.

The more prolonged the crises that occur in the countries of the Northern Triangle, and Venezuela, which the Trump Administration has politically bullied and bated into a civil war the higher the levels of displaced humanity will be, as demonstrated by the 10,000 strong convoys gathering south of Mexico.

Bouncing back

United States, apprehensions of illegal immigrants at southern border, '000

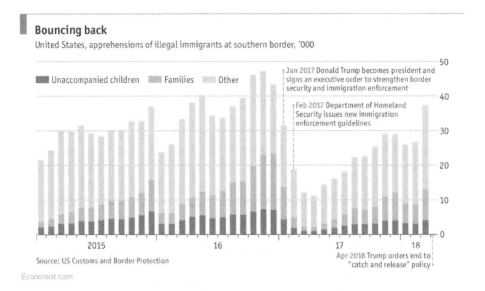

Source: US Customs and Border Protection

Economist.com

The 2019 "Convoy" from Central America.

More than 10,000 migrants request visas as "Convoy" hits Mexico. (Kinosian, 2019)

I am calling this the "Convoy" as it is a lot bigger than the "Caravan." At 10,000 strong, it dwarfs the scale of the "caravan."

At 10,000 Strong the "Convoy" dominates the "Caravan."

To stop further convoys and dam, the flood of migrants President Trump has bullied Mexico with the threat of tariffs.

Mexico has responded by sending 6,000 troops from the National Guard to the country's southern border with Guatemala. The border enforcement is aimed at cutting off the flow of migrants bound for the U.S. border.

Both President Obama and Trump have prosecuted many immigrants at the border. Trump's "Zero Tolerance" policy has inhumanly created family separations.

President Trump "Zero Tolerance" policy created family separation as a matter of standard practice. President Obama is said to have done this unintentionally.

President Trump's "Zero Tolerance" policy treats migrants from the Northern Triangle in the same way as immigrants from our neighbor Mexico. Dumping children across the border to walk 2,500-miles home! Obama put them on a plane. I can only close my eyes, take a deep breath, submerge, and hope to help immigrant children during their valiant journey.

Image Source: © Peter Lucking | contentbrandingsolutions.com

CHAPTER 7

Freedom and Justice for The Children of the Detention Camps

José sat crying by the barbwire fence; his body bent in pain and loss. His tears fell like rain from the sky. His brown eyes stung, defeated.

"Mamá... mamá, ¿dónde estás? In broken English, he moaned dejectedly, "Mamma, Mamma, where are you?"

He remembered the day so many years ago that the rain fell like tears from the sky, the wet, acidic smoke, the valley of burning shacks.

Jose fearfully sobbed; his sad brown eyes faded do embers as he remembered the haunting images of death. The men with guns were back again; this time, they were Americans.

"Mamá... mamá, ¿dónde estás? He sobbed.

His fear turned to anger.

The last soldiers had taken his sister, killed his father, and raped his mother in front of him. What would these men do?

Jose last saw his mother in the arid air of Tijuana, after days of sleeping on the hard concrete of the dusty sidewalks, and hours of standing in a line they gave up and tried to cross the border.

Sadly, they were arrested.

His Mother was snatched away from him in the dead of night. He was shoved into a van and driven for hours, and hours to a camp in the smog of California.

José broken, his dreams of freedom, liberty, and the pursuit of happiness shattered. Yes, he was fed, given a bed and a silver blanket but the inhumane life-changing way he had been treated left a stain of disgust in the young sixteen-year-old.

José had never been caged like a wild animal, stripped of all his outer clothing and personal possessions and cuffed like a thief.

José stood slowly and stared at the flag, across the detention camp, the red white and blue, the star-spangled banner of his dreams.

His mind wandered. He only wanted asylum from the horrors of Guatemala. Now he was thrown into a place that looked just like the history books he had studied. What had his teacher called it? Oh yes, Dachau!

Across the country, his mother sat waiting, sobbing, heartbroken in pain missing her son.

"José," she whispered, "what have I done."

"José," mind raced. What more could they want from a boy?

Imagine your kid was dropped off at high school and just disappeared. How would you feel?

Every person is unique; every migrant story adds to the voice that must be heard. Share your story now.

$$\$\$\$$$

The Cost of Child Detentions is $24,000 per month of taxpayers' dollars

Let's free the Children from the overcrowded tent camps by spending our dollars on helping these juvenile immigrant children and families instead of detaining them.

According to ICE FY 2018 budget (Department of Homeland Security, 2018), the average cost of detaining one adult bed per day is $133.99 before we add in all the payroll costs and operational expenses.

There is a very complicated explanation of costs, by (Benenson, 2018) but we can conclude that these costs are closer to:

- One adult bed $200 per day
- One Family bed $319 per day at a residency to keep the family together
- Tent Cities for Kids per bed $775 per person, per night!

Trump Admin's 'Tent Cities' Cost More Than Keeping Migrant Kids with Parents!

"The reason for the high cost, the official and several former officials told NBC News, is that the sudden urgency to bring in security, air conditioning, medical workers and other government contractors far surpasses the cost for structures that are routinely staffed." (Ainsley, 2018).

This is cost-prohibitive and shows the inhumanity and high cost of Trump's "Zero Tolerance" Policy. If Trump is such a great businessman, why is he spending so much of our tax dollars on inhumane detention of innocent children and the "Wall?"

Why Are Our Tax Dollars Being So Poorly Spent? It Makes No Economic Sense!

To detain a kid for one month is costing us approximately $24,000, that is $288,000 per year!

To detain a kid for one month is costing us approximately $24,000, or a total of $288, 000 per year! Complete economic madness. That cost's more than the Vice-President gets paid! No wonder he is getting a pay rise this year.

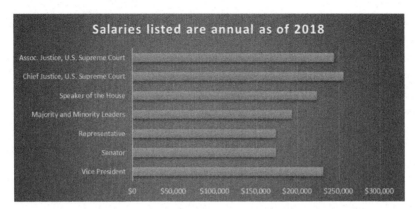

Source: Office of Personnel Management. Web: www.opm.gov/.

We need to free these kids for humanitarian reasons. However, if you are a staunch fiscal conservative, the numbers might make you consider that there might be a better way.

Sending these children and families back, to the violent Northern Triangle of El Salvador, Guatemala, and Honduras or just dumping them in Mexico is not the solution.

As an advocate for justice for Latinx immigrant children, we need to support the abused and neglected children bullied by President Trump's "Zero Tolerance" policies.

President Trump redirects the anger of his "Zero Tolerance" child detention camps by pretending to fold under pressure. With one hand, he is closing the overcrowded, razor wire enclosed cages that have raised the cries of, immorality, caused by the inhumane "Zero Tolerance" Policy."

On the other hand, Trump plans on increasing the size and number of inhuman tent camps in Florida to nearly double the capacity.

"The government plans to expand the number of children housed at a "temporary shelter" in Homestead, Fla., from 1,350 to 2,350 in January, according to a Dec. 26 letter from the Department of Health and Human Services outlining the plan." - (Jordan, Trump Administration to Nearly Double Size of Detention Center for Migrant Teenagers, 2019)

New Florida, "Temporary, Influx" Shelters Bypass Child Welfare Rules!

The new tent detention cities will be "temporary, influx" shelters on federal land. Therefore, these facilities are not subject to state regulations and inspections intended to guarantee child welfare!

The New York Times article *Trump Administration to Nearly Double Size of Detention Center for Migrant Teenagers* by Miriam Jordan Jan 15, 2019, states that. "As of Jan. 13, about 10,500 migrant minors were held in more than 100 shelters across the country overseen by Health and Human Services, down from about 14,700 in December."

These numbers are alarming. The Trump administrations Government closure of 2018-2019 caused chaos throughout the nation. Most likely, these numbers are underestimated, as many of the departments that record these numbers were working under duress.

Trump and the political posturing by all parties have left many Americans exhausted, caught between hope, and disperse.

President Trump has brought the country to a political impasse, eight hundred thousand (800,000) furloughed government workers were placed on the verge of destitution, over a "Wall!" in the 21-day shutdown of the Christmas holiday period 2018- 2019.

Are There Better Ways to Spend Taxpayer Dollars on Immigration?

The Medias Focus is Biased Both Left and Right - Some Truths Are Lost In The Exchange

---

- The wall is $5.7 billion (0.1 percent of the federal budget) an easy project to fund if one balances the payment elsewhere in the government budget.
- For the Fiscal Year FY2019, the Department of Defense' budget authority is approximately $693,058,000,000. 5.7 billion is a drop in the bucket. This is what Trump is planning to do.
- There are 700,000 DACA recipients, and another 300,000 people granted Temporary Protected Status that need solutions. They are not going away.

"President Obama granted that group temporary protection against deportation via an executive order that even he acknowledged was illegal. President Trump ended the program in advance of an

expected court-ordered shut-down, tossing the issue to Congress. He should have known better." This
opinion by Liz Peek at Fox News the heart of the issue. (Peek, 2019).

Politicians Should Solve the Innocent Children's Issues First

---

Together the parties should solve the innocent children's issues first, before tackling the larger immigration problem.

- Over 13,000 Juvenile children languish in detention awaiting Political Asylum and or the Special Immigrant Juvenile Status program.

- The judicial system needs more immigration judges; As of July 2018, 733,000 asylum request cases were pending.

- The detained migrant Children need legal representation and guardianship. After all, they are minors.

Trump is going to waste our money on expanding the juvenile detention camps. Let's solve the humanitarian problems one at a time.

Imagine you are a four-year-old child ripped from your parents' arms, enslaved in a wire cage dejected and scared. What hope is there for You?

America needs to stop sweeping the issue under the table, passing the buck to the other party. It is time to be American, charitable, compassionate, and fair. It is time to be American.

Obama and the Democratic party promised comprehensive immigration reform including protection for the DREAM'ers during the 2008 Campaign. The Democrats had the chance to pass sweeping legal legislation following the election as they controlled both houses of Congress.

I hear the Trump chant, *"They are all stone-cold criminals..."* where is the proof? (Gomez B. J., 2018)

To make matters worse in 2017, Trump's administration decided to terminate Temporary Protected Status (TPS) for Sudan, Nicaragua, Haiti, and El Salvador. Sending the decision to court.

Temporary Protected Status Designated Country: El Salvador

ALERT: On Oct. 3, 2018, in *Ramos, et al. v. Nielsen, et al., No. 18-cv-01554 (N.D. Cal. Oct. 3, 2018) (PDF, 458 KB)*, the U.S. District Court for the Northern District of California enjoined DHS from implementing and enforcing the decisions to terminate Temporary Protected Status (TPS) for Sudan, Nicaragua, Haiti, and El Salvador, pending further resolution of the case.

For additional information, please see the March 1, 2019, Federal Register Notice, specific TPS country pages available on the USCIS website, and the Update on Ramos v. Nielsen page on the USCIS website.

The Temporary Protected Status will continue as long as preliminary injunction ordered by the court in Ramos, et al. v. Nielsen, et al., No. 18-cv-01554 (N.D. Cal. Oct. 3, 2018) remains in effect.

It is time for both parties to stop squabbling and get to work. We are wasting time and money without any resolution to the humanitarian problem.

On June 20, 2018, President Trump signed an executive order that the administration claimed would "end family separations." The Executive order reads.

"Section 1. Policy. It is the policy of this Administration to rigorously enforce our immigration laws... It is unfortunate that Congress's failure to act and court orders have put the Administration in the position of separating alien families to effectively enforce the law."

Source: Read the Full Executive Order

Trump, the master of redirection, blames Congress, the Democrats, and everyone else for his actions! He should accept responsibility and be held accountable.

Unfortunately, this will not help the 2,300 children separated from their families by the US Customs and Border Protection agency under the cruel, immoral, and inhumane. "Zero Tolerance Policy."

Together let us as a nation find a just solution to free the children and families from the inhuman detention Camps.

$$$

Now you have the Facts

To detain a kid for one month is costing us approximately $24,000, that is $288,000 per year!

Please Call Your State Representatives to Congress and Politely Ask Them to Spend Your Tax Dollars on Immigration Wisely!

Arturo Jiménez

Image Source: © Peter Lucking | contentbrandingsolutions.com

CHAPTER 8

Trump Hateful Rhetoric: "Send Them Back!"

Trump has fed the American public rhetoric of divisive fabrications to promote his agenda and get their support and votes with a seemingly sympathetic, narrative of "Send the Children Back to Their Families."

The general posture of President Trump has been to feed a story that the tens of thousands of children who arrived unaccompanied to our Southern border have parents sitting on their porch swings just waiting for their children to return.

Trump has fed many well-meaning, conscientious churchgoers a story that most of the children who have arrived were the victims of sex-slave traffickers who kidnapped them from their families in Central America and brought them to the U.S.

Trump's rabble-rousing explosive narrative continues-ICE agents are the heroes, Chuck Norris Texas Ranger-style, who rescued these tens of thousands and mercifully placed them in camps to await reunification with their parents.

The story culminates the President's call for the "Wall," Trump's leaning tower of Babble. The massive separatist "Wall" built as only he can, along the entire length of the Southern land border with Mexico. The "Wall" that will keep all the sex-slave traffickers out of the United States and prevent these children from being kidnapped off of their porches.

Interestingly, Trump's divisive narrative supports mass deportation of the children back to Central America and coincides with the original policy enacted by former President Obama and Vice President Joe Biden.

The problem is that many children have no parents or family to return to because their parents are dead!

Luckily many denominations of Christian Churches have seen the light. Christian Churches have joined hands with other religions and advocacy groups and are searching for solutions, providing aid, and planning for change.

There is indeed a growing criminal enterprise of cross-border sex trafficking involving children; however, the proposition that most of the 60,000 of the children who first arrived at our border in 2014 were victims of sex-trafficking syndicates is misplaced.

Half of the children came without any parents, and the other half arrived with one parent, typically their mother. Most of the children do not know where one or both of their parents are located and have lost contact with them altogether. Furthermore, many came to the U.S. hoping to be reunited with a parent or a family member.

Carla's Story

Take the story of Carla. Her mother left El Salvador at the age of 3 to work in the U.S., leaving her and her younger sister in the care of their grandmother and their uncle. Within a year of her mother leaving El Salvador, Carla's uncle was openly killed in the street, and the authorities did nothing to the murderer.

Carla, her sister, and her grandmother became part of a fast-growing demographic in El Salvador of all-female households. These households are viewed by very patriarchal Salvadoran society as living without a male who could provide them with protection — regarded as vulnerable to the uncontrollable gangs imported from the United States.

Meanwhile, back in the United States Carla's mother had recently been granted "Temporary Protected Status" (TPS) a program that offers a temporary legal status to immigrants who cannot return to their country of origin due to ongoing armed conflict for other reasons, with permission to work in the United States. Also, Carla's mom had a son born in the U.S. and held a respectable job, which allowed her to send money back to grandma to care for Carla and her sister.

In 2014, the worst happened to the family in El Salvador. Carla's teenage sister Josephine was kidnapped and held for ransom by gangs who were aware that mom was sending money from the U.S. back to a household of a senior woman raising two adolescent girls.

Carla and her grandmother received a phone call demanding large sums of money be paid immediately for Josephine. During the call, they could hear the kidnapped sister being tortured and screaming in agony.

The family tried to scrape as much of the thousands of dollars demanded by the captors. The captors were unsatisfied that the money was not presented immediately and never contacted Carla and her family again.

The authorities took a report but never followed any leads. Why would they? Many of the authorities are under gang control, bribed to turn a blind eye. Like many others, Carla's sister Josephine was never heard from again.

Josephine became a victim of gang violence, perhaps she is still alive working off her debt in a brothel, or part of the child slave trade or a 'maquiladora' labor worker in a manufacturing plant in Ciudad Juaréz in Mexico where 1500 women and girls have been brutally murdered and dumped in the desert since 1993. Another reason not to "send kids back," across the border.

When the captors contacted Carla, she knew that she would share the same horrific fate as her sister if she remained in El Salvador.

At 15 years old, she fled her home in terror escaping the gang violence and death to begin the month-long trek out of El Salvador, across Guatemala, through the vastness of Mexico and up to the Texas border.

She was detained at the U.S. border and placed in a camp with other minors in Texas for a week. There were children of all ages from 2 years old up to 17 at the camp.

Carla held on to her hope; she knew that her mother was living and working at a ski resort in the Colorado mountains. Unlike many of the other children, Carla had a telephone number and an address of someone who had permission to live and work in the U.S.

Carla called her mother and the U.S. Department of Health, and Human Services arranged her first flight on an airplane to Denver, Colorado.

Arturo Jiménez

The Conflicting Views on Immigration in Society

"Remember the Sabbath day to keep it holy. Six days you shall labor, and do all your work; but the seventh day is a Sabbath to the Lord your God; in it you shall not do any work, you, or your son, or your daughter, your manservant, nor your maidservant, nor your cattle, or the sojourner who is within your gates; for in six days the Lord made heaven and earth, the sea, and all that is in them, and rested the seventh day; therefore the Lord blessed the Sabbath day and hallowed it." - The Old Testament, Exodus 20:8-11.

On Sunday, June 24, 2018, while Christians and Jews were flocking to their places of worship, President Donald Trump couldn't hold back.

His obsession with the invasion of the United States of America by immigrant children got the better of him.

Trump's repetitive, compulsive case for cracking down on undocumented immigrants, with an emphasis on children, brought shudders of Adolf Hitler, Mein Kampf from many followers.

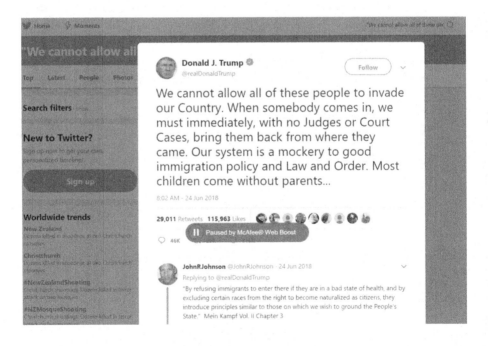

"We cannot allow all of these people to invade our Country. When somebody comes in, we must immediately, with no Judges or Court Cases, bring them back from where they came. Our system is a mockery to good immigration policy and Law and Order. Most Children Come without parents" – Donald Trump, June 2018 tweet.

The laws punishing entry and re-entry have troubling roots in white supremacy laws passed in the 1920s Today, these laws, born from a shameful legacy of white supremacist intentions, fuel a new level of trauma and horror on immigrants and communities of color under the Trump Administration's explosive nationalistic rhetoric.

White Nationalism and the "Wall"

Does President Trump's family have ties to the Ku Klux Klan (KKK)?

The historian Linda Gordon points out that Donald Trump's father Fred Trump was arrested as a young man following an altercation at a Klan march in New York City in 1927 in her book, *The Second Coming of the KKK: The Ku Klux Klan and the American Political Tradition.*

When asked about his father's KKK connection... *"Donald Trump denied that his father had had any connection to a Klan rally. "It's a completely false, ridiculous story. He was never there! It never happened. Never took place."*

The New Yorker article, *Donald Trump and the Ku Klux Klan: A History* by Evan Osnos, on February 26, 2016, is interesting reading outlining Trump's broad support among neo-Nazis, white nationalists, several white supremacists.

We know Trump is sympathetic to the white nationalist movement, "Make America Great Again" but, is he a white supremacist? On CNN, Tapper asked three times if Trump would denounce the Klan's support, and each time Trump declined.

On the anniversary of the August 2017 Charlottesville protests, where bloody clashes occurred between civil rights groups and white supremacists caring nationalist banners and Nazi flags as they brandished sticks and handguns. The Protests that ended tragically as a car rammed into the crowd of protesters killing one and injuring 19. Trump continued his twitter rhetoric yet again condoning 'all types of racism' on Charlottesville anniversary...

"You had some very bad people in that group, but you also had people that were very fine people, on both sides,"

Many White Nationalist and Trump supporters chant *"Build the Wall.:* Are they chanting from fear, hatred, or ignorance?

Please Share Your Knowledge and Opinions to Start the Immigration Discussion.

Does Trump Hate Latinx People?

Does Trump hate Latinx people? Probably, he doubled down on CNN with Erin Burnett "Some are rapist some are killers." Some people will say the video is edited... Just listen to his words. Donald Trump doubles down on calling Mexicans 'rapist...

UNIVISION and NBC have had a tenuous relationship with Trump over his derogatory Latinx rhetoric...

"At NBC, respect and dignity for all people are cornerstones of our values. Due to the recent derogatory statements by Donald Trump regarding immigrants, NBCUniversal is ending its business relationship with Mr. Trump." - Here's the statement NBC issued.

Univision CEO Randy Falco sent an internal memo explaining his decision to break ties with Trump and addressing some of the real estate mogul's accusations.

"We cannot be associated with insulting and intolerant speech that brands an entire community of Mexican immigrants in the U.S. as people who bring drugs, crime, and rape into our country....We took this action because it preserves the dignity of our community and our employees and our relationship with them," - Falco's full internal memo, June of 2015 can be read here.

Acting chief of staff Mick Mulvaney says Trump is 'not a white supremacist,' following New Zealand mass shooting. March 17, 2019.

Whether Trump is or is not a 'white Supremacist' the shooter's 74-page manifesto published before the attack praises Trump as a, "a symbol of renewed white identity and common purpose."

Trump's obsessive-compulsive comments, and tweets from March 2017 -2019 in which he described an influx of illegal immigrants as an "invasion," are so far from the truth, that I question his ability to serve all the people of the United States.

The "Wall"

Then there is the obsession with the wall! The wall that the U.S. is building!

The wall that will stop drugs! Most drugs are seized at ports of entry, not along the open border.

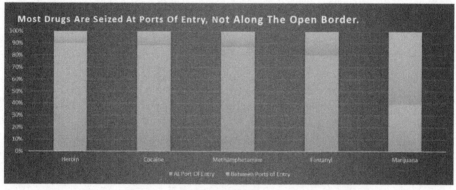

Source: U.S. Customs and Border Protection drug seizures at all borders 2019.

The wall that Mexico is building!

Trump uses rhetoric and misdirection to take the focus away from the issue of migrant children, family separations, and the true magnitude of his "Zero Tolerance" immigration policy directives. The Fact is a "wall" will not address any of the issues facing Latinx immigrant children.

Trump appears to be openly anti-Latino. Furthermore, his inhumane treatment of Latinx children and families gives us insight into his true nature, guided by a belief that people from Mexico and Central America are less than human.

An estimated 200,000 or more people per year could be prosecuted under the "Zero Tolerance policy." Jeff Sessions now the Former United States Attorney General planned to further expand mass prosecutions through "Operation Streamline," a strategy of mass hearings and mass imprisonment, with hundreds of immigrants arraigned, convicted and sentenced simultaneously in just one hearing. Already, migrant prosecutions under these unjust laws consume half of all federal prosecutions. Migration crimes, along with drug offenses, are the major contributor to a massive federal prison boom.

The federal prison boom breeds gang assimilations from "White Supremacists" to violent drug gangs like the *"Maras."* The *"Maras"* gang has grown dramatically with the feds unknowing help.

Recently the intervention of evangelical churches to assist those wanting to leave the *"Maras"* gang appears to be fruitful due to the respect of the *Mara syndicate* for those entering religious life to raise a family and work.

"Jesus rose from the dead on a Sunday (Matthew 28:1, Mark 16:2, Luke 24:1, John 20:1), so we reserve Sunday as our special day in order to commemorate his resurrection."

As Christians broke bread in remembrance of Jesus, with communion, and peace, Trump raged war on children.

Unfortunately, the Christian Broadcasting Networks, the evangelical media powerhouses have on occasion echoed Trump's words. To be fair, the Christian Broadcasting Network tries to show both sides of the immigration discussion, for example in, The Stranger' Among Us: Church Tackles Immigration. David Brody - CBN News Chief Political Analyst and Tracy Winborn try to show both sides.

Many white evangelicals have consistently upheld Trump's policies on immigration and refugees. However, many are now questioning their position, especially when it comes to immigrant children who are seeking asylum.

In 2018, 68% of White Evangelicals Thought America Shouldn't House Refugees

Source: (The Pew Research Center, 2018)

Trump rhetoric misled many to believe that separating families at the border was the right way.

Luckily many religious groups have reacted with:

"Give the members of your community a fair hearing, and judge rightly between one person and another, whether citizen or resident alien." – The Bible. Deuteronomy 1:16

Perhaps those that doubt and have no empathy should remember, the words from Deuteronomy 10:18-19 – *"For the Lord your God...loves the strangers, providing them food and clothing. You shall also love the stranger, for you were strangers in the land of Egypt."*

Many of America's ancestors were also strangers to the "New World" in the context of North America and welcomed by Native Americans. 90 Native Americans and 53 Pilgrims attended the first Thanksgiving according to the Pilgrim Hall Museum, The first Thanksgiving.

At religious gatherings across the country, pastors, priests, rabbis, and imams from other religions and denominations have delivered impassioned sermons, fiercely denouncing the humanitarian immorality of the Trump Administrations separating children from their parents at the U.S.-Mexico border.

There is a striking difference in between New Anglican Father Cameron Lemons and his wife Jenelle's observations and their compassionate actions and those of Diane Serafin Councilwoman of the City of Murrieta, a tea party organizer, and Anti-immigrant activist in Murrieta, California. Their comments are eye-opening.

"I'm concerned some of the churches, or people will start taking them in," Sarafin said. "Our government should have before they shipped them, bused them, threw them on a plane, given them medical treatment. There's too many with diseases."

Sarafin also said if churches want to show compassion, they should start with their own country.

"Okay, we're $17 trillion in debt -- I'm barely surviving myself -- and we're going to pay them to stay here and take care of them, food and welfare," she said. "Our nation can't afford it."

Source: (Winborn, 2018)

Diane Serafin fiscal concerns are valid. The U.S. continues to show no fiscal responsibility under the Trump administration. American taxpayers should be asking why the government is spending so much on X, Y, and Z and $24,000, per month per child, that is $288,000 per year on child detentions when there is a more fiscally responsible way.

To Detain A Kid for One Month Is Costing the U.S. Approximately $24,000.
That Is $288, 000 Per Year!

Note that many locals do not agree with Councilwoman Diana Serafin's, actions in Murrieta and are seeking an Outside Investigation From DOJ Regarding Murrieta Protestors and Obstruction Of Justice.

Many older white conservatives evangelical Christians are loyal to Trump and his fiery immigration policies. They turned out to support 2018 midterm elections. I ask myself why, why would Christians support Trump? Why?

Perhaps some of the older white evangelicals believe Trump will realign American politics, with the Christian Right, reasserting itself after eight years of Barack Obama.

A 2018 study published by the Public Religion Research Institute (PRRI,) suggests that many white Evangelicals don't agree with Latinx and other people of color Protestants when it comes to race and immigration.

It is healthy to have differences of position and opinion on the immigration issue. However, we should all have empathy for the innocent migrant children who have come to seek protection and asylum.

We should first solve the humanitarian children's plight and be good Samaritans, then perhaps we can discuss and resolve the immigration issues as a whole.

Trump behavior is encouraging white supremacists and unethical actions. It appears to have become acceptable to bully, malign, and slander others. Appearances lie.

"A majority (54%) of Americans say that President Trump's decisions and behavior as president have encouraged white supremacist groups, compared to just five percent who believe the president has discouraged white supremacist groups. Nearly four in ten (39%) say Trump's behavior has not affected white supremacist groups.

There are large differences between racial and ethnic groups on this issue. About seven in ten black (72%) and Hispanic (68%) Americans, compared to less than half (45%) of white Americans, believe that the president's conduct has encouraged white supremacist groups. Among white Americans, those with a four-year college degree are more likely than those without a degree to say that Trump's decisions and behavior as president have encouraged white supremacist groups (58% vs. 38%)."

Source: (PPRI, 2018) <u>Download the full PRRI report</u>

The Majority of Americans believe, "<u>Trump Has Damaged the Dignity of The Presidency</u>."

The question that every American should ask themselves is simple. Do I believe in integrity the "The American Way," and the principle of life, liberty, and the pursuit of happiness?

If you do, you should act with compassion and empathy for the migrant children, let us solve their immigration status first together as a nation. Let us recognize their innocence and need for care.

Many humanitarian religions and sects have gathered across the country, pastors, priests, rabbis, and imams to deliver impassioned sermons, fiercely denouncing the morality of the Trump Administrations separating children from their parents at the U.S.-Mexico border.

Their actions show their belief that being a human involves recognizing the sanctity and humanity of all human beings, many support DACA, and the DREAM'ers, many believe "Black Lives Matter," and immigration reform is needed.

Trump is the pied piper of Family Separations, through his "Zero Tolerance" policy. The Republican Party must choose whether or not to act like puppets on his strings.

"Send the Children Back Home to Their Families." What if No Family or Home Exist?

Politically the best way to get rid of any problem is to sweep it under the table, removing it from Americas instant political media cycle. This is exactly how Trump manipulates and misdirects the media, and this is what many politicians from both parties would like to do.

Don't believe me? Think about the Columbine High school massacre, Sandy Hook Elementary School Shootings, or more recently the 2018 Parkland shooting in Florida that left 17 people dead.

El Paso Shooting Suspect's hate-filled, anti-immigrant Manifesto Echoes Trump's Rhetoric.

Look at the recent news-At least 31 people were killed over the weekend of August 3, 2019, in mass shootings in Texas and Ohio.

"This attack is a response to the Hispanic invasion of Texas," the manifesto says... The Hispanic population is willing to return to their home countries if given the right incentive. An incentive that myself and many other patriotic Americans will provide.... such terrorist attacks will "remove the threat of the Hispanic voting bloc."

Politicians ran to Texas and Ohio in droves, just as they did to Columbine High School twenty years ago seeking political gain. They will pretend to seek change.

In the end, the politicians will shirk from solving the difficult issues that have plagued our nation for years. They wait like dusty books on a shelf till the issue dies down, repapering all shiny and new to fight another committee investigation battle.

Some Republicans relish "Sending back the children." The sad truth is they will be sending them back to a place with far worse problems than Texas or Ohio.

The moral and humanitarian issues are irrelevant. The fact that they may have no home or family to go to is irrelevant. The fact that their country is in turmoil run by gangs and thugs that the U.S. trained, backed, and supports is irrelevant.

The only relevant thing for many politicians in general is: **They came here illegally. So, throw them out, don't give them any legal representation; they are just unaccompanied Latinx kids. They can't vote, they have no say."**

Trump's rabble-rousing nationalistic Republican slogan **"LET'S MAKE AMERICA GREAT AGAIN,"** by systematically attacking people of color and for that matter anyone who disagrees with his incendiary rhetoric, **"LET'S THROW THEM OUT. SEND THEM BACK - LET'S FAIL TO HONOR DACA AND THROW THEM OUT, LET'S MAKE AMERICA GREAT AGAIN!"**

Bulling Rhetoric is Part of the U.S. War on Immigrant LatinX Children.

Trump's Republican Administration is happy to reunite detained children with their families if they agree to deportation! What type of choice is that? Oh, I forgot the slogan... "Let's make America Great Again by throwing out the Latinx children."

Fight to stay separated from your children or be deported with your children!

That is the kind of choice a dictator gives, the type of choice based on hate and racism. We are a greater nation than this.

Republicans, Democrats, Independents and Religious leaders should focus their efforts in reuniting the families, act in a humanitarian manner be a good Samaritan in helping the weak and the weary travelers displaced by the violence in the Northern Triangle.

Bob Dylan, a great social commentator who captured and reflected politics and existentialism sang, "The Times They are a-Changin'." How right he was in 1964 and how right his song is again today.

Image Source: © Peter Lucking | contentbrandingsolutions.com

SOLUTIONS

A Call for a Bipartisan Solution for Immigrant LatinX Children

Many scholars and legal professionals have proposed that we make changes to our immigration system to alleviate the harsh anti-American unhumanitarian treatment that we unknowingly hand out to the DREAM'ers growing up alongside our children and to the masses of children at our Southern border.

A growing number of people are recognizing that the Dreamers living among us are stuck in a vicious political cycle that relegates them to live in limbo as a permanent nationless underclass.

Public opinion appears to be moving towards embracing the plight of immigrant children with many embracing the cause while at the same time admitting that many Americans are still unsure how to approach the issue of adult immigrants.

I would say that this is a valid starting point. No one has all the answers, and there is little agreement about how to reform the immigration laws for the adults who arrive at our borders. Most importantly, there is a consensus that we must do something for immigrant children, and we must do it now.

That consensus still leaves many of us at a difficult juncture because very few politicians and community leaders have dedicated themselves to the task of proposing a more inclusive, or comprehensive, plan to alleviate the draconian, effect of our immigration system on children who are "scarred for life" by the severe psychological trauma they are put through.

As we witnessed, it was much easier for the Obama Administration to quietly implement the largest removal of children from our country in the history of the United States.

President Trump continues Obama's policy and publicly celebrates the caging of children while he distracts the public with his inability to provide solutions beyond building a "wall."

I would dare say that Obama's administration created the humanitarian crisis at the border while Trump's administration is continuing this crisis for political gain.

President Trump tries to spin the "Zero Tolerance" policy as a crackdown on illegal immigration.

"Under the "Zero Tolerance" policy created by Trump and Attorney General Jeff Sessions, the Department of Justice prosecutes and imprisons all migrants for migration crimes. The horrific consequences of these mass prosecutions are family separation and the transfer of children to child detention centers or federal foster programs.

The laws punishing entry and re-entry have troubling roots in white supremacy laws passed in the 1920s. These unlawful entry laws were introduced by a pro-lynching Congressman who will remain nameless who's specific intent was to exclude and incarcerate Mexican immigrants." **From the Letter Calling on Congress to Decriminalize Migration by the National Immigration Project of the National Lawyers Guild (NIPNLG).** Read the letter.

Perhaps the former president did not realize that his administration, had produced a crisis for youth countrywide in Honduras just five years earlier by assisting in the demise of their democratically elected government. Other people have offered a more sympathetic explanation that President Obama started deporting *more children than any president in U.S. history* because he wanted to appear heavy-handed to the then-Republican Party-controlled Congress to negotiate more benefits for immigrants such as the DREAM'ers who had grown up here.

I, for one, decline to participate in this revisionist practice of trying to protect the legacy of former presidents. I also refuse to advocate for only the young people who grew up in the U.S. who would benefit from the DREAM Act. All of the children, including those camped out at our borders, are DREAMERS.

Many advocates for children state that we need to stop wasting time blaming one president or another; however, all advocates agree that we must expect that all sectors of the United States, including religious groups, legal groups, average citizens and all political parties take responsibility to resolve the crisis that has developed at our border. I believe that responsibility from government officials also requires that we hold them accountable, and see that history does not repeat itself.

By understanding how President Obama and his administration created such a crisis in Honduras and how he succeeded in winning the title of *"Deporter-In-Chief"* from immigration advocates, will help us address President Trump's current actions, and fashion solutions for the future.

My opinion is that we are allowing our country's government under President Trump to make the same mistake if we do not clearly demand a policy of aid to the Central American countries to help them regain stability and assist in the improvement of their public safety, education, health and economic opportunity in their own countries.

More on this later after we look at the details of how President Trump has exacerbated the problem at the Southern Border.

The "Wall"

On one extreme, that large number of U.S. citizens that support the construction of a physical barrier along the entire Southern Border assumes that such a barrier would reduce immigration by physically stopping children and adults alike from entering the country without permission and that this would solve most of the issues with undocumented entrants.

Others believe that the construction of a wall would solve the humanitarian crisis at the border by sending a symbolic message to the world that "the door to the U.S.A. is locked."

Few of our citizens, including those that are in favor of constructing the wall know that President Bill Clinton signed the authorization of the construction of the "wall" twenty years before President Trump won the presidency.

The physical construction of a wall is rife with issues including the winding rivers and natural science of the earth, gullies ravines and mountains that provided challenges to the engineering of such a barrier. Thus, the Southern barrier has been halted at various times due to many issues beyond financing.

One issue facing the "wall's" construction is the fact that we signed treaties with Native American tribes that live on both the Mexican and the U.S. sides of the border.

Native American tribes including the Tohono O'odham, Yaquis and Kikapoo tribes, among 36 other tribes, who existed on both sides of the border since the establishment of the current line in the sand between Mexico and the U.S. in the Treaty of Guadalupe Hidalgo in 1848 and the Gadsden Purchase of 1853 are feeling the sharp pinch of family separation.

Native American tribes existed on both sides of the border; it's their land why divide them with a "wall."

Additionally, there are real concerns with environmental damage to endangered animal habitats and the jungles that are right in the path of a physical barrier. Thus, the construction of the wall has been held up by many of these concerns, some of which were taken up by various federal court oversight on Presidents Clinton, Bush, Obama and now on Trump.

Even if all these issues could be resolved, the prevention of various tunnels being excavated underneath a wall or just a ladder, a crane over the wall or any other apparatus to help people go over under and around makes such a barrier worthless.

Some migrants are paying coyotes thousands of dollars, to cross the southern border. They could fly to Canada and walk across the "wall-less" border unhindered.

How drugs and trafficking pass by ICE checkpoints is a mystery. The movement of massive amounts of drugs and human trafficking right through the ICE monitored checkpoints at the border's many ports-of-entry simply do not make the construction of a physical wall into a credible solution to the humanitarian crisis facing immigrant children today. Building a "wall" is economically and socially pointless.

Most Drugs and Trafficking Pass-through ICE Checkpoints they do not go Over, Under or Around the Wall!

Furthermore, the supposed "KEEP OUT - YOUR NOT WELCOME" message that the construction of a physical "wall" would send to the world, including the Northern Triangle of Guatemala, El Salvador, and Honduras is lost on people fighting daily for survival.

The message will continue to be lost on massive populations in those countries who continually witness U.S. interference in their attempted democratic processes, at the expense of humanity.

The countries of the Northern Triangle witness growing poverty and crime while U.S. based companies continue to their historical control (and profits from) the agricultural output by countries like Honduras while they continue to leave the citizens, especially children, at a severe loss of options except to migrate out of a need for survival.

Even worse, a devastating natural disaster caused by the drought in Guatemala has decimated the agricultural subsistence of small farmers and is exacerbating the issue of survival for many more Central Americans. These catastrophes are happening globally on an accelerated rate by climate change. Poverty and starvation will inspire more caravans as a result.

The "Wall" is a Political Stunt That is Meant to Pander to Many U.S. Voters.

The "Wall" is a political stunt that is meant to pander to many U.S. voters. It would not solve any of the above issues. To many, it would require the massive use of U.S. taxpayer resources to the tune of billions while insulting the basic sensibilities of all U.S. citizens. Perhaps the only U.S. citizens who would benefit are the private contractors that would be used to construct the wall. I am not the first person to wonder if these companies would have to rely on undocumented workers to finish the job.

Just as the Democratic Party hoped to use the false promise of DACA to pander to Latino voters in the last election, President Trump and Republican Party candidates will utilize the false promise of a "wall" to pander for reelection to white nationalists. They will use hateful incendiary rhetoric that divides a nation ironically built upon the diversity of immigrants.

Most importantly, even if the "Build a Wall" advocates were able to build an impervious barrier at a massive price tag that could handle the insurmountable geographical, environmental and symbolic tasks to completely stem the flow of illegal migration on our Southern border, then what about the over 12 million people who are already here? The "Wall" would only keep them from leaving at the end of the agricultural harvest season after they picked the beets, lettuce, and corn in Colorado and Nebraska. Likewise, the "Wall" would trap resort workers in the winter ski resorts from returning to their families in Mexico during the Spring—forcing them to birth and raise their children in the U.S.

Overhaul and Improve ICE

On the other extreme, there is a growing movement led by immigrant-advocacy groups who not only oppose the "Wall" but go much further to call for the elimination of the Immigration and Customs Enforcement arm of the Department of Homeland Security.

The "Abolish ICE" advocates point out that ICE has recently received billions of dollars for their budget (about 7.4 billion) and cannot seem to respond to President Trump's mandates to increase stormtrooper like ICE raids in the interior while detaining and guarding the children and families at the Southern Border.

Many immigration activists have pointed out; ICE has been rife with internal conflict, allegations of abuse by officers and rampant unprofessionalism—particularly by the Border Patrol that also falls under ICE's umbrella. Most of the concerns are serious faults that must be dealt with sooner rather than later.

Most U.S. citizens recognize that ICE still has an important function to guard our airports, seaports and land borders against terrorists externally and internally, violent criminals like drug traffickers, the possibility of food contamination and the spread of contagious diseases. Thus, although it might feel good to give the finger to "la Migra" as ICE has been known for many years, the "Abolish ICE" position becomes very hard to sustain especially for Middle America.

At the same time, this movement continues to grow at a faster pace than the "Wall" advocates because they have one very valid point when they ask: "Do we want those in charge of detecting and arresting drug traffickers and terrorists to handle the tens of thousands of children at the border?"

Many Americans across the entire political spectrum have begun to ask: "Is this the right agency to deal with DREAM'ers who grew up with our children and are being thrust back into immigration court by the Trump Administration?

ICE's shortcomings require a serious review and a broad overhaul while becoming more efficient in what I would call their very necessary existence. Perhaps the new moniker can be amended to read "Abolish ICE for Kids."

As George W. Bush stated on immigrants: "We ought to say thank you and welcome them."
(ANAPOL, 2018)

Some meritorious remedies that have been proposed in the recent past are: to increase our corps of black-booted asylum officers, better train those officers and, at the same time, provide them the authority to decide the merits of a person's claim right at the border upon or shortly after their arrival.

This last piece would allow those fleeing violence and persecution in their home countries through a request for asylum to bypass the long process of waiting to see an Immigration Judge in Immigration Court in the interior of the U.S. or waiting in Mexico at our Southern Border. This would allow these empowered asylum officers the ability to grant the approvable cases while saving the immigrants, our law enforcement, and the taxpayers precious time and money.

Former government officials, such as Doris Meissner who used to be the head of the Immigration and Naturalization Service or "INS," which is the predecessor to the Department of Homeland Security's ICE and USCIS branches, has proposed this exact approach for asylum seekers at the border. However, none of the former and present administration officials has proposed that we implement this policy immediately and focus on the children at our border *first*.

Everyone would agree that it makes sense to avoid expensive prolonged detention of children in burgeoning camps with the dangers of federally contracted foster care where they may be subject to physical and sexual abuse.

The Cost of Child Detentions is $24,000 per month of taxpayers' dollars.
The horrendous cost is, a child "scarred for life!"

Likewise, as is evident with the government's inability to move children out of detention under the *Flores Settlement*, that this proposal would help avoid the requirement that kids wait for and attend court dates where most of them cannot afford an attorney. Further, the current lack of well-trained, experienced, politically unbiased asylum officers has exacerbated the unnecessary separation of children from their families.

Supposedly, the *Flores Settlement* entered into by the government and the plaintiff children to a federal lawsuit was supposed to prevent children from being detained for more than 20 days; however, the government has not been able to comply with the requirement that children be moved to a "non-detained" environment. Consequently, this settlement has sent more and more children to unlicensed private foster care facilities across many states.

It is important to note that the asylum officers of today are not under the branch of ICE rather they operate under the United States Citizenship and Immigration Service (USCIS) which is also an arm of the Department of Homeland Security. Furthermore, USCIS is not charged with handling the border directly—another internal problem with the huge bureaucracy of the Department of Homeland Security, which was created after 9/11 terrorist attacks in New York in 2001.

The Border Patrol got to keep their name while the Immigration and Naturalization Service (INS) was moved completely to the new DHS branch from the Department of Justice arm of *internal* immigration enforcement. INS was then split into three different branches: ICE, USCIS and the Border Patrol within the newly minted Department of Homeland Security infrastructure. Unfortunately, the function of our immigration laws did not change in any meaningful way after the reorganization.

It almost seems like an easy fix to implement the DREAM Act that was most recently passed by the House of Representatives and allow them to earn their citizenship; however, it is estimated that only three million of the undocumented immigrants living in the United States would benefit from the DREAM Act even if it is expanded to include those Temporary Protected Status holders—many of whom are from Honduras and El Salvador. However, addressing the growing crisis facing children on the border has presented a much more complicated problem.

Decriminalization of Child Immigrant Status

Surprisingly, there are few bold proposals that provide immigrant children much hope. One such proposal comes from former Secretary of Housing and Urban Development and recent presidential candidate Julián Castro who asserts that we should decriminalize the illegal entry of so-called "illegal aliens" coming into the country.

Secretary Castro proposes that Congress should pass a law doing away with *8 United States Code Section 1325* that allows border officials the ability to charge a person, adult, or child, who has crossed the border illegally to be charged with a misdemeanor criminal charge.

Presently this criminal section is not mandatory and is not always used by the Border Patrol or ICE after detaining someone. It is the primary reason why people have come to refer to undocumented immigrants as "illegal," even though most of the border crossers are rarely charged with it. Castro proposes that we do away with this little-used law and, as he argues, unnecessary label.

Whether one disagrees or agrees with Secretary Castro, we all must recognize that he has provided the opportunity on a national stage via nationally televised presidential candidate debates for the discussion of a grand policy shift away from "thinking inside the box" of border law enforcement and the construction of a wall. His proposal moves towards viewing the significant issues facing real people rather than treating them as less than human beings, aliens.

I believe that most U.S. citizens would be in favor of this change as it applies to children (I will leave the debate about adult unlawful entry to another book by another author).

I stress that we should immediately make this g adjustment to our laws for immigrant children by completely decriminalizing arrival at our borders *by children under 18 years of age*. Secretary Castro's solution as applied to children makes all sense in the *context of children*.

A juvenile crossing the border should not be placed in the same category as an adult who commits an intentional crime. After all, even in cases of trespassing or destruction of property by minors under 18, in most of the 50 states, our colonies and commonwealths are already treated as cases of juvenile delinquency, not a crime.

What if Secretary Castro is correct with regards to children? We could take away the entire veil of calling these children "criminals" and holding them in cages. Decriminalizing immigrant children would allow us to forego making toddlers "pay" and be held accountable for actions that they don't understand.

Alleviate the Backlog of Immigration Dockets

Of course, while we want to alleviate the huge backlog of cases in the Immigration Courts, those courts could use some relief as well.

Since President Trump took office at the beginning of 2017, the court's backlog of immigrant cases has jumped over 225,000 cases. Now there are more than 850,000 on the Immigration Court's calendar.

There are currently almost 90, 000 children in court without any parents according to the Executive Office for Immigration Review's Adjudication Statistics.

There are currently almost 90, 000 children in court without any parents according to the Executive Office for Immigration Review's Adjudication Statistics/Current Representation Rates for the second quarter of 2019. Also, over 65,000 immigrant cases of adults and children were designated as "Family-unit" cases. Thus, over half of all immigration cases involve children.

- Only about 400 judges are tasked with hearing immigration court cases!
- Families and children stuck in this backlog are in for a long wait.

President Trump has borrowed a strategy from President Clinton twenty years ago by moving the most recent cases to the front of the line to clear the backlog. This is not a solution. Carlos paid the price of this very action by being pushed to the back of the line as he "aged out."

Almost every President, including Trump, have tried to hire more immigration judges; however, they cannot move quickly enough as Trump is overloading the Immigration Court system.

The Immigration Courts are not under the Department of Homeland Security like ICE and the Border Patrol. Instead, the Immigration Courts are administered by the United States Department of Justice. This is yet another branch of the President's Executive Power. The bureaucratic mess that ensues due to differing priorities, communication, and coordination between the enforcement arms and the Immigration Courts are part of the reason why the courts are overburdened and backlogged.

To make matters worse, the Immigration Courts are rife with their internal problems due to President Trump's frequent changes of his appointed Attorney Generals. No wonder immigration advocates and immigration hard-liners have scrutinized the budget of the Executive Office for Immigration Review, which is the official name of the branch of the U.S. Department of Justice that oversees the Immigration Court system.

The budget for the Immigration Courts is over one-half billion dollars per year and growing. The system is backlogged; children await their day in court for months on end.

The Solution

Secretary Castro's approach is a good starting point, but we must go further and be more intentional for children. For the most part, our juvenile delinquency courts recognize that minors cannot truly understand the consequences of their actions, with exceptions for very serious or heinous crimes.

I propose that we drastically reorganize and repurpose Immigration Courts for children. Specifically, children should only go to immigration court as a last resort and not as a starting point.

All Minors Need Guardians and Legal Representation

All minors need representation. Even in juvenile delinquency court when a minor skips school or caught shoplifting, most courts ensure that a minor has some form of adult representation. Therefore, if we are going to continue placing children in some type of immigration process, then we should provide them representation that will help the child.

- Let us treat migrant children with humanity and compassion
- Let us provide them with a guardian
- Let us provide unaccompanied minors with the council to serve their best interests
- Let us reallocate taxpayers' funds wisely

Remember that undocumented person, whether adults or minors, do not have the right to an attorney at our taxpayer's expense.

We Throw Away Taxpayers' Dollars Arbitrarily When It Comes to Immigration?

The U.S. is willing to throw away massive amounts of taxpayer dollars to fund law enforcement personnel, contract detention space, and for expensive foster care for children—but we do not provide a counsel or guardian ad litem to represent them.

The Cost of Child Detentions is $24,000 per month of taxpayers' dollars

Whether it is a parent, a guardian, or someone appointed by the court, there must be someone there to "represent" that child; they are unaccompanied minors they need accompanying and guidance.

I often wonder, what if Susana had not been available to take charge of Elaizer? Where would he have ended up? Perhaps he would have suffered abuse or been "lost" in the shuffle between ICE, the Department of Health and Human Services, and the Immigration Courts. Even worse, Elaizer could have been sent back to Guatemala and killed by the rampant gang members who threatened his life for not joining their criminal syndicate.

One thing is for sure, children, just like the little boy with sad brown eyes that I saw shackled like a slave at the beginning of my career, are forced to appear in Immigration Court and represent themselves! Could any of our children do that? Let alone a child, a minor who has suffered, is frightened, and abused? To make it worse, we may be speaking in an unknown language, English, which is just gibberish to that child.

The Child Immigration Guardians Ad Litem (IGAL's)

I propose that we focus our strained Immigration Courts on adults and create a new corps of Immigration Guardians Ad Litem (or "IGAL's") to take their place when it comes to children.

IGAL's would be trained attorneys who have experience in actual family or juvenile courts. It makes sense that if the child has an undocumented parent, then an Immigration Guardian Ad Litem could help make decisions regarding that child since the parent may have a conflict of interest in trying to present their case to stay in the U.S. It makes even more sense that children who are here without anyone to care for them, or as our government labels them Unaccompanied Alien Children or UAC's, need these IGAL's more than anyone.

A Guardian Ad Litem (G.A.L.) is best known in divorce proceedings as two parents vie for parental control. The family court judges often appoint the G.A.L. to determine the best interest of the child. The G.A.L. investigates the home situation, evaluates the school, interviews the parents, and give the judge a report on the totality of that child's circumstance. Here, the parents, the Homeland Security, the Health Human Services, (H.H.S.) officers often fail to take the best interest of these children into account in any meaningful way. They will fail to advocate for the child's legal interest.

If we are going to dedicate a portion of our taxpayer-funded immigration system to children, then let's do it right!

Let Us Provide Each Migrant Child with Legal Guardians and Representation. How will we pay for this I hear you Chant?

To pay for this system, I suggest that we do away with the Immigration Courts for children and reapportion one-quarter of the Immigration Court budget to hire trained and experienced federal Immigration Guardians Ad Litem (IGAL's) to take over the children's cases from the Immigration Court. This would free up the courts to focus on adult cases, including those where families are in court and give children much-needed advocacy.

If the IGAL is unable to resolve any situation for the child's best interest, then they should be able to turn to the immigration judge for an order to compel the government to act.

IGAL job #1 – Don't let the Children die in Custody

- The Immigration Guardians Ad Litem (IGAL's) would work with ICE and Border Patrol to ensure that the child's health and safety are being provided for by our frontline law enforcement. The first goal of an IGAL would be to ensure that we no longer have deaths of children due to lack of adequate medical care as they come into custody by our government.

IGAL job #2 – Don't Allow Immigrant Children to be Physically, Emotionally and Sexually Abused

- The IGAL would work with ICE and the Department of Health and Human Services to contact the child's parents or future guardians in the states and/or in the home country to first confirm that the child's identity and family while, at the same time, providing a check on H.H.S. administration of the basic education and medical needs.

- The IGAL would visit the foster care facilities and detention centers, have full access to visit the child and address this legal their legal and health needs.

- ILGALs would be empowered to get children like Jose and Carla the counseling and mental health services that HHS has available. The trauma of their experience would not be ignored.

IGAL job #3 – Keep Children out of Detention

- The IGAL would assist and HHS in complying with the requirement to find an alternative to detention within the 20 days laid out in the Flores Settlement.

- More importantly, an IGAL would be appointed in the first 24 hours before a child is ever separated from family or guardian before that child comes into ICE custody. More effective, efficient, and humane. No exceptions!

IGAL job #4 – Help Find the Parents and or Family

- If the child has a potential parent or guardian living in the U.S., then the IGAL can locate, contact, and screen those individuals. They would visit the home and ensure that a child is not delivered into a situation where they would suffer neglect, abandonment or abuse

- Also, the IGAL would have investigatory power to ascertain if the child was kidnapped by human traffickers and get that child back to their parents or guardians in the home country immediately--if that was in the best interest of the child.

Finally, if the child has a potential guardian living in the U.S., then an IGAL can locate, contact, and screen those individuals. Follow-up visits to the home ensure that a child is not delivered into a situation where they would suffer neglect, abandonment, or abuse.

IGAL job #5 – Help the Child Apply Asylum

- The IGAL could ensure that a child who fears to return to their country receives their initial credible fear interview and, if possible, their dispositive asylum determination (assuming we give this power to asylum officers) shortly upon entering the U.S.

- The IGAL would assist an Asylum officer from USCIS in collecting evidence for this purpose.

- If the child were lucky enough to find legal representation by a non-profit or a private immigration attorney, then the IGAL could assist or step back to allow another legal representative to prepare evidence.

IGAL job #6 – Help the Child Apply for Special Immigrant Juvenile Protection

- The IGAL would accompany the Child (UAC) to guardianship, probate or custody court and assist the child in securing the requisite order from a State Judge declaring that they were abandoned, abused or neglected by one or both parents.

The proposed IGAL's would be much more than a helping hand for ICE or a watchdog over HHS.; they would be a true legal advocate. Specifically, the proposed IGAL would be authorized to enter a local court and request the prerequisite order from the local judge for guardianship or custody status for the child to apply for SIJS and then forward that application to USCIS to get it approved.

Again, I think of Elaizer, if he had not had his aunt Susana to hire both an immigration attorney and a guardianship attorney on his behalf. He wouldn't have been able to initiate and navigate his application for Special Immigrant Juvenile Status (SIJS). Elaizer most likely would have been deported before he turned eighteen years old.

The IGAL would operate outside of the immigration courts unless the IGAL believes that their case should be referred to the Immigration Judge as a last resort. Currently, children who apply for Special Immigrant Juvenile Status like Elaizer are still forced into the court system even though they likely do not need to be there as they wait for years in a visa backlog.

Children who file for asylum protection are forced into immigration court while the asylum officers, who currently hold very limited power to decide, work through another huge backlog of political asylum applications.

Tens of thousands of children are forced to represent themselves in immigration court while they are already waiting in some other category. Also, the smaller number of children who have no applications pending are waiting for years in the Immigration Court until they are eventually told that they will have to deport back to their country voluntarily.

The idea to provide government-paid (really taxpayer-funded) attorneys for immigrants is not new. The American Immigration Attorney Association (AILA) to which I belong, has long advocated for immigrants to receive representation just like a criminal defendant is owed a public defender in criminal cases. Of course, children are not criminals.

I do agree with AILA that government-funded legal counsel will promote efficiency and fairness. It would be an ideal world if immigration attorneys like myself were no longer overworked and spread-thin as we cannot possibly take on all the immigration cases of children in Immigration Court.

My proposal is more nuanced and focuses on children rather than all immigrants.

Immigration Reform for Children First

We should put the humanitarian child immigration issues first.

There will be a difference of opinion as to how best to approach the immigration issue and where to start. I do believe that it is more than a reasonable strategy to focus on immigration reform for children first.

This proposal may be met with skepticism by some advocates on both sides of the political spectrum who want proposed solutions to apply to adults and children equally.

I am proposing that children receive vastly more consideration and legal opportunities than adults as a starting point.

Treat All Dreamers as DREAM'ers

Many people along the entire political spectrum have already agreed that the DREAM Act will alleviate the situation that has befallen so many young people in the U.S. just like Carlos and Gabriela as I detailed earlier in this book.

Back in 2007, the Democrats undermined the Republican bill based upon the argument that we needed comprehensive immigration reform that applied to adults as well as children. Now the non-comprehensive or "piecemeal" approach to the passing the Dream Act for those who arrived as children is often the entirety of the policy discussion by the immigrant advocates. Most have abandoned the demand for similar treatment for the parents of DREAM'ers *as a starting point* because we have so much agreement on the plight of immigrant children.

I suggest that we look at the situation of the Dreamers at the border in the same light as those who have grown up here—specifically that they not be treated the same as their parents. The children at the border are also Dreamers

This proposal will be met with opposition by those on the Right who will point out that we already give children extra consideration because we provide the opportunity for *Special Immigrant Juvenile*

Status (if kids can afford a couple of private attorneys), and our government attempts to comply with the Flores Settlement.

"The history of migration from the Northern Triangle, resulting from economic insecurity, seems to impede policymakers to change their thinking to meet today's realities..." (Vigaud-Walsh, 2017)

The sad fact is that most children are not allowed to apply for SIJS, and the government is failing to release children from detention. Finding representation and applying for protections are most often left to good luck or the economic means to hire both an immigration attorney and a probate/family attorney to represent a child in both Immigration Court and a local probate/family court.

Most people would struggle to pay two attorneys in two different proceedings in two different courtrooms at the same time—much less an immigrant child who may not even have a parent present in the country! Thus, the dual representation that Elaizer was afforded through his aunt Susana is the exception, not the rule. That young man is truly one of the lucky ones as the vast majority of unaccompanied minors arriving at the border will never see an attorney, never complete an application for asylum, and consequently be deported.

Both the Left and the Right will point to the lackluster Flores Settlement as if it were some *save-all for kids*. On the one hand, some have rejoiced at the victory of federal court oversight while others have thrown up their hands, acknowledging that government officials are doing their best, but failing to implement the requirement. Unfortunately, this is a good example of an unpleasant situation where the courts cannot simply order the government to accomplish what they do not have the resources to fix.

The "Abolish ICE" advocates are right about one thing: the administration of billions of dollars by both ICE and the Immigration courts is not working.

Amnesty?

Of course, all these proposals will not alleviate the situation of people who are continuing to come to our borders to escape persecution, poverty, and famine. So many people are against providing anything that appears to be an "amnesty" that will allow the people who are already here because the problem keeps coming back.

It is helpful to know that the last "amnesty" type of program by our government was passed by Congress and signed into law by Republican President Ronald Reagan in 1986 as the Immigration Reform and Control Act (IRCA).

The Immigration Reform and Control Act (IRCA) law provided a temporary legal permanent residence for two groups:

- Those who had lived in the U.S. for the majority of the'80s

- Those who had worked in agriculture as seasonal agricultural workers for ninety (90) days or more.

Both groups had to pass the history and civics exams that we normally only give to applicants for citizenship, they had to pass security and background checks and later apply to become permanent residents after receiving a temporary status.

Congress passed strict laws in The Immigration Reform and Control Act (IRCA), an amendment to the Immigration and Nationality Act of 1952. IRCA was introduced in 1986 for the first time that punished employers who continued to hire unlawful immigrant workers. The many applicants, many of which are now U.S. citizens, benefitted greatly; however, the employers in agriculture, mining, railroads, and construction, continued to hire large numbers of unlawful workers.

The large numbers of people who legalized their status under that amnesty were later replaced by more unlawful workers. Many people refuse to consider another "amnesty" type of law. Most people would favor an e*arned* legal status for adult immigrants. Rarely do we hear about programs that provide for children "first."

The U.S. Must Stop Undermining Central American Governments.
The U.S. should help Create Prosperity and Peace.

The conditions of our country's neighbors to the South have genuinely been the true reason for continued immigration. Those conditions have been shaped by our government's actions in those countries as I detailed in prior chapters. Thus, our government needs to stop interfering with the democratic processes of elections and laws of Mexico and Central America. On the other hand, we must truly assist those governments to recover their hold on public safety in those countries. The U.S.

must invest in those country's infrastructure for the creation of jobs and help grow the economies of the Northern Triangle and Mexico.

President Trump, like other presidents before him, has demanded that Mexico be a partner in this work. The migrant caravans, individuals, and even human trafficking rings have been able to cross the vast territory of Mexico to the Southern border of our country. I have already detailed how the Mexican migrant officials have been placed in charge of Central American and other refugees who are forced to wait in Mexico under Trump's so-called Migrant Protection Protocol.

The Mexican government has also created a large National Guard that has largely been deployed to the border with Guatemala to attempt to control crossings including giving Central Americans and others the "opportunity" to apply for asylum in Mexico. Unfortunately, crime in Mexico has become uncontrollable in many parts as the drug cartels have moved their operations to Mexico from the jungles of Colombia in the last 15 years.

The United States Department of State has issued travel warnings for U.S. citizens in most of the 31 Mexican states due to sustained violent crime. For Mexico to provide an alternative for refugees, particularly children, then the issues of public safety will have to be dealt with before we can expect Mexico to absorb any significant number of refugees from Central America.

AID for Rehabilitation, and Reintegration of Gang Members into Society

To be clear, many immigrants, who are deported, have not committed any crimes in the United States. Even though they could have been charged with a misdemeanor crime for entering the U.S.

However, a small percentage—much smaller in proportion to U.S. citizens—did commit crimes that resulted in incarceration. As explained previously, this small group of Central Americans who committed serious crimes are at risk to begin the cycle of being forcibly recruited to the Mara Salvatrucha gang.

The *Maras* receive free recruits upon their incarceration in California prisons, then are "trained" (in exchange for protection) while completing their sentences, and then being "placed" onto the field to work for the criminal syndicate in the illegal drug production, distribution, and transportation from Central America to the U.S. market. This "placement" occurs when the new trainees are deported by ICE, receiving free flights from the Department of Homeland Security to Central America as part of this process.

The *Maras* continue to grow every year in each of the three countries and it should be a prerogative of our government to stop the proliferation of this massive transborder crime syndicate both through prison reform here in the states as well as providing aid from our government to the Central American governments in order to rehabilitate and reintegrate those Mara's who were forced to join while in American prisons.

Numerous studies point to the Mara members themselves seeking out opportunities to leave the criminal life and start anew. These same studies point to evidence that when offered assistance, gang members were, in fact, able to leave. One of the continuing barriers to stopping this cycle is the stigmatism by Central American society and government.

Furthermore, the intervention of Evangelical churches to assist those wanting to leave the *Maras* appears to be fruitful due to the respect by the *"Maras"* syndicate for those entering religious life to raise a family and work.

I propose that our government provide additional aid to Central American governments. The aid would only be allocated for rehabilitation, retraining, and reintegration of those gang members wishing to leave the gang immediately upon their arrival via deportation from the U.S. This would require coordination of funds between churches, Central American governments, and rehabilitation/reintegration professionals to give the program the best opportunity for success.

Logically, the small, but very disruptive gang members are not the only group of deportees that need economic opportunity, including training. Therefore, our foreign aid should also be designed to assist those non-gang members who need job training and assistance.

Economic Investment in People, not Governments

Finally, U.S. aid should be designed to help the entire economies of the three nations. For instance, in Honduras, our government has assisted U.S. companies in maintaining a one crop banana economy for much of the 20th Century. There we can do ourselves a favor and invest in the development of other economic opportunities that would provide jobs and a better standard of living for Hondurans.

Governments in third world countries and banana republics along with their economies, water rights, and land use are prone to manipulation, and corruption. By investing in Mom-and-Pop Establishments, the people see the change at the grassroots level. A subsistence farmer has the economic opportunity to grow both food and financially.

Can these Mom-and-Pop establishments compete with the big box chains? Yes, if they form cooperatives following the examples set in France and other forward-thinking nations.

"Cooperative companies function in line with the principle of free enterprise, and make people their top priority, with a focus both on the long-term and on competitiveness. They have an unusual profile, combining a democratic economy and an entrepreneurial model based on fairness and social responsibility." - Le Cooperation Agricole (France, 2019)

In Guatemala, a severe drought has become the "final straw" that has sent many rural Guatemalans, particularly Mayan-speaking families, packing for the U.S. now that they are facing starvation in addition to gang terror, lack of education, and health care.

Again, the idea of providing foreign aid to address the surge in migration from Central American is not new; there are many versions and ideas that have been proposed by academics and legal advocates such as AILA. These proposals have unique approaches that all deserve consideration, such as AILA's "resettlement initiative" that calls upon our government to work through the United Nations Refugee Agency.

Most children from Central America continue to insist that they would have preferred to stay in their countries. Thus, economic aid from our government is a win-win scenario. I, like many, would like to see all of the children of the Northern Triangle stay in their countries and not have to flee into Mexico or the U.S.

Image Source: © Peter Lucking | contentbrandingsolutions.com

CONCLUSION

The Way to Help Immigrant Children

Our government's inability to address the humanitarian crisis of children at the border is now playing out in front of our eyes as our social media posts are filled with news of children dying in the custody of ICE.

Even worse, we see more and more of our neighbors tiring of the situation. It would be easy to roll our eyes, swipe down the screen of our smartphone, and watch videos of cats.

President Trump's "Zero Tolerance" of immigrant children, his inhumane family separation orders have created an environment that makes us want to turn off our television.

Furthermore, the chant of "Send Them Home!" inspired by President Trump is aimed at immigrant children as well as members of the United States Congress who speak out against his policies.

Even worse, these official policies and public encouragement of ugly nationalism by many people in the United States has incited anti-immigrant individuals to violence.

I had to review the names of the dead in El Paso, Texas, at a Walmart where twenty-three (23) people were murdered in August of 2019. A madman opened fire on innocent people, including babies, U.S. citizens, and immigrants alike, apparently to stave off a "Hispanic Invasion." I once shopped there with my wife as we came back from a trip to Mexico. I know many people who live on both sides of the border who have shopped there. Fortunately, I did not recognize any of the names of the deceased. May they rest in peace.

Thoughtful and caring people cannot sit back and blame the President, wait for elections, and assume that the problem will go away. As we know, a change in the next president's political party has little effect, if any on our treatment of immigrant children.

If we are lucky, television journalism will continue to follow the sad stories of immigrant children languishing in cages. If we are fortunate enough, a handful of investigative journalists will bring breaking stories of more immigrant children being lost and abused by an overwhelmed foster care system.

I hope to see more success stories like Carlos and Elaizer, who survived the nightmare and are now living the American Dream.

Many individuals in Middle America hope that the construction of a wall on the Southern Border will solve these issues by literally shutting the door to more children arriving in the U.S. As the argument goes, once we ensure border security, then we can solve our immigration problems at home—as if it were that simple!

I truly hope that we do not become so tired of the situation that we begin to ignore reality. I sincerely wish that readers of this book will begin the conversation about immigrant children.

It would be wonderful for our communities to interject into the conversation about quotas, amnesty, detention and removal "How about the immigrant children?"

When conversations about immigration digress into discussing criminals, terrorists and welfare recipients, I hope to hear that voice saying, "Can't we do something special for the Dreamers, the children who are here with no real choice?"

Additionally, individual citizens can demand that our leaders provide an approach that will address the problems facing immigrant children and not just appeal to the lowest common denominator. After all, the United States has the means as the most powerful nation in the world, built by and sustained by immigrants, to end this nightmare for kids.

Ending the nightmare begins with ending the war of detention, separation, abuse, and death. We have perpetuated the war on Latinx children in their home countries and at our borders.

As Mahatma Gandhi once said, "If we are to teach real peace in this world, and if we are to carry on a real war against war, we shall have to begin with the children."

Another wise leader, Nelson Mandela said: "There can be no keener revelation of a society's soul than the way in which it treats its children."

Perhaps we can end the war on immigrant children and redeem our souls.

Together Let us Find a Solution for The Children.

Arturo Jiménez

THANK YOU

We are not done just quite yet.

I want to say thank you to our conscience's readers for supporting our work by reviewing this book on Amazon.

Please share your thoughts and knowledge with your friends and neighbors.

If you are concerned about the issues of immigrant children, please visit my website and share your constructive thoughts, so that together we may find a solution.

Thank you again for your support, be part of the solution for the sake of the children.

Until next time!

Arturo Jiménez

Arturo Jiménez

ABOUT THE AUTHOR

Arturo R. Jiménez was born in 1972 and grew up with his parents, and siblings in Denver, Colorado. Inspired by the matriarch of the family his Grandmother, Abuela - Eulalia "Lily" Calderón (Lopez - maiden) December 19, 1923 - May 8, 2017, his Mother Virginia Calderón Jiménez and his father Arthur R. Jiménez.

Education: He graduated with a Bachelor of Arts in Sociology and Ethnic Studies from the University of Colorado at Boulder, and his Juris Doctor (JD) from the University of Colorado at Boulder School of Law.

Arturo is happily married to his wife Angelina and is the proud father of three children, Metzli, Leonor, and Citlamina.

Arturo is a bilingual lawyer who has practiced federal immigration law since 1998. As an Advocate, his humanitarian practice has represented thousands of individuals for over twenty (20) years in Colorado and other States.

The Immigration Law Offices of Arturo Jiménez helps unify families through spouse petitions, family immigration, naturalization, Deferred Action for Childhood Arrivals (DACA), visas for victims and deportation defense in immigration court. Most of all, they seek to support the humanitarian rights of all individuals with an emphasis on immigrant children.

Political Experience: The Hon. Arturo R. Jiménez was elected to the Denver Public Schools Board of Education and served from 2007 until 2015.

Arturo Jiménez' balanced viewpoint in an interview on FOX31, *Immigration agent, caught on disparaging camera protesters?* Arturo shows his commitment to fairmindedness, human rights, and immigration issues. "He hopes this ICE agent's unfiltered comments are not reflective of the rest of the agency's employees."

Immigration Agent Caught on Camera Disparaging Protesters.

POSTED 6:27 PM, AUGUST 24, 2018, BY CHRIS HALSNE

"What type of dialog are we looking to have?" Jiménez asked FOX31. "We can continue the rhetoric around immigration and use those kind of words, like violent and criminal, and not able to read, uneducated and kind of perpetuate that, but when you have people out and excising their First Amendment rights, we have to study that and say we really can't talk about people that way." (HALSNE, 2018)

As a member of the National Association of Latino Elected Officials' Education Leadership Institute (NALEO/NECI), he served on its National Task Force from 2010-2015.

Throughout his career, Mr. Jiménez has worked to educate our community about our nation's immigration laws.

Founder and Volunteer Experience: A founder of the Labyrinth Arts Academy, Mr. Jiménez' volunteer activities include the Ya Es Hora Citizenship Campaign; Parent Leadership Coordinator/Los Padres/Las Madres, Academia Sandoval, 2004 to 2006; Strengthening Families Parent Trainer, Latin American Research and Service Agency 1998; former Board Member of College Path Inc. at North High School, 1993 to 1995; and the Multi-Cultural Regional Prevention Center, Alcohol Abuse Prevention, 1994 to 1996. Arturo is one of the founders of the Immigration Clinic at Catholic Charities in the Diocese of Pueblo and served as the President of the Colorado Statewide Parents Coalition.

Awards: Mr. Jiménez received an award for Outstanding Contributions for the Advancement of Chicano/Chicana Students in Higher Education at the 13th Annual Colorado Statewide Parent Learning Institute 1993 and the Education Champion Award from Escuela Tlatelolco in 2011.

2016 Federico Pena Education Leadership Award by the Colorado Association of Bilingual Educators (CABE).

Arturo was awarded the 2016 Lena Archuleta Award for Education Leadership by the Colorado Latino/Latina Advocacy and Research Organization (CLLARO)

CLARO
Colorado Latino Leadership, Advocacy & Research Organization

CLLARO Announcements

Announcing the 2016 Bernie Valdez Awardees

The Lena Archuleta Education Awardee:

Arturo Jimenez, Immigration Attorney and former Denver Public Schools Board Member

The Lena Archuleta Education Award is presented to an individual who works to educate our community through research which guides policy, increases awareness, and stimulates action.

Memberships: He is a member of the Colorado Chapter of the American Immigration Lawyers Association, the National Immigration Project of the National Lawyers Guild, the Colorado and Denver Bar Associations and a past member of the National Association of Latino Elected Officials.

Arturo is passionate about his commitment to represent and unify families and children to be their voice, to be their Advocate.

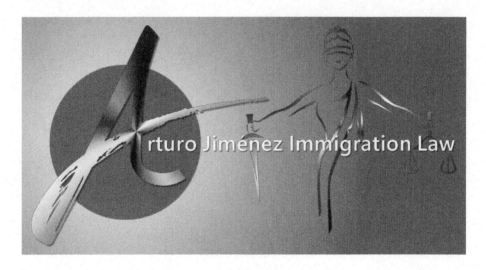

rturo Jiménez Immigration Law

Jiménez Immigration Law. Denver, Colorado https://arturojimenezimmigrationlaw.com/

Book Website http://arturojimenez.com

CONTACT ME

Press package: Can be downloaded from my website at https://arturojimenez.com/press-kit/

Booking for speaking engagements: Can be done through my contact page on my website

Image Source: © Peter Lucking | contentbrandingsolutions.com

Arturo Jiménez

WHY LATINX?

The term Latinx has become the preferred term for people to refer to themselves within the vastly diverse populations of people previously referred to as Latino, Hispanic, Latin American, and Spanish origin. It is important to understand what the term Latinx means because it was generated from within and between those communities. In this book, I focus on children from Mexico, Guatemala, El Salvador, and Honduras, who are very different in their immigration status, gender, languages, and self-identification. The term Latinx is the most inclusive and flexible term for such diverse populations.

Immigration Status

The term refers to those of Latin American descent who are both U.S. born citizens and those born outside of the United States. It normally refers to those who are living in the United States; however, it can refer to those who live in other countries in Latin America or other parts of the world. It also applies to those arriving at the U.S. borders. Importantly, Puerto Ricans are automatic U.S. citizens by birth in Puerto Rico as a U.S. citizen.

Gender

The "x" at the end has become a welcome replacement to the gender politics surrounding previous uses of "Latino/Latina" or "Latina/o" and provides a more gender-neutral term than the male-dominant "o" from the Spanish-language.

Language

The term that those in the U.S. government used 50 years ago was "Spanish-speaking" people or "Spanish-surnamed." The term Latinx refers to those of so-called Latin American descent who may speak primary languages other than Spanish such as Mayan dialects in Guatemala, English in Belize, Portuguese in Brazil and Nahuatl in Mexico.

Importantly, it encompasses many people in the U.S. of Latin American descent who speak English as their primary language and recognizes that even in other Latin American countries, many people have surnames that are other than Spanish.

Sexual Orientation and Transgendered

Likewise, the "x" also serves to be more inclusive to those of different sexual orientations and transgender individuals of Latin American descent.

Flexibility and Individualism

The "x" in Latinx allows for a growing diversity within such a non-homogenous grouping. The "x" allows for more individuality of identity by those within Latin American communities while still identifying their connection to a larger community.

You, Will, See the Various Latinx Terms Used Interchangeably at Times In This Book.

Race and Culture

Latinx people can be of indigenous, European, African, Asian or Pacific Islander origins. Also, there are many Latinx people who are of mixed origin, including those who are mixed ethnically with Anglos or White Americans. The "X" recognizes and represents the cross-cultural and cross-racial composition of Latinx peoples.

Politics

It is well recognized that Latinx people span the political spectrum both inside and outside the U.S. where Cuban Americans were generally members of the Republican Party while Puerto Ricans and Mexican Americans were generally most of the Democratic Party. Now growing numbers are Independents.

THE IMMIGRATION QUIZ
ANSWERS

1. YES, our government deports unaccompanied children.

2. President Clinton 1993 – 2001 (D) Holds the record for total deportations 12,290, 905.

3. The Dream Act proposal was introduced as a bill by Republican Senator Orin Hatch of Utah and Democratic Senator Dick Durbin 2001.

4. Over the last 18 years, at least ten versions of the Dream Act have been introduced in Congress

5. DACA and the Dream Act are different things

6. The DACA program does not currently provide permanent lawful status or a path to citizenship.

7. Honduras

8. President Bill Clinton

9. No, the children who have arrived at our Southern Border are not considered "Dreamers" by those sponsoring the DREAM ACT?

10. The Immigration Reform and Control Act of 1986—signed into law by President Ronald Reagan on November 6, 1986—granted amnesty to about 3 million undocumented immigrants in the United States

11. Democrats under Obama

12. Central America's Violent Northern Triangle: El Salvador, Guatemala, and Honduras

13. No

Arturo Jiménez

REFERENCES

Aarvik, E. (1987, Feb 2). *Award ceremony speech*. Retrieved from The Nobel Peace Prize 1987: https://www.nobelprize.org/prizes/peace/1987/ceremony-speech/

Ainsley, J. (2018, June 20). *Trump admin's 'tent cities' cost more than keeping migrant kids with parents*. Retrieved from NBC News: https://www.nbcnews.com/storyline/immigration-border-crisis/trump-admin-s-tent-cities-cost-more-keeping-migrant-kids-n884871?utm_source=newsletter&utm_medium=email&utm_campaign=newsletter_axiosam&stream=top

American Immigration Council, A. (2015). *A Guide to Children Arriving at the Border: Laws, Policies and Responses*. Na: American Immigration Council. Retrieved from https://www.americanimmigrationcouncil.org/sites/default/files/research/a_guide_to_children_arriving_at_the_border_and_the_laws_and_policies_governing_our_response.pdf

ANAPOL, A. (2018, August 2). *George W. Bush on immigrants: 'We ought to say thank you and welcome them'*. Retrieved from The Hill: https://thehill.com/blogs/blog-briefing-room/372882-george-w-bush-on-immigrants-we-ought-to-say-thank-you-and-welcome

Ann Frank House. (2019, March 13). Retrieved from Ann Frank .org: https://www.annefrank.org/en/anne-frank/go-in-depth/why-did-hitler-hate-jews/

Avalos, J. R. (2008, May 29). *Obama's Promise (May 2008) Video Clip*. Retrieved from Jorge Ramos: https://www.jorgeramos.com/en/obamas-promise-may-2008/

Bader, H. (2009, Aug 29). *Obama to Cut Off Aid to Honduras, Based on Legal Mistake and Misreading of the Law*. Retrieved from Competitive Enterprise Institute: https://cei.org/blog/obama-cut-aid-honduras-based-legal-mistake-and-misreading-law

Barrett, D. M. (2007, May 08). *Congress, the CIA, and Guatemala, 1954*. Retrieved from Central Intelligence Agency: https://www.cia.gov/library/center-for-the-study-of-intelligence/kent-csi/vol44no5/html/v44i5a03p.htm

BBC. (2015, February 26). *Guatemala ex-President Alfonso Portillo freed from US jail*. Retrieved from BBC world News: https://www.bbc.com/news/world-latin-america-31633785

Becerra, B. (2018, June 10). *La ACNUR manifiesta alarma por el aumento del desplazamiento de refugiados en México*. Retrieved from El Sol de San Juan del Río: https://www.elsoldesanjuandelrio.com.mx/mexico/la-acnur-manifiesta-alarma-por-el-aumento-del-desplazamiento-de-refugiados-en-mexico-1751910.html

Behar, A. (2013, Feb 14). *CNN*. Retrieved from Study the use of nanoparticles in food: https://www.cnn.com/2013/02/14/opinion/behar-food-nanoparticles/index.html

Benenson, L. (2018, May 9). *The Math of Immigration Detention, 2018 Update: Costs Continue to Multiply*. Retrieved from The National Immigration Forum: https://immigrationforum.org/article/math-immigration-detention-2018-update-costs-continue-mulitply/

Beristain, C. M. (1998, April 24). *Guatemala: never again*. Retrieved from Forged Migration Review: https://www.fmreview.org/fmr-3/beristain

Booth, W. (2012, January 2). *In Mexico 12,000 killed in drug violence in 2011*. Retrieved from The Washington Post: https://www.washingtonpost.com/world/in-mexico-12000-killed-in-drug-violence-in-2011/2012/01/02/gIQAcGUdWP_story.html?noredirect=on

Boutros-Ghali, B. 1.-2.-G. (1995). *The United Nations and El Salvador, 1990-1995. The United Nations Blue Books Series Volume IV*. Retrieved from United Nations Digital Library: https://digitallibrary.un.org/record/198261

Brown University. (1986, Na NA). *Understanding the Iran-Contra Affairs: Nicaragua Timeline*. Retrieved from Brown Edu: https://www.brown.edu/Research/Understanding_the_Iran_Contra_Affair/timeline-nicaragua.php

Bureau of Justice Statistics. (2012). *Survey of State Criminal History Information Systems, 2012*. Washington, D.C: U.S. Department of Justice Office of Justice Programs.

Caldwell, L. M. (2018, May 7). *The Wall Street Journal*. Retrieved from Stiffened U.S. Approach to Illegal Border Crossings Will Separate Families: https://www.wsj.com/articles/trump-administration-to-step-up-prosecution-of-border-crossing-parents-1525708761?mod=article_inline

cganemccalla. (2011, May 2). *How The CIA Helped Create Osama Bin Laden*. Retrieved from NEWSONE: https://newsone.com/1205745/cia-osama-bin-laden-al-qaeda/

Chodron, P. (2016, July 14). *19 Ways to Awaken Your Heart*. Retrieved from UPLIFT: https://upliftconnect.com/awaken-your-heart/

CIA. (2018, NA NA). *The World Factbook*. Retrieved from Central Intelligence Agency: https://www.cia.gov/library/publications/the-world-factbook/geos/co.html

CIA Helped To Mine Ports In Nicaragua. (1984, April 7). Retrieved from The Washington Post: https://www.washingtonpost.com/archive/politics/1984/04/07/cia-helped-to-mine-ports-in-nicaragua/762f775f-6733-4dd4-b692-8f03c8a0aef8/?noredirect=on&utm_term=.993827ed6aca

Clinton, H. (2016, April 11). *TRANSCRIPT: Hillary Clinton meets with the Daily News Editorial Board, April 9, 2016*. Retrieved from NEW YORK DAILY NEWS : https://www.nydailynews.com/opinion/transcript-hillary-clinton-meets-news-editorial-board-article-1.2596292

Cohen, G. T. (2014, April 6). *More Deportations Follow Minor Crimes, Records Show*. Retrieved from The New York Times: https://www.nytimes.com/2014/04/07/us/more-deportations-follow-minor-crimes-data-shows.html

Congress. (2009-2010, March 26). *S.729 - DREAM Act of 2009*. Retrieved from Congress.gov: https://www.congress.gov/bill/111th-congress/senate-bill/729

Copp, T. (2018, October 29). *President Trump orders 5,200 active-duty troops to US-Mexico border*. Retrieved from Military Times: https://www.militarytimes.com/news/your-military/2018/10/29/trump-orders-5200-active-duty-troops-to-us-mexico-border/

Country Studies. (1986, NA NA). *The Rise of the FSLN*. Retrieved from This website contains the on-line versions of books previously published in hard copy by the Federal Research Division of the Library of Congress as part of the Country Studies/Area Handbook Series sponsored by the U.S. Department of the Army between 1986: http://countrystudies.us/nicaragua/12.htm

CQ Almanac. (1983, Na Na). *Nicaragua Covert Aid Issue Compromised*. Retrieved from QC Press: https://library.cqpress.com/cqalmanac/document.php?id=cqal83-1198446

CQ Researcher. (1939 - 2019, Na Na). *United States Trade with Latin America*. Retrieved from CQ Researcher: https://library.cqpress.com/cqresearcher/document.php?id=cqresrre1939101000

Dade, C. (2012, December 24). *Obama Administration Deported Record 1.5 Million People*. Retrieved from National Public Radio: https://www.npr.org/sections/itsallpolitics/2012/12/24/167970002/obama-administration-deported-record-1-5-million-people

Danner, M. (1993, December 6). *THE TRUTH OF EL MOZOTE*. Retrieved from The New Yorker: https://www.newyorker.com/magazine/1993/12/06/the-truth-of-el-mozote

Department of Homeland Security. (2012, Na Na). *Instructions for Consideration of Deferred Action pdf*. Retrieved from NATIONAL IMMIGRATION LAW CENTER: https://www.nilc.org/wp-content/uploads/2017/12/i-821dinstr.pdf

Department of Homeland Security. (2016, Accessed January 2019 9). *Southwest Border Unaccompanied Alien Children Statistics FY 2016*. Retrieved from U.S. Customs and Border Protection: https://www.cbp.gov/site-page/southwest-border-unaccompanied-alien-children-statistics-fy-2016

Department of Homeland Security. (2018, Na Na). *Department of Homeland Security U.S. Immigration and Customs Enforcement Budget Overview*. Retrieved from Department of Homeland Security: https://www.dhs.gov/sites/default/files/publications/ICE%20FY18%20Budget.pdf

Department of Homeland Security. (2019, Aug 6). *Southwest Border Migration FY 2019*. Retrieved from U.S. Customs and Border Protection: https://www.cbp.gov/newsroom/stats/sw-border-migration

Deseret News. (1989, October 11). *BUSH AGREES TO DRUG SUMMIT; 7 KILLED IN MEDELLIN SHOOTINGS*. Retrieved from Deseret News: https://www.deseretnews.com/article/67475/BUSH-AGREES-TO-DRUG-SUMMIT-7-KILLED-IN-MEDELLIN-SHOOTINGS.html

DHS. (2018, NA NA). *U.S. Border Patrol Southwest Border Apprehensions by Sector FY2018*. Retrieved from DHS - U.S. Customs and Border Protection: https://www.cbp.gov/newsroom/stats/usbp-sw-border-apprehensions

DHS. (2019, NA NA). *Temporary Protected Status*. Retrieved from U.S. Citizenship and Immigration Services: https://www.uscis.gov/humanitarian/temporary-protected-status

DHS, D. o. (2016, Na Na). *Table 39. Aliens Removed Or Returned: Fiscal Years 1960 To 2016*. Retrieved from U.S. Department of Homeland Security: https://www.dhs.gov/immigration-statistics/yearbook/2016/table39

Diplomatic Dispatches. (2011, June 19). *A Selection From the Cache of Diplomatic Dispatches*. Retrieved from The New York Times: https://archive.nytimes.com/www.nytimes.com/interactive/2010/11/28/world/20101128-cables-viewer.html?hp#report/cables-09TEGUCIGALPA645

El Tiempo. (1975, July 28). *El TIEMPO page 27*. Retrieved from Google News: https://news.google.com/newspapers?nid=N2osnxbUuuUC&dat=19750728&printsec=frontpage&hl=es

Espada, R. (2012, July 11). *Recommendations of the Government of Guatemala for the Experiments Practiced with Humans in Guatemala*. Retrieved from The City Project: https://www.cityprojectca.org/blog/archives/14924

France, A. C. (2019, Aug 8). *The agricultural cooperatives family*. Retrieved from La Cooperation Agricol: https://www.lacooperationagricole.coop/en/agricultural-cooperatives-family-france-and-worldwide

Freidel, F. S. (2002, October 8). *Calvin Coolidge - Exert from Presidents of the United States of America*. Retrieved from The White House: https://www.whitehouse.gov/about-the-white-house/presidents/calvin-coolidge/

Friedman, M. (2015, November 17). *Brennan Center for Justice*. Retrieved from Just Facts: As Many Americans Have Criminal Records As College Diplomas: https://www.brennancenter.org/blog/just-facts-many-americans-have-criminal-records-college-diplomas

Gallucci, M. (2018, May 28). *The Struggle to Make Diesel-Guzzling Cargo Ships Greener*. Retrieved from spectrum.ieee.org: https://spectrum.ieee.org/transportation/marine/the-struggle-to-make-dieselguzzling-cargo-ships-greener

García, M. R. (2013, December Na). *First, Do No Harm: The US Sexually Transmitted Disease Experiments in Guatemala*. Retrieved from US National Library of Medicine National Institutes of Health: https://www.ncbi.nlm.nih.gov/pmc/articles/PMC3828982/

Gelatt, J. (2006, August 1). *Congressional Republicans Continue Field Hearings on Immigration, Introduce New Immigration Reform Proposal*. Retrieved from Migration Policy Institute MPI: https://www.migrationpolicy.org/article/congressional-republicans-continue-field-hearings-immigration-introduce-new-immigration

Gilbert, D. (1988, p.164). *Sandinistas : The Party and the Revolution*. Cambridge, Mass, USA: Basil Blackwell, Inc.

Gilder Lehrman. (2018, Na Na). *Henry Kissinger and American Foreign Policy*. Retrieved from The Guilder Lehrman Institute of American History: http://ap.gilderlehrman.org/history-by-era/seventies/essays/henry-kissinger-and-american-foreign-policy

Gomez, B. J. (2018, Dec 6). *President Trump calls caravan immigrants 'stone cold criminals.' Here's what we know*. Retrieved from USA Today: https://www.usatoday.com/story/news/2018/11/26/president-trump-migrant-caravan-criminals/2112846002/

Gomez, G. K. (2018, May 17). *Trump ramps up rhetoric on undocumented immigrants: 'These aren't people. These are animals.'*. Retrieved from USA TODAY: https://www.usatoday.com/story/news/politics/2018/05/16/trump-immigrants-animals-mexico-democrats-sanctuary-cities/617252002/

Gómez, M. (2003, p.139). HUMAN RIGHTS IN CUBA, EL SALVADOR AND NICARAGUA A SOCIOLOGICAL PERSPECTIVE ON HUMAN RIGHTS ABUSE . NewYork: Routledge.

Gorden, M. (2018, Sept 12). *Tent city's closure saving Maricopa County millions*. Retrieved from azfamily: https://www.azfamily.com/tent-city-s-closure-saving-maricopa-county-millions/article_5a7c5c36-c2f4-5c88-8271-e593c612730d.html

Graham, M. (2014, July 25). *Child Deportations: How Many Minors Does the U.S. Actually Send Home*. Retrieved from Bipartisan Policy Center: https://bipartisanpolicy.org/blog/us-child-deportations/

Graham, M. (2014, July 25). *Child Deportations: How Many Minors Does the U.S. Actually Send Home?* Retrieved from Bipartisan Policy Center: https://bipartisanpolicy.org/blog/us-child-deportations/

Graham, M. (2014, July 25). *Child Deportations: How Many Minors Does the U.S. Actually Send Home?* Retrieved from Bipartisan Policy Center: https://bipartisanpolicy.org/blog/us-child-deportations/

Grandin, G. (2016, March 10). *Before Her Murder, Berta Cáceres Singled Out Hillary Clinton for Criticism*. Retrieved from The Nation: https://www.thenation.com/article/chronicle-of-a-honduran-assassination-foretold/

Grandin, G. (2016, August 9). *Hillary Clinton's Embrace of Kissinger Is Inexcusable*. Retrieved from The Nation: https://www.thenation.com/article/hillary-clintons-embrace-of-kissinger-is-inexcusable/

Grandin, G. (2016, March 3). *The Clinton-Backed Honduran Regime Is Picking Off Indigenous Leaders*. Retrieved from The Nation: https://www.thenation.com/article/the-clinton-backed-honduran-regime-is-picking-off-indigenous-leaders/

Guardian News. (2018, June 19). *Children separated from parents cry at US detention center – audio*. Retrieved from The Guardian: https://www.theguardian.com/us-news/video/2018/jun/19/children-separated-from-parents-cry-at-us-detention-centre-audio

Guatemala Human Rights Commission, G. (2010). *US Assistance to Guatemala*. Washington: Guatemala Human Rights Commission http://www.ghrc-usa.org/. Retrieved from PRESS ROOM.

H.R.2419 - Intelligence Authorization Act for Fiscal Year 1986. (1985, April 12). Retrieved from Congress.gov: https://www.congress.gov/bill/99th-congress/house-bill/2419

HALSNE, C. (2018, August 24). *Immigration agent caught on camera disparaging protesters?* Retrieved from Fox 31 Denver: https://kdvr.com/2018/08/24/immigration-agent-caught-on-camera-disparaging-protesters/

Hammilton. (2017, December 3). *The cold-blooded Cocaine Godmother of Colombia invented the motorcycle drive-by shooting that killed her*. Retrieved from The Vintage News: https://www.thevintagenews.com/2017/12/03/cocaine-godmother-of-colombia/

HHS. (2015, Na NA). *HHS FY2015 Budget in Brief - Administration for Children and Families (ACF): Discretionary - ACF Discretionary Budget Overview*. Retrieved from HHS : https://www.hhs.gov/about/budget/fy2015/budget-in-brief/acf/discretionary/index.html

HHS-ORR. (2019, Feb 2). *Unaccompanied Alien Children Released to Sponsors By State*. Retrieved from Office of Refugee Resettlement: https://www.acf.hhs.gov/orr/resource/unaccompanied-alien-children-released-to-sponsors-by-state

Historian, T. O. (1977-1988, Na Na). *Central America, 1977–1980*. Retrieved from Department of the State : https://history.state.gov/milestones/1977-1980/central-america-carter

History. (2019, 3 18). *Iran-Contra Affair*. Retrieved from History: https://www.history.com/topics/1980s/iran-contra-affair

Hudson, M. (2011, November 11). *Despite lack of support from "reformers," Arturo Jimenez's brand of reform rings true*. Retrieved from Colorado Politics: https://www.coloradopolitics.com/opinion/despite-lack-of-support-from-reformers-arturo-jimenez-s-brand/article_3d1883b7-4f2e-5809-ba9e-cc538e45f872.html

ICE. (2014). *ICE Enforcement and Removal Operations Report*. Washington: U.S. Immigration and Customs Enforcement.

Immerman, R. (1982). The CIA in Guatemala: The Foreign Policy of Intervention. Austin: University of Texas Press.

Immigration Task Force. (2014). *Child Migration by the Numbers*. Washington: Bipartisan Policy Center bipartisanpolicy.org. Retrieved 2019, from https://bipartisanpolicy.org/wp-content/uploads/sites/default/files/BPC%20Immigration%20Task%20Force%20-%20Child%20Migration%20by%20the%20Numbers%20June%202014.pdf

INS. (1999, NA NA). *1999 Statistical Yearbook of the Immigration and Naturalization Services*. Retrieved from U.S. Department of Justice, Immigration and Naturalization Service: https://www.dhs.gov/sites/default/files/publications/Yearbook_Immigration_Statistics_1999.pdf

ITEP. (2017, March 2). *Undocumented Immigrants' State & Local Tax Contributions*. Retrieved from Institute on Taxation and Economic Policy: https://itep.org/immigration/?gclid=EAIaIQobChMI_v-clavx4wIVD__jBx0FYACPEAAYASAAEgJ1GPD_BwE

Jordan, M. (2019, Jan 17). *The New Your Times*. Retrieved from Family Separation May Have Hit Thousands More Migrant Children Than Reported: https://www.nytimes.com/2019/01/17/us/family-separation-trump-administration-migrants.html?rref=collection%2Ftimestopic%2FImmigration%20Detention&action=click&contentCollection=timestopics&region=stream&module=stream_unit&version=latest&contentPlacement=3

Jordan, M. (2019, Jan 15). *Trump Administration to Nearly Double Size of Detention Center for Migrant Teenagers*. Retrieved from The New York Times: https://www.nytimes.com/2019/01/15/us/migrant-children-shelter-tent-city-tornillo-homestead.html?rref=collection%2Ftimestopic%2FImmigration%20Detention&action=click&contentCollection=timestopics&region=stream&module=stream_unit&version=latest&contentPlace

Jordan, M. (2019, Jan 15). *Trump Administration to Nearly Double Size of Detention Center for Migrant Teenagers*. Retrieved from The New York Times: https://www.nytimes.com/2019/01/15/us/migrant-children-shelter-tent-city-tornillo-homestead.html?rref=collection%2Ftimestopic%2FImmigration%20Detention&action=click&contentCollection=timestopics&region=stream&module=stream_unit&version=latest&contentPlace

KAPLAN, R. (2014, June 30). *Obama's illegal immigration plan alarms migrant childrens advocates*. Retrieved from CBS News: https://www.cbsnews.com/news/obamas-illegal-immigration-plan-alarms-migrant-childrens-advocates/

Kelly, J. (2014, June 25). *HHS Ready to Spend on Unaccompanied Minors: We Need Beds Now*. Retrieved from The Chronical of Social Change, Children and Youth Front and Center: https://chronicleofsocialchange.org/featured/hhs-ready-to-spend-on-unaccompanied-minors-we-need-beds-now

Kinosian, M. B. (2019, January 23). *More than 10,000 migrants request visas as caravan hits Mexico*. Retrieved from The Washington Post: https://www.washingtonpost.com/world/the_americas/more-than-10000-migrants-request-visas-as-caravan-hits-mexico/2019/01/23/340169b8-1f2b-11e9-a759-2b8541bbbe20_story.html?utm_term=.c70b618567b7

Kinzer, S. (2018, April 1). *Efraín Ríos Montt, Guatemalan Dictator Convicted of Genocide, Dies at 91*. Retrieved from New York Times: https://www.nytimes.com/2018/04/01/obituaries/efrain-rios-montt-guatemala-dead.html

Klein, H. S.-J. (1999). The Atlantic Slave Trade. Cambridge: Cambridge University Press.

Lind, D. (2014, July 29). *14 facts that help explain America's child-migrant crisis*. Retrieved from Vox: https://www.vox.com/2014/6/16/5813406/explain-child-migrant-crisis-central-america-unaccompanied-children-immigrants-daca

Lind, D. (2018, June 21). *What Obama did with migrant families vs. what Trump is doing*. Retrieved from Vox: https://www.vox.com/2018/6/21/17488458/obama-immigration-policy-family-separation-border

LOPEZ, A. G.-B. (2016, December 16). *U.S. immigrant deportations fall to Lowest level since 2007*. Retrieved from Pew Research Center: http://www.pewresearch.org/fact-tank/2016/12/16/u-s-immigrant-deportations-fall-to-lowest-level-since-2007/

LOPEZ, J. M.-B. (2014, July 22). *Children 12 and under are fastest growing group of unaccompanied minors at U.S. border*. Retrieved from Pew Research Center: http://www.pewresearch.org/fact-tank/2014/07/22/children-12-and-under-are-fastest-growing-group-of-unaccompanied-minors-at-u-s-border/

Malkin, E. (2011, October 20). *An Apology for a Guatemalan Coup, 57 Years Later*. Retrieved from The New York Times. https://www.nytimes.com/2011/10/21/world/americas/an-apology-for-a-guatemalan-coup-57-years-later.html

Martin, D. (2003, April Na). *Immigration Policy and the Homeland Security Act Reorganization: An Early Agenda for Practical Improvements*. Retrieved from Migration Policy Institute: https://www.migrationpolicy.org/research/immigration-policy-and-homeland-security-act-reorganization-early-agenda-practical

Maslin, S. E. (2016, December 13). Remembering El Mozote, the Worst Massacre in Modern Latin American History. Retrieved from The Nation: https://www.thenation.com/article/remembering-el-mozote-the-worst-massacre-in-modern-latin-american-history/

Mcclendon, C. H. (2017, April 5). Christians remain the world's largest religious group. Retrieved from Pew Research Center: http://www.pewresearch.org/fact-tank/2017/04/05/christians-remain-worlds-largest-religious-group-but-they-are-declining-in-europe/

Meislin, R. (1982, Dec 19). *U.S. MILITARY AID FOR GUATEMALA CONTINUING DESPITE OFFICIAL CURBS*. Retrieved from New York Times: https://www.nytimes.com/1982/12/19/world/us-military-aid-for-guatemala-continuing-despite-official-curbs.html

Merchant, C. L. (2018, June 20). *No clear plan yet on how to reunite parents with children*. Retrieved from PBS: https://www.pbs.org/newshour/nation/no-clear-plan-yet-on-how-to-reunite-parents-with-children

Morris, J. (2017, August 19). *Top 10 Disturbing Facts About Los Zetas*. Retrieved from Listverse: http://listverse.com/2017/08/19/top-10-disturbing-facts-about-los-zetas/

Mount Holyoke Colledge. (2018, Na Na). *Guerrilla and Paramilitary Groups*. Retrieved from Drug Trafficking in Colombia: http://www.mtholyoke.edu/~macne22k/classweb/traffickingincolombia/page3.html

Muzaffar Chishti, &. S. (2017, January 26). *The Obama Record on Deportations: Deporter in Chief or Not?* Retrieved from Migration Policy Institute: https://www.migrationpolicy.org/article/obama-record-deportations-deporter-chief-or-not

Newsroom Panama. (2013, February 18). *US responsible for death of Omar Torrijos, - former militar...* Retrieved from Newsroom Panama: https://www.newsroompanama.com/news/panama/us-responsible-for-death-of-omar-torrijos-former-militar newsroom@denverpost.com. (2009, December 21). *Political activist pleads guilty in window-smashing.* Retrieved from Denver Post: https://www.denverpost.com/2009/12/21/political-activist-pleads-guilty-in-window-smashing/

Nick Penzenstadler Steve Reilly David Wilson Karen Yi Pim Linders John Kelly Jeff Dionise. (2016, Ongoing Na). *Donald Trump: Three decades 4,095 lawsuits.* Retrieved from USA TODAY: https://www.usatoday.com/pages/interactives/trump-lawsuits/

Obama, P. (2014, Nov 20). *Remarks by the President in Address to the Nation on Immigration.* Retrieved from The White House: https://obamawhitehouse.archives.gov/the-press-office/2014/11/20/remarks-president-address-nation-immigration

OECD. (2018 , Sept 14). *Social spendingPublic, % of GDP, 2016 or latest available.* Retrieved from OECD Data: https://data.oecd.org/socialexp/social-spending.htm

Official Website of the Department of Homeland Security. (2018, Na Na). *Special Immigrant Juveniles.* Retrieved from Department of Homland security : https://www.uscis.gov/green-card/sij

Official Website of the Department of Homeland Security. (2019, March 21). *Temporary Protected Status Designated Country: El Salvador.* Retrieved from The Department of Homeland Security: https://www.uscis.gov/humanitarian/temporary-protected-status/temporary-protected-status-designated-country-el-salvador

panelists, T. t. (2004, December 4). *Impact and Repercussions: U.S. Military Aid to Colombia.* Retrieved from Carnegie Council for ethics in International Affairs: https://www.carnegiecouncil.org/publications/articles_papers_reports/190

Peek, L. (2019, Jan 21). *Fox News.* Retrieved from Two years of Trump hatred and Democrats' 'resistance' has accomplished what, exactly?: https://www.foxnews.com/opinion/liz-peek-two-years-of-trump-hatred-and-democrats-resistance-has-accomplished-what-exactly

PolitiFact. (2019, March 22). *Promises about Immigration on The Obameter.* Retrieved from PolitiFact: https://www.politifact.com/truth-o-meter/promises/obameter/subjects/immigration/

Posey, S. S. (2009, December 9). *Mexico: The War with the Cartels in 2009.* Retrieved from World View: https://worldview.stratfor.com/article/mexico-war-cartels-2009

POST, T. D. (2016, May 6). *Political activist pleads guilty in window-smashing.* Retrieved from The Denver Post: https://www.denverpost.com/2009/12/21/political-activist-pleads-guilty-in-window-smashing/

PPRI. (2018, October 29). *Partisan Polarization Dominates Trump Era: Findings from the 2018 American Values Survey.* Retrieved from PPRI: https://www.prri.org/research/partisan-polarization-dominates-trump-era-findings-from-the-2018-american-values-survey/

Preston, J. (1987, June 10). *PANAMANIANS RIOT AFTER ACCUSATIONS.* Retrieved from Washington Post: Julia Preston

Renwick, R. C. (2018, June 26). *Central America's Violent Northern Triangle.* Retrieved from Council on Foregn Relations: https://www.cfr.org/backgrounder/central-americas-violent-northern-triangle

Report: Americas and Caribbean top global murder rates. (2011, October 7). Retrieved from CNN: https://www.cnn.com/2011/10/07/world/un-homicide-report/

Robertson, L. (2018, June 28). *Illegal Immigration Statistics.* Retrieved from FactCheck.org: https://www.factcheck.org/2018/06/illegal-immigration-statistics/

S.1615 - Dream Act of 2017. (2017, July 26). Retrieved from Congress.gov: https://www.congress.gov/bill/115th-congress/senate-bill/1615

Sacchetti, S. H. (2018, May 7). *Sessions vows to prosecute all illegal border crossers and separate children from their parents.* Retrieved from The Washington Post: https://www.washingtonpost.com/world/national-security/sessions-says-justice-dept-will-prosecute-every-person-who-crosses-border-unlawfully/2018/05/07/e1312b7e-5216-11e8-9c91-7dab596e8252_story.html?noredirect=on&utm_term=.1d4045d0bf55

Smith, K. (2019, Jan 25). *NEWS*. Retrieved from CBS News: https://www.cbsnews.com/news/tijuana-port-of-entry-san-ysidro-allows-20-immigrants-claim-asylum-immigration-advocates-2019-01-25/

Spetalnick, M. (2007, January 19). *Bush, Mexico's Calderon to work on immigration*. Retrieved from Reuters: https://www.reuters.com/article/us-bush-mexico/bush-mexicos-calderon-to-work-on-immigration-idUSN0943134520061109

Stahl, J. (2019, July 26). *Top CBP Officer Testifies He's Unsure if 3-Year-Old Is "a Criminal or a National Security Threat*. Retrieved from SLATE: https://slate.com/news-and-politics/2019/07/cbp-chief-brian-hastings-family-separation-judiciary-hearing-not-mueller.html

State, U. D. (2018, Na Na). *Central America Regional Security Initiative*. Retrieved from Central America Regional Security Initiative: https://www.state.gov/j/inl/rls/fs/2017/260869.htm

Strange, H. (2013, July 16). *Profile: the brutal cartel boss who took sadistic killing to new levels*. Retrieved from The Telegraph: https://www.telegraph.co.uk/news/worldnews/centralamericaandthecaribbean/mexico/10182371/Profile-the-brutal-cartel-boss-who-took-sadistic-killing-to-new-levels.html

Stratfor. (2009, March 30). *Mexico Security Memo: March 30, 2009*. Retrieved from World View Stratfor: https://worldview.stratfor.com/article/mexico-security-memo-march-30-2009

The Center for Justice Accountability. (2017, March 31). *THE GUATEMALA GENOCIDE CASE*. Retrieved from The Center for Justice & Accountability: https://cja.org/what-we-do/litigation/the-guatemala-genocide-case/

The New York Times Editorial Board. (2019, Jan 17). *The Lost Children of the Trump Administration*. Retrieved from The New York Times: https://www.nytimes.com/2019/01/17/opinion/family-separation-border-trump.html?rref=collection%2Ftimestopic%2FImmigration%20Detention&action=click&contentCollection=timestopics&region=stream&module=stream_unit&version=latest&contentPlacement=2&pgtype=coll

The Pew Research Center. (2014, July 22). *Children 12 and under are fastest growing group of unaccompanied minors at U.S. border FACT TANK NEWS IN THE NUMBERS*. Retrieved from FACT TANK NEWS IN THE NUMBERS: https://www.pewresearch.org/fact-tank/2014/07/22/children-12-and-under-are-fastest-growing-group-of-unaccompanied-minors-at-u-s-border/

The Pew Research Center. (2018, May 24). *Republicans turn more negative toward refugees as number admitted to U.S. plummets*. Retrieved from The Pew Research Center: http://www.pewresearch.org/fact-tank/2018/05/24/republicans-turn-more-negative-toward-refugees-as-number-admitted-to-u-s-plummets/

The U S Cittizenship and Immigration Services. (2012, June Na). *Consideration of Deferred Action for Childhood Arrivals (DACA)*. Retrieved from Official Website of the Department of Homeland Security: https://www.uscis.gov/archive/consideration-deferred-action-childhood-arrivals-daca

The White Huse Press Release. (2005, November 28). *President Discusses Border Security and Immigration Reform in Arizona*. Retrieved from George W Bush-whitehouse.archives: https://georgewbush-whitehouse.archives.gov/news/releases/2005/11/20051128-7.html

Times. (1977, November 6). *U.S. FOOD AID SEEN HURTING GUATEMALA, Page 51*. Retrieved from The New York Times Archives: https://www.nytimes.com/1977/11/06/archives/us-food-aid-seen-hurting-guatemala-donations-sent-after-1976-quake.html

Tobia, P. J. (2014, June 20). *No country for lost kids*. Retrieved from RMPBS: https://www.pbs.org/newshour/nation/country-lost-kids

Transcript. (2006, May 15). *Bush: U.S. 'a lawful society and a welcoming society'*. Retrieved from CNN.com: http://www.cnn.com/2006/POLITICS/05/15/bush.immigration.text/index.html

Transcript. (2006, May 15). *Bush's Speech on Immigration*. Retrieved from The New York Times: https://www.nytimes.com/2006/05/15/washington/15text-bush.html

Truth, Lies and El Salvador March 16, 1993, Page 20. (1993, March 16). Retrieved from The New York Times: https://www.nytimes.com/1993/03/16/opinion/truth-lies-and-el-salvador.html

U.S. Customs and Border Protection. (2019, Na Na). *Customs and Border Protection*. Retrieved from Official website of the Department of Homeland Security: https://www.cbp.gov/newsroom/stats/sw-border-migration

United Nations High Commissioner for Refugees. (2015, October NA). *Women On The Run* . Retrieved from United Nations High Commissioner for Refugees: https://www.unhcr.org/5630f24c6.pdf

United Nations Office on Drugs and Crime. (2012, Na Na). *2011 Global Study on Homicide*. Retrieved from UNODC : https://www.unodc.org/unodc/en/data-and-analysis/statistics/crime/global-study-on-homicide-2011.html

Vigaud-Walsh, F. (2017, November 29). *DISPLACEMENT AND VIOLENCE IN THE NORTHERN TRIANGLE*. Retrieved from Refugies International: https://www.refugeesinternational.org/reports/2017/11/27/displacement-and-violence-in-the-northern-triangle

White House Press Release. (2006, June 8). Remarks by President Bush *and President Michelle Bachelet of Chile - The Oval Office*. Retrieved from U.S. Department of State: https://2001-2009.state.gov/p/wha/rls/prsrl/2006/q2/67723.htm

Winborn, D. B. (2018, July NA). *The 'Stranger' Among Us: Church Tackles Immigration*. Retrieved from CBN: https://www.cbn.com/giving/special/SBDVDClub.aspx?intcmp=A_FUND:ROS:PREVID:PREVID:AHG54655

Woodrow Wilson Center. (2017, Jan 11). *The Northern Triangle of Central America: Violence, Security, and Migration*. Retrieved from Woodrow Wilson Center: https://www.wilsoncenter.org/event/the-northern-triangle-central-america-violence-security-and-migration?gclid=EAIaIQobChMIh5b1wq2n4AIVibbACh3bwAXpEAAYASAAEgKXXfD_BwE

Yuhas, A. (2016, March 20). *US-Cuba relations: timeline of a tangled history*. Retrieved from The Gardian: https://www.theguardian.com/world/ng-interactive/2016/mar/20/us-cuba-relations-history-timeline

Zunes, S. (2016, March 14). *The US role in the Honduras coup and subsequent violence*. Retrieved from National Cathlic Reporter: https://www.ncronline.org/blogs/ncr-today/us-role-honduras-coup-and-subsequent-violence

Arturo Jiménez

BOOK SYNOPSIS

The politicians have failed the DREAM'ers and DACA recipients; they are living a nightmare. One knock on the door away from deportation.

Our southern borders are overrun by asylum seekers; migrants fleeing violence, corruption, kidnapping, rape, rampant crime, human trafficking, and human rights abuses that few of us can imagine, let alone survive through.

Arturo Jiménez, an experienced family Immigration Lawyer, humanizes the issue, utilizing stories of his clients to help us understand the causes and effects of the migration of Latinx children and families from The Violent Central Triangle of El Salvador, Guatemala, and Honduras, and the surrounding states of Nicaragua and Mexico to the United States.

This book looks at the effects of American Foreign Policy and U.S. National Interests in Latin America and the associated human rights abuses which cause the migration of asylum seekers to the U.S. Southern border.

Arturo takes us on a personal journey to explore how the U.S. treats migrant asylum seekers, DREAM'ers, and DACA recipients. Arturo searches for the truth without religious or political bias sharing his firsthand experiences, insights, knowledge, and findings to help us come up with solutions, to start the consensual discussion of Immigration reform.

The immigration issue will shock you, have you in tears, of anger and sorrow. Whether you are a Democrat or a Republican the *DREAMers Nightmare: THE U.S. WAR ON IMMIGRANT LATINX CHILDREN* will shatter your beliefs, enlightening you with the knowledge to share with others so together we can make a beneficial change.

If you think you are an expert on immigration, take the "Immigration Quiz."

Made in the USA
Coppell, TX
24 October 2019